THE INSURRECTIONIST

THE INSURRECTIONIST

Major General Edwin A. Walker and the Birth of the Deep State Conspiracy

PETER ADAMS

LOUISIANA STATE UNIVERSITY PRESS ★ BATON ROUGE

Published by Louisiana State University Press
lsupress.org

Manufactured in the United States of America
First printing

DESIGNER: Michelle A. Neustrom
TYPEFACE: Minion Pro
PRINTER AND BINDER: Sheridan Books, Inc.

Jacket photograph: Walker in the custody of federal marshals after his arrest at Ole Miss, October 1, 1962. (AP Photo)

LIBRARY OF CONGRESS CATALOGING-IN-PUBLICATION DATA

Names: Adams, Peter, 1953– author.
Title: The insurrectionist : Major General Edwin A. Walker and the birth of the deep state conspiracy / Peter Adams.
Other titles: Major General Edwin A. Walker and the birth of the deep state conspiracy
Description: Baton Rouge : Louisiana State University Press, [2023] | Includes bibliographical references and index.
Identifiers: LCCN 2023004003 (print) | LCCN 2023004004 (ebook) | ISBN 978-0-8071-7992-5 (cloth) | ISBN 978-0-8071-8050-1 (pdf) | ISBN 978-0-8071-8049-5 (epub)
Subjects: LCSH: Walker, Edwin A. (Edwin Anderson), 1909–1993. | Right-wing extremists—United States—Biography. | United States. Army—Officers—Biography. | John Birch Society. | Racism—United States—History—20th century. | Conspiracy theories—Political aspects—United States. | United States—Politics and government—1945–1989.
Classification: LCC E840.8.W34 A6 2023 (print) | LCC E840.8.W34 (ebook) | DDC 973.92092 [B]—dc23/eng/20230425
LC record available at https://lccn.loc.gov/2023004003
LC ebook record available at https://lccn.loc.gov/2023004004

For my children, Genevieve and Elliot,
and my grandchildren, Owen and Margot.

May you all live in interesting times.

CONTENTS

Illustrations follow page 108.

ACKNOWLEDGMENTS

As with any writing project, there are those to whom I am indebted for their sound advice and encouragement. A biography of Major General Edwin A. Walker, an odd and troublesome character of the 1960s, was clearly overdue, especially given the political events of the past several years and the questions about the future of American democracy.

As historians, we search the past for clues to the origins of current debates and crises. For a brief period, Edwin Walker was a notorious figure of the militant Right. Describing his career and distorted ideology is my small contribution to putting the events of the present in their historical context. A successful biography should present new information about its subject or offer a unique perspective on what has already been written about a period of history. I hope I have done both. Any errors of fact or interpretation are entirely my own.

I am particularly grateful to Rand Dotson and LSU Press for seeing the potential in this biography, as well as the editorial team that worked to put this manuscript in its final form. Todd Manza and Catherine Kadair provided much-needed edits. I am also grateful for the assistance of Marisa Jefferson and Aryn Glazier of the University of Texas Dolph Briscoe Center for American History. They navigated me through the extensive Walker papers, providing me with the materials I needed in order to bring this enigmatic character into sharp focus. Rick Mikulski and Rosie Liljenquist at William and Mary as well as Tricia Gesner of the Associated Press were particularly helpful in tracking down crucial images.

Additionally, the following libraries and sources were invaluable: the Library of Congress; Hathi Trust; the John F. Kennedy Library; the Dwight D. Eisenhower Library; Mississippi State University Libraries Special Collections;

University of Mississippi Libraries; Mississippi Department of Archives and History; Emily Ward at the University of Arkansas Libraries Special Collections; the Johns Hopkins University Digital Collection; American Jewish Historical Society Archives; Old Dominion University Library; and the city libraries of Birmingham, Cincinnati, Milwaukee, Palm Beach, Tampa, Houston, Jackson, and Dallas.

I extend my thanks to Maura Olson, one of my most promising students, for her assistance in research, as well as my colleagues and friends Alicia DeFonzo, Sheri Reynolds, and Joyce Hoffmann. Once again, my lifelong partner, Maureen, has had to live with another writing project. She made valuable changes and suggestions for the first and final drafts, discovering the errors that missed my eyes. She continually urged me to write in a style that would appeal to a broad audience, because Walker's story, hopefully rescued from obscurity, is indeed a cautionary tale for our times.

THE INSURRECTIONIST

Introduction

> Unhappy is the land in need of heroes.
>
> —BERTOLT BRECHT

In the 1964 political thriller *Seven Days in May,* an American general, played by Burt Lancaster, leads a military coup against a president he naively believes sold the country out to the Soviet Union. As the plot against the government unfolds, the president tells his close aides in the White House that his greatest fear is realized. A nation confronted with a Cold War crisis and a web of conspiracy theories looks for a "man on a white horse."

In a brief moment, the audience is reminded that this fictional coup d'état is never too far from what could happen under the right conditions. The embattled president says that for some Americans, that savior on horseback was "a Senator McCarthy, for others it was a General Walker." Joseph McCarthy's name is remembered as the sinister face of an anticommunist hysteria that dominated American politics during the 1950s. The General Walker referred to is Major General Edwin A. Walker, the subject of this biography.

More than a half century before the January 6, 2021, attack on the US Capitol, Walker was charged with insurrection against the federal government. He was arrested on orders from the attorney general's office after he led, in a sea of Confederate flags, a deadly riot against the first African American attempting to register as a student at the University of Mississippi.

A half century before QAnon, Walker spoke darkly of the "control apparatus"—deep state actors in the State Department, the Pentagon, and throughout the government working with coconspirators in the Kremlin and at UN headquarters to create a one-world government. "Every American citizen is a target of infiltration and subversion," he said.[1] Here was a commander of US troops on the front lines of the Cold War in Germany advancing conspiracy theories of the John Birch Society well beyond the limits of believability. In Congress, Walker's case raised concern that high-ranking officers in the army and navy were engaging in political activities at the ideological nether regions. President John F. Kennedy took the issue seriously, urging that *Seven Days in May*, first published as a novel in 1962, be made into a movie as a warning that Walker and others in uniform peddling conspiracies of the radical Right were a threat to democracy.[2] The liberal *Christian Century* cautioned that if this militarism went unchecked, "we shall drift into dictatorship."[3]

Through the 1950s and into the early 1960s, Americans witnessed the threat of nuclear war, the Cuban Revolution that put Fidel Castro into power, and a challenge to white supremacy in the South. For some, it was a time of uncertainty and fear. Among the leaders of the ultra Right, the answers were easy—a hidden conspiratorial network. It is a reductionism common to a vast spectrum of extremism: a belief that every major change in society has a simple cause and a simple solution.[4]

It was during these transformative years that Edwin Walker became a hero of the most radical elements of the American Right, which was "sweeping like a prairie fire across the South and West," in the words of Fletcher Knebel, author of *Seven Days in May*.[5] Walker's prominent role in the right-wing ecosystem of the 1960s was highlighted in a December 1961 *Newsweek* examination of extremism, which featured his picture on the magazine cover with the headline "Thunder on the Right." Walker's appeal was his credentials as both an uncompromising southern segregationist and an heir to Joseph McCarthy's anticommunism.

In the wake of the Supreme Court's *Brown v. Board of Education* ruling in 1954, states' rights and state sovereignty became convenient dog whistles for preserving segregated schools and the South's structural white supremacy. Walker was the keynote speaker at a Citizens' Councils national leadership conference in 1963, presenting his case that the Supreme Court, under Chief Justice Earl Warren, was an arm of federal tyranny.

That fear of impending tyranny from Washington was the connecting tissue between the segregationist Citizens' Councils and other corners of the extreme Right. For those in the John Birch Society, this distrust of government manifested in opposition to Medicare, international treaties, UN membership, and federal aid for education. To the Birchers, the Democratic Party of the New Deal and John F. Kennedy's New Frontier was socialism, and socialism was communism.

Visions of a Great Conspiracy

These factions of American conservatism inhabited a darkened corner of unreality, envisioning one great plot by traitors at every level of government, the churches, universities, and even the PTA, with plans to mix the races and turn America over to their masters in the Kremlin. Medford Evans, who was one of Edwin Walker's closest confidants and, like Walker, a member of both the Citizens' Councils and the John Birch Society, called integration "communism in action."[6]

Joseph Lowndes, in his *From the New Deal to the New Right,* concludes that the antigovernment sentiment that guided the Birchers also served as an intellectual gloss for the emerging modern conservatism around William F. Buckley's *National Review.*[7] Buckley defended a philosophy of unfettered capitalism as well as hostility to egalitarian impulses. This small government conservatism of Barry Goldwater's 1964 campaign for the White House and Ronald Reagan's presidency, with their focus on low taxes and limits to social programs, shared the ultra Right's rejection of federal efforts to create a more just society.

While Buckley attempted to excommunicate the Birchers from what he termed responsible conservatism, the antigovernment ideology remained a common denominator of both the moderate and the ultra Right. Texas historian John Huntington, in his *Far-Right Vanguard: The Radical Roots of Modern Conservatism,* makes the case that Buckley's and Reagan's modern conservatism was erected, at least in part, upon a foundation established by groups like the John Birch Society.[8]

In the alternate reality of the right-wing fringe, however, there were those who viewed the Birchers as all talk and no action. Robert Bolivar DePugh, who led an underground antigovernment militia known as the Minutemen, was unambiguous about his intention: "Traitors beware! Even now the cross-hairs are on the back of your necks."[9] Edwin Walker mixed freely but discreetly among some of these more violent factions of the Right. Following his arrest for inciting a riot at the University of Mississippi campus, the FBI was concerned that Walker was providing financial support to well-armed Minutemen cells in Texas.

Although DePugh imagined himself the commander of an army of suburban warriors, there was a paper-thin delineation between the rhetoric of the Birchers and the Minutemen. Both were convinced that the time was fast approaching for an apocalyptic battle against Chinese soldiers in United Nations uniforms training across the Rio Grande. Walker gave voice to these delusions, and as a decorated senior officer who had served courageously in two wars, he was deemed credible by those on the far edges of conservatism.

Walker also gave voice to violent factions of the Ku Klux Klan, who differed from the Citizens' Councils only in tactics. Robert Shelton, the imperial wizard of the United Klans of America, offered Walker a white robe and an exalted title to head his operations in Texas. Walker declined the overture. He preferred to stand in the shadows of the "Invisible Empire," lending his advice and strategy learned in the course of a thirty-year military career.

Even the most radical of the violent ultras looked to Walker as their would-be fuehrer—the anti-Semitic National States' Rights Party praised him. But Walker rejected the invitation when a close friend with ties to the American Nazi Party sought to enroll him in their ranks. The swastika-wearing Nazis were a bridge too far for General Walker. He had served in the elite First Special Service Force in World War II, leading a predawn mission to take out German positions on islands off the French coast in preparation for one of the largest amphibious landings of the war.

While many on the extreme Right had hopes that Walker would lead a movement that could unite their disparate forces, he turned out to be a disappointment. He spoke the language of extremism but offered little in terms of ideas. He was an intellectually hollow character, only adept at projecting the fantasies of the ultras, with his imposing six-foot-three figure, dark suit, and white Stetson hat. Any political ambitions Walker had were stillborn in 1962, when he ran unsuccessfully for Texas governor. Despite his fiery rhetoric, Walker was an abysmal public speaker, and many conservatives found Walker "too esoteric for their taste."[10]

In addition, the mercurial Walker was not above physically assaulting news reporters. Attorney General Robert Kennedy considered Walker unstable enough to commit him briefly to a psychiatric hospital, following Walker's arrest at the University of Mississippi. Walker was a loner, reclusive in the years after he was gone from the headlines, holding tight to a secret double life, until one night in a darkened Dallas park. Walker's arrest for public lewdness essentially outed him as a deeply closeted gay man. This "most eligible bachelor" at the officers' club could be markedly defensive about his marital status. At a time when suspicions of homosexuality would destroy a military or government career, Walker was especially cautious, always portraying an image of hypermasculinity.

Although Walker appears, Zelig-like, at major historical moments, this is mainly the result of happenstance, as an unwitting actor. He was Lee Harvey Oswald's first target before assassinating President Kennedy. As a result, Walker was questioned by the Warren Commission and under scrutiny for his participation in a raucous demonstration against Adlai Stevenson's visit to Dallas only a month before Kennedy was murdered.

Walker was a reluctant commander of soldiers thrust into the center of the fight to admit African American students to Central High School in Little Rock, Arkansas. Walker was ordered by President Dwight Eisenhower to escort the Little Rock Nine to the schoolhouse door in the face of a taunting and vicious mob. It was ironic for this white supremacist to ensure the safety of the Little Rock Nine, but Walker was first and foremost an obedient soldier. In many ways, Edwin Walker did not drive events but was swept up in them.

Walker's complex story is evaluated as an anticipation of today's rise of authoritarianism and the assault on democratic institutions. The conspiracy theory and the "big lie" are the authoritarian's most potent weapons, and Walker was adept at using them. Before the advent of "fake news," Walker alleged that the nation's news media was hiding the truth of Soviet infiltration in every corner of our lives. Writing in 1961, journalist Alan Barth observed that the 1960s opened with "widespread fear arising out of real and imagined perils." This, he said, was not conducive to the rule of reason.[11]

In a 1961 memo to Attorney General Kennedy, labor leader Victor Reuther raised concerns that radical Right dominance of the radio was responsible for this widespread fear of conspiracies. As Nicole Hemmer notes in *Messengers of the Right,* the conservative movement was skilled at broadcasting its outlandish views to a significantly large audience.[12] It was a phenomenon going back to the Depression, when Father Charles Coughlin delivered his pro-fascist speeches to almost 30 million weekly listeners as the famed "radio priest." Additionally, right-wing periodicals proliferated in the 1960s as they received funding from wealthy donors. In the 1970s, direct mail pioneers like Richard Viguerie "created hair-on-fire fund-raising letters about civilization on the verge of collapse" to a bulging list of subscribers.[13]

Among the Right's media moguls were Texas oil millionaire H. L. Hunt; former dean of the Notre Dame Law School, Clarence Manion; and Dan Smoot. Hunt's *Facts Forum* and *The Manion Forum* were particularly influential. With virtually unlimited funds, Hunt could air his *Life Line* radio show on hundreds of stations regardless of its popularity. Hunt's *Facts Forum* pumped millions of dollars into conservative organizations, and his son Bunker Hunt, by far the John Birch Society's largest benefactor, also helped finance George Wallace's 1968 presidential campaign. As one member of Congress quipped, the expensive television and radio time purchased should "convince anyone that this is no pitiful group of bearded nuts grinding out handbills in a basement."[14]

They were also adept at grinding out letters to Capitol Hill—thousands, in well-organized campaigns. California senator Thomas Kuchel estimated that he received as many as six thousand letters a month from members of radical Right groups, "self-appointed saviors . . . preying profitably on the fears of Americans."[15] *The Manion Forum,* bankrolled by listener donations and subscriptions, could be heard on 270 radio stations and, as of 1962, seen on nearly fifty television stations.[16] Manion, who held a leadership position in the John Birch Society, also published and distributed Goldwater's *Conscience of a Conservative,* which was ghostwritten in 1960 by Buckley's brother-in-law, L. Brent Bozell.[17] The American Right of the 1960s was something of a family affair.

Dan Smoot, a former FBI agent and Dallas-based broadcaster, was far more articulate than Walker, but like Walker, Smoot created a fantasy that

America was secretly run by what he called the "invisible government." This interlocking directorate was just as extensive as Walker's "control apparatus." Here was the Council on Foreign Relations as orchestra leader directing a cabal that included major foundations, newspapers, TV networks, and both political parties. Whether it was the invisible government or the control apparatus pulling the strings behind a veil of secrecy, it was a frightening vision. In Smoot's dystopia, there were "a few sinister people . . . at the top of the pyramid [who] want America to become part of a worldwide socialist dictatorship under the control of the Kremlin."[18]

It is no wonder that Smoot was identified by one member of Congress as among the fright peddlers who "would create distrust of the president, the armed forces, the Supreme Court, Congress, the State Department, and our government generally."[19] Distrust of our elections would have to wait another sixty years. Smoot also used his weekly *Dan Smoot Report* to defend Walker, calling him a prime target of the "intellectual mafia."[20] That intellectual mafia, of course, referred to CBS, Walter Cronkite, syndicated columnist Drew Pearson, and the liberal elite of the Kennedy administration with their Ivy League degrees. These were the adversaries of real Americanism. It was an opinion shared by Buckley's very erudite *National Review,* Billy James Hargis's Christian Crusade, and the Dixie-playing radio show *Citizens' Council Radio Forum,* which featured interviews with Edwin Walker and his fiercest champion in the Senate, Strom Thurmond.

Tulsa evangelist Hargis provided Walker a platform to address the fundamentalist Right, giving him top billing as a featured speaker at his Christian Crusade Leadership School. Birch Society leaders Kent and Phoebe Courtney also gave Walker top billing at their Conservative Society of America conferences, on their radio program, and in publications. The Courtneys not only ardently promoted Walker's speeches and pamphlets in their *Independent American* but also encouraged readers to support Walker as a candidate for president.

Conspiracies, a sense of lost status, and even of betrayal, marked the height of the Cold War. Edward Miller, in his definitive biography of John Birch Society founder Robert Welch, *A Conspiratorial Life,* writes, "These were not usual times . . . Americans were anxious . . . They were getting ready to 'duck and cover' in the event of a nuclear attack from the Soviet Union that might come at any moment."[21] Walker, Welch, Hargis, and DePugh with his Minutemen were nourished by this fear and anxiety. As Miller notes, the conspiratorial style of politics that these men articulated remains potent today in the age of Donald Trump, Alex Jones, and Marjorie Taylor Greene.[22]

Just as Walker imagined a fast-approaching "worldwide supergovernment" planned behind the closed doors of UN headquarters, so too does today's extreme Right posit conspiracies about secret bases of black helicopters ready to swoop down, seize Americans' guns, and end US sovereignty. Instead of radio, the militant Right today exploits social media to deliver its refashioned brand of fear.

In their 1965 study of radical Right ideology, published in the *Journal of Politics,* Gilbert Abcarian and Sherman M. Stanage identify several key features. One is the uniquely American principle of the centrality of the individual, embraced by the traditional and libertarian Right. Any form of collectivism, Welch said, "is a European cancer" that leads to tyrannical government.[23] Goldwater, who failed to make extremism more palatable to the American voter, relied on the same rhetoric, saying, "The collectivists have not abandoned their ultimate goal—to subordinate the individual to the state."[24]

Abcarian and Stanage also point to fundamentalism as a core belief—that we must return to eternal truths, both biblical and secular. On the religious side, that can mean a literal interpretation of the Bible; on the political side, the call is for a return to authentic Americanism and constitutional originalism.[25] Walker and Billy James Hargis together embodied both the secular and the religious fundamentalist idea. In 1963, they joined forces, embarking on a cross-country speaking tour with dire warnings about political and moral decay.

Consequently, Abcarian and Stanage identify another pillar of the Rightist framework: the nation must be purified of this moral and political rot, which will lead to the restoration of an American golden age. The Far Right of the 1960s, like its current incarnation, idealized the past. To Walker and his followers, "Make America Great Again" would refer to the years before Franklin Roosevelt, or a time before lawless youth, decadence in the arts, and "perversion," as one group put it. The answer was "a great cleansing" and a "return to the sacred heritage of traditional Americanism."[26]

Those who flocked to Walker's side believed they were losing the battle to restore a vanishing moral and political order. It was "a long twilight struggle," Walker said, and time to save America was running out.[27] Major General Edwin A. Walker's career on the outskirts of American political discourse starts in Little Rock, when the nation faced the challenge of dismantling a house divided by race.

1

From Anzio to Little Rock

Edwin Walker was an unknown figure on the American Far Right when he took command of the US Army Military District of Arkansas in July 1957. It was only two months before Little Rock became the site of a major test of the modern civil rights movement. President Eisenhower insisted that Governor Orval Faubus comply with the law to allow nine African American students attend all-white Central High School. Although he was a staunch segregationist, Walker was an obedient soldier, a lesson first learned during his years at West Point. He waited dutifully in the background, prepared to follow orders from the president to ensure the safety of the Little Rock Nine.

Thrust unwillingly into the center of a dramatic confrontation over school integration, Walker for the first time publicly expressed absurd and dangerous white supremacist views that drew concern from journalists and army leaders.

In Walker's imagination, integration was a communist plot and part of a strategy to dilute the white race in preparation for a one-world government. Walker saw the world through the lens of an epic and imminent battle. He was a frequent speaker at groups like the Little Rock Kiwanis Club and the Reserve Officers Association, saying the war against communism "is on and everybody is in it." There was no room for negotiation and no coexistence on the battlefield, he said, referring to his wartime experience in Korea.[1]

Arkansas journalist Harry Ashmore recalled that his conversations with Walker over drinks "began to raise my hair." Ashmore described Walker as "a tall handsome bachelor . . . [with] a distinguished career as an artillery man in Korea." When taking command of his troops, "Walker's comportment . . . was a model of aloof correctness." Ashmore was alarmed when Walker spoke of his political views and "began to pass on to me . . . extreme right wing tracts devoted to the Communist conspiracy presumed to be controlling the government of the United States." This unidentified "they" in what later became known as the deep state was responsible, Walker said, for placing him in a position to advance the communist agenda to mix the races through school integration. Ashmore said he brought these disturbing notions to the attention of a general he knew at the Pentagon during a visit to Washington. Ashmore described it as "a public relations time bomb ticking away in the Little Rock command post."[2]

While Walker's service in World War II and Korea was well respected, he was certainly viewed as more than just mildly eccentric—one reason he was assigned to the backwater of the Arkansas Military District. During the crisis that unfolded in late September, Walker's superiors knew the usually inarticulate general should never stand before the television cameras. He was instructed to make no statements to the press.[3] As Ashmore recounted, a press office in Walker's headquarters "did the talking."[4]

The road to Little Rock had started three years earlier with a unanimous Supreme Court ruling that "separate but equal" was anything but equal and was unconstitutional. The court's 1954 *Brown v. Board of Education* decision overturned the 1896 Supreme Court ruling that codified the Jim Crow system of separating the races in public transportation, accommodations, schools, and just about every corner of public life.

Brown v. Board of Education would propel a civil rights movement already beginning to challenge segregation throughout the South. A year later, in a subsequent opinion referred to as *Brown v. Board of Education II,* Chief Justice Earl Warren ordered the district courts and local school authorities to take appropriate steps to integrate public schools in their jurisdictions "with all deliberate speed." In the summer of 1955, the National Association for the Advancement of Colored People (NAACP) sent out word to its members to petition local school boards to desegregate. As a result, 170 school boards in seventeen states received transfer requests from Black parents asking that their children be sent to currently all-white schools.[5] Opening Central High School to the Little Rock Nine would now test Eisenhower's commitment to racial equality. Though he was not a segregationist, Eisenhower was cautious when it came to civil rights and race issues. Integration moved slowly in postwar

America, but it received its first push with President Harry Truman's executive orders in 1948, which ended segregation in the armed forces.

The Eisenhower administration preferred to ignore the race issue as much as possible. During the Eisenhower years, Black employment in the federal government remained low.[6] As president, he was silent on the murder of Emmett Till in 1955, nor did he offer support to Rosa Parks that same year in the Montgomery, Alabama, bus boycott. Eisenhower met with civil rights leaders only once in his eight years in office, but he did respect the Constitution and the Supreme Court's interpretation of the Constitution. It was that, he said, "or we shall have chaos."[7]

To his credit, Eisenhower did order the integration of public facilities in the nation's capital, and on September 9, during the height of the Little Rock crisis, he signed the Civil Rights Act of 1957. It was the first federal civil rights legislation since Reconstruction, establishing a Civil Rights Division in the Department of Justice. The law also gave the federal government the power to enforce voting rights, a measure that was diluted by southern Democrats in Congress.[8] In the final analysis, Eisenhower walked a delicate balance; he was deeply conflicted, wanting to uphold the Supreme Court's decision but not to run the risk of alienating his southern friends and supporters.[9]

School integration in the southern states would not come easily or peacefully, as white resistance gained traction. Several southern governors adopted interposition resolutions that essentially declared that a federal law could be declared null and void. In 1956, under the leadership of segregationist senators Strom Thurmond of South Carolina and Walter George of Georgia, eighty-two House members and nineteen senators signed the Southern Manifesto denouncing the *Brown* decision as an abuse of judicial power.

The Citizens' Councils: "The Uptown Klan"

Just weeks after *Brown v. Board of Education,* the first of many local Citizens' Councils was formed in Indianola, Mississippi. From there, Citizens' Councils took root in every southern state, with 250,000 members in just two years. The Citizens' Councils billed themselves as respectable middle-class people from your small-town Rotary, church, or business community, not like the violent Klan. It could be considered "KKK light," or as some put it, the "uptown Klan."[10] Citizens' Council propaganda, which included a radio program billing itself as "the American viewpoint with a southern accent," portrayed desegregation as a "second vicious Reconstruction."[11] Even as General Walker would command US soldiers to protect the Little Rock Nine, his sympathies lay with the Citizens' Councils; he would later be a featured speaker on their Dixie-playing radio program and represent his home state of Texas in a Citizens' Council leadership conference.

An early test of the *Brown* decision came in February 1956, when Autherine J. Lucy, a Black graduate student, enrolled in the University of Alabama. However, after a violent mob attacked several buildings on campus, Lucy was suspended under the pretense that her own safety was in jeopardy. Eisenhower's attorney general, Herbert Brownell, expected that "a clash of historical importance was inevitable" between the president and political leaders in the South.[12]

Arkansas was a more moderate southern state than Alabama when it came to race relations, and the city of Little Rock already was moving in a progressive direction, motivated by ambitions to be a regional business hub. A city of about 117,000 in 1957, Little Rock had integrated buses and some motels and restaurants. Even Governor Faubus was regarded as more moderate on race issues than other southern governors and won a reputation as a southern-style populist during his first term. Colorfully described by *Time* magazine as a "slightly sophisticated hillbilly," Faubus was born in a village so far back in the Ozarks that the first paved road to the outside world was not completed until 1949.[13]

By the middle of 1957, the mood was shifting away from progressive politics. As the Citizens' Council was gaining adherents in the state, Faubus, up for reelection in 1958, was being pushed further to the right. To win another term, Faubus needed the segregationist vote, but he was well aware that the admission of nine Black students to Central High at the opening of the 1957 school year promised a violent reaction. As the first day of classes approached, Superintendent of Schools Virgil Blossom was threatened to the point of sending his family safely out of town.[14]

The Little Rock Nine were carefully selected by the school board as the first students to begin the process of integrating Central High School. They were chosen not only for their academic records but also for the lighter shade of their skin.[15] In August, the segregationist Mothers' League of Central High lost its case in court to block integration. On September 2, just two days before the doors to Central High opened, Governor Faubus ordered the National Guard to take over the building, citing "imminent danger of tumult [and] riot,"[16] but his true intent was to use the Guard to prevent the Little Rock Nine from entering the school. The next day, September 3, as many as two hundred National Guard troops encircled the building. The school board asked for a delay in admitting the students, but Federal District Judge Ronald Davies ordered desegregation to go forward.[17]

On the morning of September 4, when the Little Rock Nine showed up for class, led by Daisy Bates, the head of the Arkansas NAACP, they were met by a mob surrounding the school and blocking them from entering. It was on that morning that one of the students, fifteen-year-old Elizabeth Eckford, was spat upon and listened to taunts of "lynch her" as she held her books close to her chest. As the crowd of almost three hundred became more unruly and protected by Faubus's National Guard troops, the Little Rock Nine retreated.[18]

As tensions heightened, the school board went to court on September 5 to request a temporary suspension of the integration plan. That was rejected, but out of fear for the children's safety there would not be another attempt to enter the school for two weeks.[19] Meanwhile, Governor Faubus was losing ground as the Justice Department found there was no justification for calling out the National Guard. It was simply done to obstruct court orders and was not intended to protect lives and property.[20]

In a telegram to the president, Faubus said that integration was proceeding in the state's colleges and some public schools but had to go slowly, warning, "It is impossible to integrate some of our schools at this time without violence." Any blood that may be shed, Faubus wrote, "will be on the hands of the federal government." He also claimed he was being hounded by the FBI, that he was about to be taken into custody, and that his telephone was tapped.[21] All this was subterfuge, Eisenhower told the governor. In a terse reply, he said, "The only assurance I can give you is that the federal Constitution will be upheld by me by every legal means at my command."[22]

Just before 9:00 on the morning of September 14, the two met privately at Eisenhower's vacation retreat in Newport, Rhode Island. Faubus asked for "breathing room"—a delay to try to resolve the issue peacefully.[23] There would be little breathing room for the governor, however, and in the end Faubus assured Eisenhower that he would comply with the integration order. As *Time* magazine reported, "There were smiles and handshakes for the camera, then politely worded, carefully prepared statements." Eisenhower told the press he was confident the governor would "give his full cooperation in carrying out his responsibilities." Faubus issued his own statement that "the people of Little Rock are law-abiding, and I know that they expect to obey valid court orders. In this, they shall have my support."[24]

Despite his assurance to the president that the integration of Central High School would proceed, Faubus had no intention of yielding without a fight. It was a matter of federal overreach, his lawyers said. "The governor will not concede that the United States can question his discretion and judgment as chief executive of a sovereign state."[25] On September 20, Judge Davies ordered the National Guard removed and the admission of the Little Rock Nine to Central High. Faubus withdrew the guardsmen and promised that state and local police would maintain order. Eisenhower expressed confidence that the citizens of Little Rock would "vigorously oppose any violence by extremists."[26]

That same day, General Edwin Walker took his strategy, code-named Operation Plan No. 1, to the Pentagon in anticipation of a decision at the White House to deploy federal troops to Little Rock. Walker wanted a minimum number of army and federalized National Guard units under his command, and he made it clear that machine guns were to be left behind.[27] Walker also made a stop in Little Rock to assess the layout of the city. Dressed in civilian clothes, he circled the school until he was questioned by an Arkansas state trooper, who asked for some identification. After a brief argument, Walker finally identified himself by name, rank, and serial number.[28] One question that remained was the reliability of the ten thousand Arkansas National Guard troops if called upon to enforce the law. To get a sense of where the Guard stood, Army Chief of Staff General Maxwell Taylor ordered a survey that found widespread opposition to enforcing an order to integrate Central High School.[29]

Walker's Orders: Use Army Paratroopers as a Last Resort

On Sunday, September 22, the day before the Little Rock Nine were to make another attempt to take a classroom seat, Taylor gave Walker his final orders. The Arkansas National Guard, under federal control, would be prepared to enforce the court's order to escort and protect the students if violence broke out. Regular army troops would be there only as a backup, as a last resort. That role would be assumed by the 101st Airborne Division out of Fort Campbell, Kentucky. The paratroopers of the 101st could move quickly if needed. Walker, concerned that the sight of Black troops of the 101st could add fuel to the fire, directed the commander to keep any Black soldiers out of sight if the paratroopers were called into action.[30]

When the Little Rock Nine arrived on campus on Monday, September 23, as many as one thousand protesters easily smashed through the police barricades and raced toward the school entrance. Several journalists were assaulted, including three Black newsmen.[31] It was no spontaneous demonstration, said Little Rock mayor Woodrow Wilson Mann; it was well organized "by professional agitators [with] a concerted plan of action."[32] The nine Black students attended only three classes. With the mood outside still ugly by noon, Assistant Police Chief Gene Smith ordered his officers to escort the students out through a side door and into waiting squad cars.[33] The mob had won the first day's battle; it had "tasted blood and liked it," according to one report.[34] The *New York Times* called those outside the school "these creatures of unreason."[35]

Eisenhower, betrayed by the governor, was now faced with a decision. Should he use federal forces to carry out the court's order? The president recognized that the rule of law was at stake. Later that day he issued a proclamation ordering anyone engaged in preventing the students from entering Central High to "cease and desist."[36] Just an hour later, Army Secretary Wilber Brucker and Attorney General Brownell began to prepare for what they believed would be the inevitable use of force.[37] In addition, there was the question of America's image abroad, or as Eisenhower said, feeding "the mill of Soviet propagandists."[38] That evening, as army counterintelligence characterized Little Rock as "tense," Walker began to consider tactics.[39]

By 7:30 Tuesday morning, city police were encircling Central High with barricades, but as school opened, nine people were arrested, two of them armed. As many as forty-five were charged with vandalism in other parts of town. The Little Rock Nine would stay away again as Black leaders feared for the children's lives.[40]

Mayor Mann appealed to the White House to intervene. Conditions in Little Rock were "out of control . . . People are converging on the scene from all directions," he wrote. Describing a brawl on the streets and an overwhelmed police force, he said "the immediate need for federal troops is urgent."[41] In his recollection of the Little Rock events, journalist Ashmore wrote that with the violence allowed by the governor, the city "became the symbol of brutal, dead-end resistance to the minimum requirements of racial justice."[42] Mann knew the damage could be devastating to a city that aspired to attract investment. The city was growing, with a newly opened industrial district, but violence at the high school was sure to put a brake on businesses seeking to make a home in the state capital. Mann himself had been threatened earlier in the month with a cross burning on his lawn.[43]

Eisenhower knew it was time to act. Without a show of force, the crisis could fester and embolden other southern governors to defy court orders. He swiftly federalized the ten thousand troops of the Arkansas National Guard and dispatched one thousand troops of the 101st Airborne Division, the Screaming Eagles. They reached Little Rock by nightfall in twenty-six army vehicles.[44] In an address to the nation that evening, Eisenhower put the blame on "demagogic extremists" from outside Little Rock. He was clear that federalized guardsmen and paratroopers from the 101st under General Walker's command would not replace local law enforcement or assume the responsibility of running the city's school board.[45]

Predictably, Faubus called Little Rock "an occupied territory . . . by the naked force of the federal government." In a television address, he compared Walker's troops to the Soviet tanks rolling through Budapest just a year earlier, and even to the Nazi occupation of Paris. To Faubus, General Edwin Walker was commanding an invading force "against a defenseless state." As a southern governor, Faubus used the argument of states' rights to reject the Supreme Court ruling, and he took direct aim at Little Rock mayor Mann and the reporting of Harry Ashmore, which he called "slanted and distorted." These are the men, Faubus said, "who have sought to advise the president's palace guard."[46] Eisenhower's position from the beginning of the crisis was unambiguous: "Mob rule cannot be allowed to override the decisions of our courts."[47]

As soon as the president called out the 101st from Fort Campbell and federalized the Arkansas Guard, Walker was thrust into the position of quelling an insurrection on American soil. With the National Guard out of the hands of the governor, Walker could call on any Guard unit he would need to ensure the safety of the students. Reporting directly to General Taylor, Walker was instructed to use the absolute minimum force and "if he can get by with just standing there, so much the better."[48] Walker and his superiors in the Defense Department wanted to keep the 101st paratroopers back, shifting most of the burden of keeping the peace to the Arkansas Guard. Taylor told Walker, "the President of the United States is watching your move personally. Make it expeditious."[49]

Walker did press the Pentagon to send military police to Little Rock not uniformed paratroopers. "I had hoped and prayed," he said years later, "that the army would not become involved in that nonmilitary issue."[50] The army defended its use of the paratroopers, saying they could be quickly mobilized.[51] Although he objected to the president's order to deploy the army, Walker was a soldier first, recognizing his duty to carry out the will of the commander in chief. In orders to his troops, Walker was explicit that they were to "assist the civil authorities and not to interfere with them. Our personal conduct should be exemplary."[52] Walker carried out his orders with military efficiency, receiving praise from the national press.

By early morning Wednesday, September 25, about three hundred soldiers of the 101st, equipped with bayonets fixed to M-1 rifles, and gas masks, ringed the school, a five-story building on a campus occupying six city blocks. At the same time, Walker pored over maps and aerial photos of the campus and neighboring streets.[53] Walker instructed the soldiers that they were to line the streets at intervals of three yards and were to disperse any group of more than three adults within a mile of the school. Yet civilians were to be treated politely and addressed as "sir" and "ma'am" at all times.[54] Walker also ordered his men not to step onto private property even as hecklers taunted the soldiers from front lawns and porches near the school. Walker also wanted any African American troops out of sight and stationed at the armory.[55]

Walker Warns Students: Obey the Law, No Exceptions

With the campus quickly secured, Walker was ready to address the students in an assembly. Only about half of the 1,900 students came to school that morning, passing through a cordon of troops. Walker took to the stage for what was described as "a lecture on civics," a statement carefully scripted by Pentagon public affairs the night before.[56]

Walker started by reminding the students that the *Brown* decision found that segregated schools violated the Fourteenth Amendment, which guarantees equal protection, adding that every citizen has an obligation to obey the laws, "whether we approve of them personally or not. There can be no exceptions." In a deliberate and clear tone, he told students, "I intend to use all means necessary to prevent any interference" with the admission of the Little Rock Nine to class.[57]

To one newspaper's editorial board, Walker's stern message to the high school was "an undignified spectacle . . . warning [students] to behave, leaving an implied 'or else.'"[58] However, Walker's demeanor revealed something very different—a displeasure with deploying US soldiers, with bayonets fixed to their rifles, on the streets of an American city. He sounded apologetic at times, telling the students that his troops "are here because they have been ordered to be here." It was clear neither he nor the men under his command were there for moral reasons. Walker also tried to calm the fears of some at the sight of well-armed soldiers. "'They have been carefully instructed not to molest any law-abiding citizen."[59]

Bringing the Little Rock Nine to Central High later that morning had the feel of a well-prepared military operation as Walker dispatched an army station wagon flanked by two jeeps packed with troops to pick up the teenagers at the home of Daisy Bates. The caravan sped to the school to avoid possible snipers. Walker deployed a helicopter above as well. At 9:25 a.m. the students and their thirty escorts of the 101st were met at the steps of Central High School by about 1,500 protesters. Soldiers would be stationed outside every classroom but could enter only if the teacher called for help. Each of the Little Rock Nine was assigned a soldier to accompany them between classes.[60]

On that first day, Walker also had to respond to a bomb threat at about 11:00, evacuating the school for thirty minutes. Soldiers also seized eight individuals and turned them over to the local police. Walker was seen as a tough but fair military officer. School superintendent Blossom was impressed with his "erect, West Point bearing . . . efficient and direct who evoked loyalty in those around him."[61] Responding to reports of scuffles and rock throwing outside the school, Walker was clear and admittedly intimidating, saying, "There will be none when I get through."[62]

Although Walker and others in the Defense Department thought it best to limit the military's role in what was a domestic crisis, Walker's show of force that first day worked. By early Thursday morning, September 26, Walker had reduced the number of troops outside Central High from 319 to 270. He also decided to rely mostly on federalized National Guard members and had the paratroopers stationed out of sight inside a stadium behind the school. Walker also wanted to ensure that Arkansas guardsmen under his command, who may have objected to desegregation, were obeying their orders. After all, only a couple of weeks prior, these same guardsmen were blocking the entrance to Central High, preventing the Little Rock Nine from starting their first day of classes.[63]

The opening days of school also had their share of baseless rumors. Faubus alleged that soldiers were leering at girls on the athletic field and that some were inside the girls' locker rooms under the pretense of protecting the Little Rock Nine. He said that a number of female students were the target of "remarks" by troops in the corridors. The governor was catering to the fears of defiled southern womanhood, employing the incendiary language of race and gender.[64] In his television address on September 26, Faubus spoke of "sharpened, naked bayonets on the backs of school girls." He also falsely claimed that "teen-age school girls have been taken by the FBI and held incommunicado for hours."[65] FBI Director J. Edgar Hoover accused Faubus of spreading lies.[66]

In a letter addressed to Walker as "commander of occupation troops," Faubus asked the general to send in members of the Women's Army Corps to police the halls, "rather than the male soldiers armed with rifles, bayonets and billy clubs." Walker returned Faubus's letter unopened, leaving it up to Secretary of the Army Brucker to reply, saying the governor "stooped to making a vulgar charge." Brucker said an investigation found "no shred of evidence" to support Faubus's accusations. To Brucker, the governor was acting out of desperation in "an unworthy attempt to defame our American soldiers at Little Rock."[67] In a subsequent exchange between Faubus and Brucker later that month, Faubus again referred to Walker as a commander of occupation forces. Brucker told the governor he was replying reluctantly, "in view of your malicious disrespect to General Walker."[68]

When asked to show proof that soldiers were leering or invading the privacy of female students in their locker room, Faubus could only point to a picture of a paratrooper walking past girls playing softball, saying it was "an indication" that something could have happened.[69] Central High School teachers were largely divided on the subject of integration but overall were committed to teaching, whether the students were Black or white. To one Central High administrator, "education was our major responsibility and integration a secondary problem . . . My immediate goal was having the Black children in school as just ordinary children."[70]

Teachers seemed more unified in their opinion that armed paratroopers on the streets of Little Rock was an unnecessary display of force. Walker, to some, was a tyrant who intimidated the students with his tough talk about staying out of the way of his soldiers. One teacher referred to Walker's speech to the students about obeying the law as "a browbeating and we were stunned. It was actually impossible to believe that an American General was standing there talking to an American audience."[71] Another teacher, a chemistry instructor, referred to the general's "brutal talk."[72]

Georgia Senator: Walker's Tactics like Hitler's Storm Troopers

Predictably, Walker was criticized by some southerners in Congress for what they perceived as a heavy-handed approach. An Alabama congressman said troops under Walker's command attacked innocent bystanders. Georgia senator Richard Russell went a step further, saying Walker's soldiers held bayonets to the throats of unarmed citizens and absurdly comparing Walker's tactics to "the totalitarian police state methods [of] Hitler's storm troopers."[73]

Eisenhower shot back, saying, "I fail to comprehend your comparison of our troops to Hitler's stormtroopers," but assured the Georgia senator that the secretary of the army would look into any charges of "wrong-doing" under Walker's command.[74] Even four years later, Senator Russell would refer to Walker's tactics as arbitrary and intimidating. As a man, he said, Walker was "ruthless, opinionated and overbearing."[75] Brucker called these charges of brutality "loose and irresponsible," saying in one instance a protester tried to wrestle a gun from one of the soldiers, who was justified striking the man in the head with the rifle butt.[76]

Walker, who was a reluctant enforcer of the court's desegregation order, also took a beating in the conservative southern press. Under the headline "Bayonets at Their Throats," the *Dallas Morning News* called Eisenhower's response at Central High School "Reconstruction II." To these Texas editors, Washington viewed the South as "satellite provinces compelled by military force if necessary." As for Dallas, if "Walker and his self-called 'Battling Bastards of Bastogne' are flown in here, the bitterness engendered will flare up all over Texas."[77] The Memphis daily called on Walker to refrain from what it called "the promiscuous use of bayonets and rifle butts."[78]

Almost a full year after the crisis, Amis Guthridge, an Arkansas attorney running for Congress, demanded an investigation into Walker's actions in the days before the troops were deployed. The politically ambitious lawyer, who counted the Citizens' Council as a client, accused Walker of "casing" Central High School to prepare a "coldly calculated plot for federal troops to invade." Ashmore found Guthridge's claim ludicrous. Of course, reconnaissance would be a "normal procedure" for a senior army officer who might be leading a military operation.[79] Walker dismissed Guthridge with a terse "I'm not interested in what he says."[80]

Starting on Friday, September 27, Walker began scaling back his forces and gave permission for a football game and dance to take place as scheduled. He allowed off-duty soldiers to attend the game as well, without incident. By Monday, September 30, normal traffic patterns were restored, troops were without gas masks, and their bayonets were sheathed. Walker was feeling confident that the worst was over and handed over student discipline problems back to school administrators.[81] On October 1, Walker removed all of the remaining paratroopers, about two hundred men, and replaced them with guardsmen to patrol outside and inside the school. Walker predicted the change would be smooth and that the guardsmen, none of whom were from Little Rock, would perform their duties as well as the men of the 101st. Reassuring the city, Walker said with confidence, "Everything is in first rate order."[82]

However, the move was a mistake, as violence quickly erupted. A few students took advantage of the gaps in security and bullied the Little Rock Nine with shoving and threatening language. Some of the guardsmen, clearly hostile to the Black students, ignored this rising harassment. There was concern the Little Rock Nine would withdraw, handing a victory to Faubus and segregationists throughout the South. It was also clear that Faubus had no intention of maintaining order at Central High after federal protection was removed.[83]

On Thursday, October 3, with no other choice, Brucker ordered Walker to bring the soldiers of the 101st back to duty inside and outside the school building and to take more assertive measures to protect the children. Feeling the pressure from Washington, Walker also instructed his troops to be proactive—to "prevent disorder" instead of simply maintaining order.[84]

Walker also called for student bullies to be treated as adults when apprehended.[85] It was a strategy not just to quell a mob but also to make it clear the Little Rock Nine were well protected. NAACP leader Daisy Bates said she received reassurances from Walker that the students would be safe from harassment.[86] They would be escorted to the entrance of the school by National Guard troops, and from there the 101st would be responsible for their safety.[87]

The strategy worked and the situation slowly improved; by October 16, Walker reduced the presence of the 101st Airborne in Little Rock by half, to five hundred soldiers.[88] On November 7, he withdrew the hallway guard and the patrols around the school. Twenty days later, the remaining troops of the 101st Airborne had departed, leaving a federalized Arkansas National Guard presence in Little Rock of about four hundred men.[89]

Throughout that school year, the Little Rock Nine were subject to daily harassment and taunting. There were numerous bomb threats and the discovery of a homemade explosive in a student locker.[90] Walker believed that the school board would not take on more responsibility for protecting the students at Central High as long as a National Guard presence remained. Consequently, on April 24, Walker withdrew guardsmen entirely from the campus without incident.[91]

As graduation day approached, it became apparent that there were serious threats against graduating senior Ernest Green. Walker was reluctant for his National Guard troops to play a role in protecting Green, feeling that any considerable show of force would provoke a confrontation. On May 27, 1958, with Reverend Martin Luther King Jr. in the audience, the sixteen-year-old Green became the first Black student to graduate from Central High School.[92] Two days later, the last National Guard troops, defederalized and returned to the control of the state, pulled out of Little Rock.[93]

With the withdrawal of the National Guard, the Mothers' League of Central High School celebrated what they called Liberation Day. To these hardcore segregationists, Harry Ashmore and the *Arkansas Gazette* were traitors, turning over their operations to "hordes of foreign left-wing correspondents."[94] Faubus also saw the dark hand of the foreign press as the source of Little Rock's troubles. These foreign communists, he said, were in Arkansas to "foment race trouble."[95] Faubus was kind to Walker as the months passed. He had earlier castigated Walker as the head of an occupation force, but he and the soldiers under him were not to blame for the mistakes of politicians.[96]

While Walker was praised for his professionalism, he privately expressed the most abhorrent and explicitly racist ideas. He wove together an intricate fable that the Soviet Union, allied with "communist sympathizers" and traitors inside the government, was masterminding school integration. It was all part of a secret plan to subject the United States to a one-world dictatorship enforced by Asian and African soldiers.

As with any good conspiracy theory, there is a central place for the ambiguous term *brainwashing*. Walker believed the American public was being brainwashed to accept integration and was oblivious to the secret workings of the communist puppet masters. At Little Rock, the segregationist Citizens' Council tapped into these deepest fears, warning of "cunning methods to brainwash you into accepting racial integration by theaters, radio, television, athletic events, newspapers and magazines."[97]

After the troops left Little Rock, Walker repeatedly said that he regretted his role as commander of US soldiers in a "nonmilitary adventure." Decisions made in Washington, he said, were "contrary to my personal wishes," and on August 4, 1959, Edwin Walker submitted a letter of resignation to Secretary of the Army Brucker and General Lyman Lemnitzer, the newly appointed army chief of staff. Walker said that while he had looked forward to his next assignment, to the Seventh Army Europe, he could no longer be effective in the face of what he termed "a fifth column" responsible for appeasing the Kremlin and desegregating southern schools. "I have no further desire for military service with this conspiracy and its influences on the home front," he said.[98]

In a conversation that lasted about thirty minutes, Brucker told Walker that resigning would tarnish the career of a "courageous military leader with a fine record." Brucker denied Walker's request with the assurance that he could do more good fighting communism on the dividing line of the Cold War as commander of the 24th Infantry Division at Augsburg.[99] It was an assignment far from the battle lines of racial integration, but Walker's relocation to Augsburg would be his last military assignment in a career that had spanned most of his adult life.

An Early Start to a Military Career

Edwin Anderson Walker was born November 10, 1909, in Center Point, Texas, a small town about sixty miles west of San Antonio. Still a frontier town when Walker was a child, Center Point had a population of about five hundred. Walker described a happy childhood on a small but prosperous farm. It was a place where one's livelihood was at the mercy of weather that could at times "unleash great devastation."[100]

From the start, Walker was on the path to a military career. He graduated from the New Mexico Military Institute, a prep school that led him to West Point. Walker received a recommendation from Texas senator Morris Sheppard, a progressive Democrat who is most remembered as the "father of Prohibition," introducing the Eighteenth Amendment in Congress. Walker showed little promise at West Point, ranking in the bottom third of the class of 1931. An imposing figure at six foot three, Walker was an expert polo player, making the West Point team and earning a spot on the US Army team from 1934 to 1936.[101]

With the outbreak of World War II, Lieutenant Colonel Walker volunteered for hazardous duty with the First Special Service Force. With about

2,500 men, this elite combat unit was an early forerunner of the Green Berets. It was made up of Americans and Canadians, entrance standards were stringent, and the training was rigorous, including hand-to-hand combat, sabotage operations, airborne assault, night missions, and parachute jumping. Members also were trained by Norwegian instructors to survive and ski in difficult winter conditions.[102] Walker proudly stated, "there was never a force as highly selective as this one."[103]

Training in the forests near Helena, Montana, many of the volunteers were men accustomed to a rugged life—lumberjacks, forest rangers, hunters, and even gold prospectors. In addition, Canadian soldiers were a perfect fit, with experience in wintry conditions.[104] Walker's favorite expression, one newspaper reported, was "Check," "a word he snaps to indicate a mission has been accomplished or that he understands his orders." In a story that sounds more like the creation of a military myth, Walker's first airplane jump as a paratrooper started with a question, asked as he held his parachute: "How do you put this thing on?" Trained in artillery, Walker knew little about parachuting. After a five-minute demonstration, he climbed into the plane, jumped, landed safely, and turned to his subordinate with a simple "Check."[105]

The First Special Service Force was divided into three regiments, with Walker taking command of the Third Regiment. On August 15, 1943, Walker's men landed on the island of Kiska in the Aleutians to counter a Japanese attempt to attack North America. However, upon arriving at the desolate island, they discovered that the Japanese had already fled.[106]

When General Eisenhower ordered the commandos transferred to Italy in November 1943, Walker led his regiment through tough mountain terrain up the Italian Peninsula. Mostly at night, with a cold rain and limited visibility, they scaled Monte La Difensa in December. It was a major hill blocking the Fifth Army's advance, and it had few man-made trails. The men of the First Special Service Force endured constant enemy artillery fire, and in some cases, as fog lifted, they were engaged in close combat. For six days they held out atop Monte La Difensa.

In February 1944, they were at the Anzio beachhead, holding six miles of front against the Germans for ninety-nine days.[107] It was at Anzio that the First Special Service Force earned its nickname, "the Devil's Brigade," for its fierce night raids in blackened faces. Seizing key bridges south of Rome, and at one point taking two hundred German prisoners, they entered the city with other allied units on June 4, 1944.[108] One canceled operation—considered a suicide mission—was Operation Plough, a parachute jump into Norwegian territory to demolish hydroelectric plants.

Leading a Late-Night Assault on the French Riviera

The Devil's Brigade's last mission, on August 14–15, 1944, was the opening shot of a massive amphibious landing in southern France, code-named Operation Dragoon. Dragoon, like the Normandy invasion ten weeks earlier, was critical to the allied victory in Europe. Second in scope to the landing at Normandy, Dragoon involved an allied force of 300,000 men, a thousand ships, and several thousand combat aircraft. One of the goals was to seize the ports of Marseilles and Toulon. Eisenhower needed the major port in Marseilles to bring in American troops and supplies. The Dragoon landing would also liberate the southern two-thirds of France and advance up the Rhone valley to link with armies in the north.[109]

General Robert Frederick, who until this time had headed the First Special Service Force, was now called to lead the paratroopers on the day of the landing, and in turn, he handed a vital commando operation to Walker. Walker, now a colonel, would spearhead a predawn mission, making a surprise assault on the Hyeres Islands off the French Riviera. The seizure of the islands would open the way for the Seventh Army's landing at daybreak, August 15, along a forty-five-mile stretch of the Côte d'Azur from Saint-Raphael to Saint-Tropez.[110]

Shortly after midnight on August 14, Walker directed two thousand soldiers, faces blackened against the night with burnt cork, for the first blow against entrenched German positions. In rubber boats and kayaks, they came ashore on two small islands of the Îles d'Hyères, just five miles off the coast and west of the assault beaches.[111] Walker was supplied with intelligence from the French Underground and aerial photos that showed the Germans had a position on the Île du Levant, the easternmost island, which was only about a mile from one end to the other. The Germans were equipped with artillery that could pose a particular threat to troop transports offshore.[112]

Walker chose the side of the Île du Levant with the most difficult and dangerous terrain, steep cliffs and ravines. Some of his soldiers objected, calling it unacceptably risky. Walker told them the Germans would never suspect an attack from that end of the island and would likely have only a small force deployed there.[113]

Walker oversaw the operation from a command ship as about 1,300 men began scaling the cliffs of the Île du Levant. Another seven hundred were going ashore on another island, Port-Cros. They carried daggers for the quiet execution of enemy sentries. The artillery revealed in photos turned out to be drainpipes disguised to look like three menacing gun barrels. Walker's commandos succeeded in surprising a German garrison of about two hundred men taking cover in a cave on the western tip of the island.[114] One war correspondent described the assault as "Indian-style warfare . . . unusual for its emphasis on stealth rather than overwhelming firepower."[115]

Walker felt that continuing the mission was not worth the risk, that the islands were not much of a threat to Operation Dragoon. He reportedly signaled his superiors in the Seventh Army: "Two islands totally useless. Enemy batteries, dummies. Request permission, immediate departure."[116]

Three days after the massive amphibious landing, the German Army in southern France was breaking apart. Thousands of German prisoners were taken by the Free French. By August 27, Toulon was in allied hands, and Marseilles followed soon after. The entire Mediterranean coast of France was under allied control by September 9 as they moved north to join the Normandy invasion force.[117] Recalling his wartime experiences, Walker described the Devil's Brigade as "one of the finest ski, mountain, amphibious, and airborne commando units [which fought] with purpose, destroying the enemy."[118]

The First Special Service Force was officially disbanded on December 5, 1944, and by V-E Day Walker was in Oslo, overseeing the surrender of 300,000 Wehrmacht soldiers. Walker's efforts in World War II earned him the Combat Infantryman's Badge, the Senior Paratrooper Badge, the Silver Star, the Bronze Star with Oak Leaf Cluster, the French Croix de Guerre, the Norwegian Order of St. Olav, and the Order of the British Empire.[119]

Walker returned to the United States in January 1946, to the Army Field Artillery School at Fort Sill, Oklahoma. Later that year, Greece was engaged in a civil war as communist forces proclaimed a provisional government in the northern mountains. Preventing a communist takeover of the country fell to the United States and President Harry Truman's policy of containment through large-scale military and economic aid. Walker headed to the Pentagon at the opening of the civil war to manage the Defense Department's Greek Operations Desk, also making an official visit to Greece and Turkey.[120]

The Greek civil war was one of three Cold War battlegrounds that helped shape Walker's view that the West was locked in a fight for survival against an international, monolithic communist enemy. The second and third were in Asia—the Korean War and the defeat of Chiang Kai-shek's Nationalists in China. From 1951 to 1953, Walker was in Korea, leading a regiment and as an adviser to the Republic of Korea's First Corps. Walker also served as a deputy to the commanding general for prisoner-of-war affairs.[121]

The war began in June 1950, when North Korean forces crossed the 38th Parallel to invade the South. The Korean War was the first war in which the United Nations played a role, with sixteen countries sending troops, but the United States contributed 90 percent of the total and sustained more than 54,000 combat deaths. Walker saw some of the worst of the fighting, including the bloodletting at Heartbreak Ridge in September 1951, where he led artillery troops of the Second Division. They fired a record 22,000 rounds every twenty-four hours for fourteen straight days.[122]

The Korean War ended in a stalemate with the country divided. That outcome and the United Nations role in the war became an obsession throughout Walker's career. It was proof in his mind that America had been stabbed in the back by a communist-controlled UN in league with traitors inside the State Department.[123] Recounting his experience in Korea, Walker said even before deployment he was concerned that the war would not be prosecuted to total victory; "I had no interest as part of an occupation force. The general feeling [in the Defense Department] was that the war might end next week, or next month, which obviously would mean no victory."[124]

For Walker, "stalemate became a substitute for victory," and he called the North Korean prisoner of war cages a "monument to the censorship of victory on the field of battle."[125] In Walker's view, Douglas MacArthur, the almost mythic figure in the Pacific War against Japan, was denied victory in

Korea. MacArthur, who led UN forces during the first nine months of the war, ordered his troops, positioned at the 38th Parallel, to march up to the Yalu River at the Chinese border. He proposed a strategy to destroy bridges between China and North Korea, bomb military installations in Manchuria, and give the go-ahead to Chinese Nationalist troops to stage an assault against the mainland from Taiwan. President Truman sought a truce with the North and rejected MacArthur's plan to widen the war into China. MacArthur persisted, contending that China would lose in an all-out conflict.[126]

Contrary to orders, MacArthur issued a demand for immediate communist surrender. It did not end there. MacArthur was waging his fight in the court of public opinion, striving to forestall a settlement short of military triumph. On April 5, 1951, Republican Joseph W. Martin read on the floor of the House of Representatives a letter from MacArthur essentially charging the Truman administration with appeasement in Korea. On April 8, the Joint Chiefs of Staff endorsed a recall of MacArthur, citing the necessity of having a commander who supported the administration's policy on the war, and on April 11, Truman relieved MacArthur of his command.

Walker Calls MacArthur's Recall Truman's "Clown Trick"

Walker defended MacArthur's position against a truce, claiming that the communist North could have been defeated if MacArthur had been allowed to pursue the enemy. "We had the enemy on the run . . . We could have easily gone to the Yalu and stayed there." Walker also was convinced that China would not have been drawn into a conflict with American forces and that the war could have been won without the use of nuclear weapons. To Walker, the fear of a wider Asian war was a "fictitious and false assumption."[127]

Walker said North Korean forces were emboldened when Truman called General MacArthur back to Washington. "I watched the enemy increase the fury of his assaults . . . and the complete disintegration of [our troops'] morale." In what was often a deeply emotional tone in his writing, Walker said he led his soldiers to battle but "out of their sight, I wept over their predicament." As a military adviser to the South Korean First Corps, Walker recalled working "long nights in a hut high in the mountains overlooking the beautiful Sea of Japan, helping my Korean friends build an army in our image." It was clear, in Walker's opinion, that Syngman Rhee, a dictator who hindered efforts to end the war with a truce, was "a great anticommunist patriot."[128]

In Walker's conspiratorial fantasies, MacArthur had been punished by a president likely duped by a fifth column operating secretly inside the government. "At the fork in the road . . . MacArthur turned Right. A nation and its policy turned Left, betraying all of its friends in an invisible scheme—global conquest."[129] Years later, in typically caustic language, Walker referred to Truman as one who "pulled the greatest clown trick ever" in calling MacArthur back.[130]

Returning from Korea in July 1953, Walker was sent to the 82nd Airborne Division at Fort Bragg in North Carolina, but within two years he was back in Asia, this time Taiwan, as a senior military adviser to Chiang Kai-shek's Nationalist army. With Mao Zedong's victory in the Chinese civil war in 1949, Chiang Kai-shek's government and 2 million people fled to Taiwan. A divided China became a major theater in the Cold War.

By 1954, tensions were mounting between mainland China and Taiwan over the strategically significant Dachen Islands, and Quemoy and Matsu in the Taiwan Strait. In September, mainland Chinese forces began an air assault on the islands, which were controlled by the Nationalist army. In January 1955, Congress passed the Formosa Resolution, which gave President Eisenhower authority to defend Taiwan and the offshore islands, but little was done to support Chiang Kai-shek's desire to rule a unified China.

Walker was among those who believed that Chiang Kai-shek was betrayed in the same way that MacArthur had been denied victory in Korea. Truman looked at the balance of forces in China in 1949 and concluded that there was little they could do, short of intervention, to defeat Mao. Walker accused Truman of giving up on Chiang Kai-shek even as the Nationalist forces were anxious to engage the enemy. Using a term that he repeated later in defending his position that even nuclear war was an option, Walker said Chiang was a victim of "censorship of action."[131]

Career military men like MacArthur and Walker, who experienced the years leading to Pearl Harbor, believed that once one is committed to battle, there is no choice but victory. Walker would take that position, along with other war hawks, during the Vietnam War. Walker went so far as to suggest that US forces should have pushed the Soviets out of Berlin after the victory against Germany, or stopped the construction of the Berlin Wall even at the risk of a World War III. "We did not take advantage of all our soldiers' victory . . . and all of our sacrifices . . . in deference to the enemy, the Kremlin." Summits with the Soviets, going back to Yalta and Tehran, only proved, in Walker's mind, that coexistence is not an alternative to war.[132]

Returning to the United States from Taiwan, Walker would spend the next decade constructing a complex tale of a "control apparatus" inside the government that was acting in the interests of the United Nations in its secret plan to create a communist world government. Having his resignation from the army turned down after Little Rock, Walker was put in charge of the 24th Infantry Division, on the dividing line of the Cold War in Europe. His battle with the deep state had just begun.

2

Pro-Blue and the Red Conspiracy

With Little Rock behind him, Walker headed to Augsburg, a German city in the southern region of Bavaria. In the sixteenth century it ranked as one of the centers of European business and banking. Ravaged by a February 1944 British and US bombing campaign, Augsburg is one of those towns where street crews still find the occasional unexploded remnant of the war. Arriving at Augsburg in late October 1959, Walker took command of the 24th Infantry Division with its 750 officers, twelve thousand soldiers, and more than nine thousand dependents. Referred to as the "Shield of Bavaria," the 24th was considered among the top two best-run divisions in Europe, with its expert marksmen carrying home army awards for rifle and pistol championships.[1]

Walker came to the 24th with a plan. He started a rigorous, and somewhat unpopular, daily physical fitness program for the troops. The Bavarian winter of 1960 was particularly harsh, but Walker's men won praise for a NATO exercise in subzero temperatures. Walker was at the top of his game, clearly on his way to another star on his uniform. He maintained what the army called a high standard of readiness, with four hundred troops prepared to deploy at a moment's notice to anywhere in the world.[2]

The soldiers of the 24th were nicknamed "Taromen" for the division's taro leaf symbol. *Taro Leaf* was also the name of the base newspaper, and that's where General Walker's troubles began.

Aside from raising the bar on physical fitness, Walker had a second initiative—indoctrinating his troops about the threat of international communism. Only a month after taking command, Walker set up his Special Projects Office, dedicated to what he viewed as the cornerstone of winning the Cold War, psychological warfare. By October 1960, he inaugurated a series of lectures named Pro-Blue, carrying a startling warning of a plot to turn America over to communist masters in the Kremlin and their coconspirators in Washington.[3] In Walker's estimation, a treasonous US foreign policy since Franklin Roosevelt's presidency had allowed the "giant Frankenstein monster" of communism to slowly swallow large areas of the globe, with America the inevitable prize.[4]

Most Americans were unaware of this threat, he said, and part of the problem was that US soldiers were not getting the truth from their commanders. In base libraries like the one at the 24th Infantry Division, they were fed Leftist materials that "encourage accommodation with the enemy." Even *Stars and Stripes,* to Walker, was slanted to the left,[5] so he started filling the shelves with books with a distinctly conservative message, such as J. Edgar Hoover's analysis of communism, *Masters of Deceit.* A book by the head of the FBI would not raise any eyebrows, but one book did: *The Life of John Birch,* by Robert Welch.

Welch was the founder, and some would say dictatorial leader, of the John Birch Society, an organization that peddled the communist conspiracy to lengths that were well beyond the bounds of mainstream conservatism. Walker was still in Arkansas when he joined the John Birch Society in 1959, just a year after Welch opened his headquarters in Belmont, Massachusetts.

Born in 1899 and a graduate of the University of North Carolina, Welch made his fortune as an executive at a candy company best known for Junior Mints and a caramel on a stick called the Sugar Daddy. He made one run for political office—in 1950, for lieutenant governor of Massachusetts—but lost, and for a time in the 1950s he served as a vice president of the National Association of Manufacturers. *Time* magazine described Welch as "a balding, deceptively mild-mannered, retired businessman."[6]

Yet this soft-spoken candy maker was convinced that it was only a matter of time—maybe just a year or two—until the United States would be enslaved under a worldwide communist government operated from Moscow. Welch named his John Birch Society in honor of a Baptist missionary from Macon, Georgia, who was killed in China by communist partisans shortly after V-J Day. "He was the first casualty of World War III," Welch said, and for the Birchers, World War III was just getting started.[7]

As the Cold War and Fidel Castro's revolution in Cuba raised fears of a nuclear holocaust, the John Birch Society gained membership quickly between 1958 and 1961. Though Welch kept membership numbers and the names of prominent members secret, estimates ranged from twenty thousand to well over fifty thousand Birchers in more than one hundred chapters in thirty-four states.[8]

The Birchers had a simple answer to every debate in American politics—it was the work of international communism. It drove the civil rights movement and the Supreme Court ruling on school prayer. It led to divorce, inspired rebellious youth, and sold pornography. Even abstract art was suspect. Communist conspirators were behind fluoride in the water. Fluoridation was not an answer to tooth decay but an attempt by Moscow to impair Americans' ability to think, therefore making them more susceptible to communist propaganda.

The conspirator, Welch said, may be disguised as a patriot, a respected leader in labor, law, education, or "pose as a humanitarian liberal," without the slightest visible trace of any communist connection.[9] The John Birch Society, of course, would ferret them out and save America from the clutches of international communism. Most outlandish of Welch's fantasies was that President Dwight Eisenhower was a "dedicated conscious agent of the communist conspiracy." In his first tract, *The Politician,* written in 1954, Welch referred to "Eisenhower and his communist bosses . . . taking over our whole government, right under the noses of the American people."[10]

A military hero and popular president working for Moscow? That was enough for most conservatives. By 1961, the National Association of Manufacturers publicly distanced itself from Welch. Even such a dedicated anticommunist as J. Edgar Hoover was skeptical about Welch's aims. "Attributing every adversity to communism is not only irrational," Hoover said, "but contributes to hysteria and fosters groundless fears."[11] To those who wrote to Hoover for his opinion of the Birchers, he sent his pamphlet titled "Let's Fight Communism Sanely."[12]

A Barrage of Extremist Propaganda

Walker's Pro-Blue program was taken right out of the John Birch Society playbook, and that attracted the attention of a newspaper that was already feuding with Walker. *Overseas Weekly* broke the story in April 1961 under the headline "Military Channels Used to Push Birch Ideas." In its exposé of Pro-Blue, *Overseas Weekly* wrote that Walker was using his authority as commander and editor of the base newspaper, *Taro Leaf*, to subject his troops to a "propaganda barrage on the philosophy of the controversial John Birch Society."[13]

According to *Overseas Weekly*, the John Birch Society magazine *American Opinion* was available in the base library and on newsstands. Birch speakers William Schlamm and Edgar C. Bundy were invited to address the 24th Infantry Division. Schlamm advocated a preventive war against the Soviet Union, a dangerous departure from official Washington policy. Bundy, who wrote *Collectivism and the Churches*, claimed that American churches were infiltrated by communists. The list of Pro-Blue activities that would put Walker in hot water with the Pentagon included an essay contest with the subject "How to Stop Communist Infiltration of the Government."[14] In another case, he approved a skit taking a poke at Eisenhower for negotiating with the Soviet Union. An Eisenhower–Khrushchev summit was labeled a "submit" conference. The president's postwar diplomacy with the Soviet Union would always be suspect in Walker's mind. Eisenhower's presence in Moscow's Red Square in August 1945, reviewing a parade with Josef Stalin, was enough for Walker to declare that the architect of D-Day was not on the side of American "superpatriots."[15]

Although a 1958 National Security Directive encouraged commanders to educate their troops about communism, Walker's hysterical tone in Pro-Blue lectures went too far. In a chilling statement for a military leader, Walker charged that those who were not prepared for this life-and-death struggle with communism were guilty of treason. "The communists," he said, "have a savage plan of liquidation for a vanquished America."[16]

Particularly disturbing to officials in the Defense Department and in Congress were two Pro-Blue initiatives that were clearly political and a violation of army regulations. Just a month before election day 1960, Walker ran a front-page editorial in *Taro Leaf* urging troops and their families to consult a spiral-bound index before voting for senatorial and congressional candidates. Prepared by the Washington-based Americans for Constitutional Action (ACA), the index used a score sheet to rate candidates on their positions on the hot-button issues dear to Walker and the John Birch Society. The ACA index made its rounds throughout right-wing circles, appearing in Dan Smoot's *Report* and H. L. Hunt's *Life Line,* but in striving for respectability, the ACA boasted of a number of prominent Americans on its board, including former president Herbert Hoover and former New Jersey governor Charles Edison, the son of Thomas Edison.[17]

In typical fashion, Walker sounded a five-alarm emergency, saying the outcome of the 1960 election "will affect the future history of the world," with communist subversion making headway to turn America into "a pit of hell." Soldiers and their dependents were also given a phone number that connected to Walker's Special Projects Office. Callers could get more information on how the ACA rated candidates on their stance in eight broad areas, such as confronting communism, national security, or how candidates viewed the roles of government and the private sector. As soldiers, Walker said, "our weapons are not confined to those of physical warfare . . . The most important weapon of all—a mind capable of voting wisely."[18]

For the election of 1960, the ACA gave favorable marks to fourteen senators and 108 representatives they felt were hard-line enough on the communist threat. Presidential candidate John F. Kennedy was clearly soft on communism to the ACA, rating just an 11 out of 100.[19] Arizona congressman Morris Udall found Kennedy's zero rating on national security disgraceful, as he and other congressional liberals saw the ACA as a vehicle for advancing an extremist agenda. In 1963, the zero ACA rating for Speaker of the House John McCormack was so "patently ridiculous," according to one congressman, that Herbert Hoover, himself an ACA trustee, told McCormack he was distressed by the false implication that the Speaker was not a fiscal conservative.[20]

Former admiral Ben Moreell said he founded the ACA to "combat the shift to socialism" and "safeguard the God-given dignity of the individual."[21] Moreell, who headed a steel company, might be better known as the father of the Navy Seabees. He was also an author of tracts opposed to rent control, civil rights legislation, raising the minimum wage, federal funds for school construction, public television, and compulsory participation in Social Security, all of which were steps toward the "welfare state." As one member of Congress concluded, "the ACA is opposed to being in the twentieth century."[22]

Despite the ACA's claims that it was not a front for the Birchers, it was clearly in line with Welch's and Walker's views—"doing the devil's work in

American politics," in the words of California congressman Ronald Brooks Cameron. Addressing the House of Representatives in May 1963, several days before the ACA's Washington awards ceremony, Cameron said the organization was well funded by John Birch Society members, who accounted for more than a fifth of the $100,000 contributed in the three months before the 1962 midterm elections.[23]

Some of Robert Welch's inner circle were instrumental in funding the ACA, including Edison, who was both ACA treasurer and a member of the advisory committee of *American Opinion.* It was a "strange interlocking relationship" between people active in both the Birch Society and the ACA. In an impassioned appeal to fellow congresspeople to reject the ACA and refuse invitations to attend their Washington awards event, Cameron said, "Birch leaders are ACA leaders, Birch money is ACA money, Birch ideology is ACA ideology. It is not the conservatism acceptable to the American people."[24]

By urging soldiers under his command to consult the records of political candidates, Walker was disobeying army regulations. High-ranking officers are prohibited from using their considerable authority to influence the way their troops should vote. Just as egregious a violation of military conduct was Walker's January 1960 address to two hundred soldiers and their families at a meeting of the base PTA. Walker's address was explicitly political and extremist, saying Harry Truman, former secretary of state Dean Acheson, and Eleanor Roosevelt were communist sympathizers.[25] Walker's choice of the PTA fit neatly into a John Birch Society strategy. To the Birchers, parent–teacher association chapters were a perfect opportunity for Far Right indoctrination. Welch urged his followers to infiltrate and take control of their local PTA, a tactic that was particularly strong in the South and the West during the early to mid-1960s.[26]

A PTA with a right-wing agenda was in a good position to influence the rising number of suburban households to oppose government programs and civil rights legislation. In 1962, the New Mexico PTA convention was interrupted by heated debate over benign resolutions for federal aid to education or mental health programs, both anathema to the radical Right.[27] Welch viewed these debates as a battle with socialists—from the top of the organization down to the local level—for the hearts and minds of the "good people" who joined their hometown PTA.[28] In Congress, Morris Udall called Welch's tactics subversive, in that he was "advising his followers *not* to come out openly but to work through fronts to infiltrate the PTA."[29] The Far Right assault was so well coordinated that the president of the national organization warned local PTA leaders that they were a target of extremists bent on disrupting what would ordinarily be an evening of moms and dads discussing the new chemistry lab.[30]

At Augsburg, Walker became involved in evaluating the textbooks children were reading at the schools within his command. "I do not intend to see the soldiers' sons being taught one thing when the soldier is pledged to die for another."[31] Major Arch Roberts, who served under Walker in Augsburg and was the author of much of the Pro-Blue program, saw the United Nations Educational, Scientific and Cultural Organization (UNESCO) behind the training of young teachers, especially those graduating from Columbia University, to indoctrinate American schoolchildren to "forget love of their own country for loyalty to the world organization."[32]

At the core of the radical Right's communist fantasies was the belief that while the Soviet Union was the external threat to the free world, there was a more insidious threat: beware of hundreds of communists embedded in key federal departments and agencies, secretly pulling the strings of American foreign and domestic policy in the service of the Kremlin. Exposing this invisible government throughout Washington, even in the Pentagon, was front and center for the John Birch Society's *American Opinion* magazine: "We implore our readers to take the warning literally . . . We are faced with an open conspiracy."[33]

Walker's Deep State: The Control Apparatus

General Edwin Walker was a vocal exponent of this early incarnation of the conspiratorial deep state, which he called the "control apparatus." Those we think control our government, Walker said, are different from the ones we cannot see. This control apparatus, he said, deliberately enabled the Soviet Union to exert its influence throughout the world and was now threatening the very existence of the United States.[34] In some cases, he said, the actors are conscious agents of Moscow, or they are career diplomats in the State Department or civilian policy makers in the Pentagon who naively believe that peaceful coexistence is possible. Only men—such as himself—in uniform understand what is really happening.[35]

The conspirators in this deep state were not the only traitors; they were aided by thousands of pastors in every denomination and the majority of the press. Among Walker's "left-wing-controlled" journalists were Walter Cronkite and Eric Sevareid of CBS News as well as famed broadcaster Edward R. Murrow, who had challenged Joe McCarthy a decade earlier. To Walker, the press was conducting a propaganda war, seeking to keep Americans in the dark about the invisible enemy.[36]

It was the press that had exposed America's failures in the race to the moon, while "alleged Soviet successes are fabulously publicized," Walker said. The Russians should congratulate the *New York Times,* NBC, and CBS for making Sputnik one of the "greatest triumphs of psychological warfare."[37] Walker even alleged that the Soviet space program might be a hoax. Russian images of the moon, he claimed, were "very likely pictures out of our own *Popular Mechanics.*"[38] And it was the traitorous press that was responsible for distorting America's values overseas by not showing the "true image of a Christian free country."[39]

To Wisconsin senator William Proxmire, Walker's allegations were simply "a ridiculous absurdity." Proxmire called Walker "tragically and pitifully misinformed" and said that the fight against communism was too important to be left up to "the demagogues and the morons." In a lengthy speech in Congress, Proxmire said he was troubled that an American general was questioning the loyalty of the president, the commander in chief.[40] Walker's delusions seemed to have few bounds, as he said more than half of the American public is "communist influenced," including the fertile minds of youth.[41] FBI Director Hoover, who kept a lengthy dossier on Walker through the 1960s, said "self-styled experts on communism" were putting out erroneous information "tailored to echo personal idiosyncrasies."[42] The *New York Times* editorialized that Walker and the Birchers were "lost in a world of fantasy, finding communists everywhere, even under the bed."[43]

Walker's Pro-Blue pronouncements from Augsburg came as the Kennedy administration was dealing with Cold War crises from Berlin to Cuba to

Southeast Asia. The president was continuing negotiations started by Eisenhower to get a nuclear test ban treaty with Nikita Khrushchev. Learning of the *Overseas Weekly* exposé, Kennedy, worried about political extremism in the upper echelons of the military, called for an investigation.[44] Coincidentally, the *Overseas Weekly* story ran the very week of the disastrous Bay of Pigs invasion of Cuba, when about 1,400 anti-Castro guerrillas failed to initiate a counterrevolution. Kennedy was on the defensive against critics on the right as he took the blame for not ordering air strikes, leading to a humiliating defeat. To Walker, that day was "a death sentence for Cuban patriots."[45]

In a press conference during the week he ordered the Walker investigation, Kennedy told reporters that the general and his allies in the John Birch Society should focus their attention on the rise of communist aggression in Southeast Asia and not "the loyalty of President Eisenhower, President Truman, or Mrs. Roosevelt, or myself." The president told reporters that despite considerable obstacles to a nuclear test ban treaty with the Soviet leader, he had instructed negotiators in Geneva to "press on."[46] Yet here was a high-ranking officer of the army telling his troops that any arms control deal with Moscow only strengthened the hands of the Communists. The Limited Nuclear Test Ban Treaty was eventually signed, in 1963, after eight years of talks between the superpowers, but Walker was dead set on preventing any détente, even if it meant overstepping his bounds as a uniformed officer.

Walker indeed had stepped well beyond army regulations. On April 17, 1961, just four days after the *Overseas Weekly* hit the newsstands, Walker was summoned into the army's Heidelberg headquarters, relieved of his command, and demoted to a staff job. The major general was now working at the level of a colonel.[47] Walker also lost the chance to become commander of the VIII Army Reserve Corps at Austin, Texas, along with any possibility of earning a third star on his uniform. Several days later an army investigation was started, led by Lieutenant General Frederic J. Brown, the acting inspector general. Another of Walker's superiors, Lieutenant General Harrison Davidson, advised Walker to be "candid and complete" when questioned.[48]

As Brown conducted his investigation, Walker was anything but candid, answering many questions with a curt yes or no. In some cases his answer to a question was so unclear that it had to be repeated. His reply was often a defiant "I have nothing to add, sir." Walker also invoked the military equivalent of the Fifth Amendment. Article 31 of the Uniform Code of Military Justice allowed Walker to refuse to answer a question if his response might be self-incriminating.[49]

Defending Pro-Blue, Walker strenuously denied that his aim was to advance the John Birch Society. He was a committed anticommunist even before joining the Birchers, saying he had spent some of his own money alerting people about the danger from Russia. Calling Pro-Blue an "educational program," Walker objected to those who used the term *indoctrination.*[50] It was designed, he insisted, to teach impressionable young minds the virtues of patriotism, citizenship, and moral principles.[51] More than that, he called Pro-Blue "character guidance" and said that molding a corps of Christian warriors led to a decline in delinquency, higher morale, and even an uptick in church attendance. He was equally proud of marching his men through Munich in a NATO parade "with flags flying and armor bristling."[52]

On June 12, at the conclusion of Brown's investigation, Walker was given a verbal admonishment, essentially a dressing down by General Bruce Clarke, commander in chief, US Army Europe. Because it was not entered as a written part of his military record, the admonishment was the lightest rebuke Walker could have received. Yet it was a humiliating experience for a man who was part of one of the elite fighting forces of World War II to be told that his "improper actions reflected unfavorably upon you, this command, and the US Army." Walker was also reminded that he had failed three times to heed the warnings of superiors about engaging in overtly political activities.[53] Clarke said that while Walker had an outstanding military record and that "no one can question General Walker's sincerity of purpose," he did conduct activities on base "that were contrary to the long-standing customs of military service."[54]

Outright Attacks on Democracy

Brown's report noted that several Pro-Blue materials distributed to the troops, including *The Life of John Birch,* were "nonfactual, biased and inflammatory." Guest speakers, such as Schlamm and Bundy, were also flagged by the inspector general as making remarks that were extremist in nature.[55] A particular concern to army investigators was a John Birch Society pamphlet, *The Pentagon Case.* Part of the Pro-Blue reading list, it was a critique of the military leadership and could lead some soldiers to question their loyalty to the chain of command. This kind of literature, said Brown, was destructive to morale.[56]

Drew Pearson's "Washington Merry-Go-Round" was one of Capitol Hill's most widely read political columns, and Walker's troubles were a frequent subject. Pearson noted that some of the Pro-Blue speakers made assertions about Protestant clergy and the Supreme Court "that could only be described as crackpot." As for Walker's use of *Taro Leaf* to advance his political agenda, Pearson said some articles amounted to "outright attacks on democracy."[57] In particular, one Birch Society article reprinted in *Taro Leaf* asserted that American democracy was well on its way to becoming a "mobocracy." The United States, the article concluded, is "a republic not a democracy. Let's keep it that way."[58] If the disturbing content of Pro-Blue was not enough, the inspector general found that some of Walker's lectures became "heated and intense, with the use of excessively strong language."[59]

One of Walker's strongest defenders in the Senate, Arizona's Barry Goldwater, thought the inspector general's report had nothing more damning than Walker's rough language. "I have been in the army. I have used excessively strong language," Goldwater said. As the GOP's candidate for president in 1964, this equally tough-talking Westerner promised to stare down the leaders in the Kremlin. With regards to Walker, Goldwater warned of reaching the point "where we have a bunch of namby-pambies as our generals."[60] To the inspector general, the word that more accurately described Walker was "eccentric." That prompted South Carolina senator Strom Thurmond to respond, "God knows, I wish we had more Americans who are eccentric if they are the type of General Walker."[61]

The army's chief legal officer, Major General Robert McCaw, saw a more serious problem than mere eccentricity. By urging his troops to consult the Americans for Constitutional Action index, Walker had used his rank as commander to influence soldiers and their families how to cast their vote, which was a clear breach of Army Regulation 355-5: "Editorials concerning political campaigns, and editorial comments, analyses or interpretations . . . will not appear in authorized Army newspapers."[62]

Additionally, Walker ran up against the Hatch Act and similar statutes that protect federal employees from political coercion in the workplace. Walker may have broken a law that prohibited using his official authority to interfere in the outcome of an election. For that, Walker could face jail time.

As McCaw stated that the editorial in the *Taro Leaf* directing troops to the ACA index did violate army regulations and provisions of the Hatch Act, Walker dug in his heels, saying that his intent in publicizing the ACA index was only to encourage those in the 24th *to* vote. "I urged the soldiers to think for themselves. I never pressured any of them" to vote for one candidate or political party over another. Accusations of breaking the law were "a slander on my character and reputation," Walker said.[63] Drew Pearson wrote that this was patently false; it was a definite case of disregarding the rules and federal law, but the army ended up handling Walker "with kid gloves."[64]

While Pearson called for stricter punishment than a simple dressing down, the Pentagon leadership recognized that a trial would be a prolonged undertaking with intense and emotional publicity likely unfavorable to the government. A conviction would by no means be a certain result. On the other hand, some senior officers in the Defense Department felt that Walker's immediate reassignment before the results of the official army investigation unfairly judged him as guilty of a crime. To them, *Overseas Weekly* was accorded more decency than a battle-tested veteran.[65]

Adding to the dilemma, McCaw said that many of the witnesses to Walker's Pro-Blue program "were already claiming recollection difficulties." The bottom line to the army was that it would be difficult to win a case, and even if they did, the punishment would be no more than a reprimand, given Walker's "brilliant combat record and sincerity in attempting to fight communism."[66] Secretary of Defense Robert McNamara agreed, saying the military had more pressing national security issues and that he feared a trial would be an unnecessary distraction.[67]

To those who believed in the strict separation of the armed forces from partisan politics, Walker's Pro-Blue was more than troubling. It was dangerous. An editorial in the *New York Herald Tribune* called it "repugnant to our democratic heritage . . . that a military officer should attempt to impose his own political philosophy upon citizens entrusted to his command."[68] However, the editors of the *New York Mirror* felt that Walker was unfairly treated—and silenced—*because* of his political views. They asked why an officer's preference for his own country over Soviet Russia should be a crime.[69] The cold warriors of the *New York Daily News* wondered why the army did not hold *Overseas Weekly* to the same scrutiny.[70]

With a circulation of about fifty thousand and available on newsstands near US bases throughout Europe, *Overseas Weekly* was controversial in its own right. The tabloid was so well known for its coverage of scandals and vice that some servicemen referred to it as the "*Oversexed Weekly.*" In Walker's estimation it was "the most perverted and corrupt reporting ever devised."[71] He alleged the "subversive and immoral" *Overseas Weekly* was intent on forcing him out from the very beginning of his command. The newspaper was an agent of the Left, he said, with the express purpose of tearing down the work his Pro-Blue was doing to make the soldiers of the 24th into disciplined fighters. The newspaper was provoking enlisted men to undermine the authority of army leadership—stirring up "mutinous feelings," he said. Walker's sharp indictment did not hold up in an Army Intelligence review of *Overseas Weekly*, which found nothing about the newspaper that would be deemed subversive or a threat to national security.[72]

Walker Declares War on *Overseas Weekly*

Then there was the issue of payback—a vendetta, Walker said—by its editors and by one reporter in particular. He said that shortly after arriving at Augsburg, both he and the newspaper's editors recognized each other as "natural enemies." The editors compiled a dossier of his statements that could be magnified and distorted, Walker said.[73]

About four months before the *Overseas Weekly* story on Pro-Blue, Siegfried Naujocks, a West German journalist, questioned troops about Walker's mental health. Walker already had a reputation for impulsive and erratic behavior. When Naujocks told several soldiers he had a medical report that showed Walker was suffering from a brain tumor, Walker barred Naujocks from the base and required any other *Overseas Weekly* reporters to have an army escort when visiting the 24th.[74]

Overseas Weekly editor John Dornberg raised the stakes when he made it clear that either Naujocks would be allowed on base or the newspaper would expose Pro-Blue as a John Birch Society program. It was nothing short of blackmail, Walker said. To make matters worse, Walker remarked, "We have communists and we have the *Overseas Weekly.* Neither one is one of God's blessings to the American people." This was enough for Dornberg, and he sued for slander.[75]

Dornberg lost his case, and by mid-May 1961, the general took the offense and sued Naujocks for slander. Walker won in a Frankfurt court when Naujocks was unable to produce the medical report he said proved that Walker was suffering from a brain tumor. In addition, an army doctor testified that Walker was in good health.[76] Four days after the verdict, Naujocks resigned from the newspaper. *Overseas Weekly,* Walker said, was from the beginning intent on the "sabotage and infiltration of my training program."[77]

Walker was not through with *Overseas Weekly,* asking the army chief of staff to remove the newspaper from base newsstands, but the request was denied.[78] Walker was not alone in wanting to ban the newspaper. Starting in 1953, *Overseas Weekly* was distributed in Europe through an arrangement with the much-respected *Stars and Stripes.* In May of that year, *Overseas Weekly* was banned at some bases in Europe for its criticism of army policies and for stories and pictures that by today's standards would be considered G-rated.[79] In October 1960, an air force installation in Spain tried to remove the paper, but in each case, after threats of legal action, *Overseas Weekly* was returned to newsstands.[80]

Citing press freedom, the *Washington Post* asked whether complaints about sexy pictures were just an excuse to get *Overseas Weekly* off the newsstands when in fact it was the newspaper's "persistent reporting" that some base commanders wanted suppressed. Further, the *Post* editorial praised *Overseas Weekly*'s journalistic tenacity. "The *Overseas Weekly*'s trouble is not the girlie pictures that can be pinned up but the reporting of facts of military life that can be pinned down."[81]

Press freedom was not the issue for Walker's defenders in Congress. Texas Representative O. C. Fisher said Naujocks was seeking, and in some cases paying for, damaging information with the sole purpose of smearing the general and the US Army. Thurmond held up a copy, asking his fellow senators if a "picture of almost naked women" was healthy for "our men overseas who are already lonesome."[82] Fisher pointed to one story about British strip clubs in the Soho district of London, "with explicit details, extent of stripping and the like." It was a sleazy tabloid that specialized in "debauchery," Fisher said. Arkansas congressman Dale Alford would pull no punches, alleging that Naujocks had been a Nazi propagandist during the war, a charge that was not substantiated.[83]

Salacious reporting about London strip clubs was of little interest to army brass. They objected to stories that put American GIs in a bad light, depicting them as rowdy and disrespectful to Germans. The newspaper portrayed American soldiers as brutal and criminal, stirring German resentment against the American presence, Walker said. Allegations that *Overseas Weekly* wanted to drive American forces out of Germany would be difficult to explain, given the newspaper's dependence on American servicemen for its revenue.[84] *Overseas Weekly* editor Dornberg defended the paper as "a free and uncensored" voice available to American military personnel in Europe.[85]

Drew Pearson compared Walker's fight with *Overseas Weekly* with that of another general a decade earlier. Lieutenant General Donald Booth, as commander at Okinawa, pressured the *Okinawa Star* to fire one of its editors. Booth disapproved of reporting about protests by Okinawans over the firing of test missiles from the island. Booth also threatened to bar the newspaper from post exchanges as a way to put it out of business if they printed any stories about the persistent problem of prostitution. Pearson said Walker used the same tactics against *Overseas Weekly* to censor stories that were not favorable to his command, but he said *Overseas Weekly* "had the courage to go ahead with the [Pro-Blue] exposé."[86]

With news that Walker was in hot water with the army, his defenders made their displeasure clear to congressional offices. Letters and telegrams poured into Senate offices in what appeared to be an organized campaign. Armed Services Committee chairman Richard Russell of Georgia said he received as many as 1,200 of them. One claimed that Walker had been "throttled" because he stood up for "good old-fashioned American guts."[87] Those who called themselves "Friends of Walker" sent out equally emotional appeals for money to cover his legal fees. Soliciting contributions, a Midland, Texas, orthodontist saw the general as "a bolt of lightning [who] has started a fire that will burn the Godless communists from our country and the world."[88] Walker himself pointed to past praise from Secretary of the Army Wilber Brucker during his command at Little Rock. After visiting the 24th in July 1960, Brucker had told Walker, "I have the deepest admiration for the manner in which you are carrying out your responsibilities," pointing to enhanced physical training and troop readiness.[89]

Prior accolades were not enough to save his job and reputation. However, Walker's removal apparently had little effect on the soldiers; as one officer put it, the news "went in one ear and out the other" as far as the average enlisted man was concerned.[90] There also were those in the 24th who registered their disagreement with the way the army handled Walker's dismissal. The wife of one officer called the *Overseas Weekly* article part of "an organized smear campaign" and said Walker was popular among the troops even after some grumbling about his tough morning workouts.[91] Richard Flynn, who worked on Walker's special projects staff, said, "We all needed to boost our moral values and that's what Walker was trying to do." Flynn, who was responsible for stocking the base library with copies of *American Opinion*, also pushed back on those who accused Walker of using his authority as the commanding officer to recruit his soldiers to the John Birch Society. "He didn't push Birch stuff on his troops. He put the information on the barrelhead and let them choose."[92]

For those who took Edwin Walker's side, his only mistake was his zealotry,[93] and it was that zealotry that elevated Walker to the level of a spiritual leader in the minds of his acolytes. A certain cult of personality made Walker into a crusader riding into battle against overwhelming odds and the absolute evil of communism.

Walker was building "spiritually motivated fighters for freedom," said Congressman O. C. Fisher, who was among the Texans behind their native son. It was no surprise that the Texas Senate passed a resolution asking the Department of Defense to return Walker's command. The legislators referred to Walker's military record in two wars and his "unshakeable loyalty to his beloved United States of America."[94] Senator John Tower, elected in May 1961 to Vice President Lyndon Johnson's Senate seat, was also in Walker's camp, at least until Walker's verbal flubs on Capitol Hill made the general a political liability to mainstream conservatives. The Walker case led to three sets of congressional hearings between September 1961 and April 1962.

In early September 1961, Secretary of Defense Robert McNamara was called before a Senate panel to explain Walker's treatment by the army. Recognizing divisions in both Congress and the Pentagon, McNamara straddled the fence. He called out *Overseas Weekly*'s sensationalism, saying it was "repulsive" and that the newspaper did attack Walker "viciously."[95] But the general's case was about a uniformed officer going well beyond what is allowed in troop education. To McNamara, it was regrettable to see a talented combat officer publicly reprimanded, but "each man is responsible for his own behavior."[96]

In the packed Senate hearing room, Walker's supporters interrupted loudly in some cases, prompting Senator Russell to threaten to have them removed. When he was asked whether Walker's disregard of army regulations was an intentional move to usurp civilian control of the military, McNamara took the cautious approach, telling senators that Walker only made a mistake in judgment. He was, for all his faults, "a patriotic, highly motivated individual."[97]

"Free from the Power of Little Men"

Edwin A. Walker realized he would fade into obscurity with a new assignment managing troop training in faraway Hawaii, but the defrocked general had other ideas. On November 2, 1961, Walker submitted his resignation, giving up a $12,000 annual pension. He could now enter the political arena unrestrained, as a civilian. "I am absolutely [an] uncensored, unmuzzled citizen . . . It will be my purpose as a civilian to attempt to do what I have found it no longer possible to do in uniform."[98] The editorial board of the *New York Times* welcomed Walker's resignation from the military, writing, "Any officer who wears the uniform of his country must accept certain inhibitions upon his conduct and the free expression of his own views. The general had clearly stepped across the line that distinguishes soldier from politician."[99]

In Walker's view, his long military career was no longer useful to save America from the enemy. To his mind, he claimed, "we are at war, we are infiltrated, we are losing that war every day."[100] In a speech in Chicago three months later, Walker said, "My aim and purpose has not changed. This is to keep the American eagle flying and not see it caged or become a dead duck."[101]

Not everyone in the top echelons of the Defense Department was eager to let him go. General George Decker, who served as chief of staff of the army, said he had confidence in Walker's ability and urged him to remain in the armed forces. He told Walker it would be "in the best interests of all" if he moved to another command, but Walker was through. Walker, said Decker, "was a rather strong-willed person."[102] In a parting statement to Congress, Walker declared that in resigning he was now "free from the power of little men," free to continue his personal fight against the communists at America's doorstep. "I have no desire for compassion or sympathy," he said, and accepting retirement with its benefits "would be a compromise with my principles."[103]

Yet the general was not free from the power of Congress and would soon be summoned to appear on Capitol Hill as some asked, Why was a decorated military veteran of two wars silenced? Others, however, would ask, How can we ensure civilian control of the military? By mid-November, shortly after his resignation, Walker began mounting a defense through a new venture, the American Eagle Publishing Company. It was basically a Dallas printing company run by one Robert Surrey, whose political affiliations included American Nazi leader George Lincoln Rockwell.[104]

Taking a hysterical tone that confirmed the worst fears of his friends in Washington, Walker accused the Defense Department of conducting a purge because it had been hijacked by communists intent on muzzling senior officers and advancing a "no-win" Cold War policy. In his American Eagle pamphlets *The Military Purge* and *The Victory Purge,* he labeled it all a plot, of course, by a "political commissariat to control the thoughts, beliefs, and objectives of the soldiers, sailors, and airmen."[105] The army, Walker said, was to become "a tool of the police state," and as for the American people, they were being brainwashed—a term Walker used often.[106] In the estimation of one journalist, this was astonishing and disturbing language of thought control and Red forces prepared for imminent warfare.[107]

To make matters worse, Walker was set to embark on a speaking tour, and it looked like he was considering a run for political office. Senator Tower, as well as Walker's attorneys, tried to talk him into lying low until after he testified before Congress. Walker was not doing himself any favors when he was unplugged as he was a poor speaker and oftentimes combative. Congressman Samuel Devine of Ohio expressed concern that Walker's enemies in Washington were trying to portray him as a potential dictator or "a little psycho." It was a tactic helped by the general's own erratic behavior.[108]

Despite the words of caution, Walker went ahead, encouraged by those who saw him as a lone voice in the wilderness sounding the alarm of a grave threat to America as a free nation. His speaking engagements attracted sizeable crowds, standing ovations, and some people with signs urging him to run for Texas governor or even president. Walker was defiant, saying, "I was charged with nothing, I was found guilty of nothing and I was punished for nothing."[109]

General Clyde J. Watts was Edwin Walker's lawyer, closest adviser, and friend from prep school days. Throughout Walker's career, Watts came to his defense inside and outside the courtroom. As Walker basked in the applause from adoring fans from Los Angeles to Dallas, Watts applied some much-needed damage control. Watts said critics ignored Walker's "wonderful combat record comparable to that of any General in any Army of the world." And as for those who questioned his irrational fears of a "Washington–Moscow plan" for a world government, Watts appeared to be in full agreement with his client. "Our problem is that we do not have enough Ed Walkers who have the conviction to look this Godless enemy in the eye."[110]

Watts drew a comparison between Walker's treatment and that of two other military leaders, Billy Mitchell and, especially, Douglas MacArthur. In 1925, General William (Billy) Mitchell publicly blamed navy leaders for the tragic crash of the airship *Shenandoah* that killed fourteen crew members. Mitchell said that certain admirals as well as members of the army's general staff were incompetent and criminally negligent by not giving greater consideration to the anxieties of the pilots. "It was almost treasonable," Mitchell said. He was a zealous advocate for investments in aircraft and could see, fifteen years before Pearl Harbor, that a victory over Japan would be won by air power. Mitchell was court-martialed for his accusations, but MacArthur did cast the only vote against conviction.[111] Like Walker, Mitchell resigned from the armed forces and continued to speak out. Sounding a lot like Walker, he said, "I became so fed up with the way things were being conducted that I thought I could do more outside the service than inside it."[112]

Watts also compared the army's decision in Walker's case to President Truman's recall of Douglas MacArthur from command of American forces in Korea. Like MacArthur, who had wanted to win the war by bringing the fight to China and was recalled for it, Walker believed he was being silenced for calling for total victory over the Soviet Union. In resigning from the army, Walker said he and MacArthur were treated ruthlessly for "daring to speak the truth . . . In defeat, I am in good company."[113]

While MacArthur had always held firm to the belief that uniformed officers answered to the civilian leadership in the Pentagon and White House, Korea was a turning point. MacArthur questioned whether "the members of our armed forces owe primary allegiance to those who temporarily exercise the authority of the [president] rather than to the country and its Constitution."[114] This was a central point for Walker as well. Truman's "appeasement" in Korea, he said, was now Eisenhower's and Kennedy's appeasement in arms negotiations with the Soviet Union.

When asked about Walker, Truman simply said, in the plain-speaking style of the former president, that he "talked out of turn and he got just what was coming to him, just like MacArthur did." Truman said MacArthur and Walker were free to express their view of the battlefield, but "when a man is in the military service, the President of the United States is his commander-in-chief and he takes orders." When questioned by reporters about Walker's claim that he was being censored, Truman bluntly replied, "I'd have muzzled him if I were president."[115]

In April 1962, a year after the *Overseas Weekly* story became front page news, Walker testified before a specially convened Senate committee. It was the first time for the public to see Walker up close, and to many, his performance raised questions about his mental stability. Walker was supposed to appear in late 1961, but senators were divided over a number of procedural matters, including semantics.

Walker's allies prevailed to scrap the negative-sounding Senate "investigation" for the more neutral "inquiry." The fact that Walker was evasive with the army inspector general also led Strom Thurmond to persuade the committee to give Walker more time to prepare. Months before, Senate staff had reviewed hundreds of pages of documents and visited several military installations.[116] Mississippi senator John Stennis, who chaired the proceedings, promised a serious discussion of the facts "conducted in an atmosphere of calm" and promised to bar any "spotlight-grabbing" personality clashes.[117] Although friendly to Walker, Stennis cautioned that the public remarks of military officers should be consistent with policy coming out of the White House. America's allies and adversaries alike should not get confusing messages from the military and civilian leadership, but censorship of the views of men in uniform should "be within reason and not based on caprice or pettiness."[118]

On the first day of the hearings, Walker took an hour to read his thirty-one-page opening statement. Described as "trim and taciturn," Walker could barely express himself. Flanked by his lawyer, Clyde Watts, and Medford Evans, a leader of the John Birch Society, Walker seemed over his head when questioned. Watts and Evans frantically scribbled answers on index cards or whispered in Walker's ear. At one point an exasperated Nevada senator Howard Cannon told Walker, "If you don't mind . . . I would like to have your views and not those of Dr. Evans or Mr. Watts."[119]

Walker went on the offense early, producing letters from top military leaders, including General Lyman Lemnitzer, who praised the Americans for Constitutional Action voting index.[120] When pressed by Senator Henry Jackson of Washington State about whether he would object to officers consulting the liberal Americans for Democratic Action political index, Walker said "that would be their right and they certainly could do it."[121] Yet Walker defended his decision to use only a conservative political index, saying that troops in Europe had plenty of access to liberal or "Leftist" reading material, such as *The Nation, New Republic,* and *Bulletin of the Atomic Scientists* magazines stocked in base libraries. Walker falsely claimed that these highly respected magazines "follow the Communist line."[122]

In a terse exchange with Walker, Senator Cannon asked if President Kennedy's 11 percent rating on the conservative index implied that Kennedy, as senator, voted "against the constitutional principles of our government 89 percent of the time?" In one of his exasperating nonanswers, Walker's reply was that the numbers were open to anyone's interpretation.[123]

Throughout the questioning, Walker held to his stark and simple good-versus-evil view of the world. Walker told of a complex network—the control apparatus that had forced him out of his command. "The real control apparatus will not tolerate militant anti-communist leadership."[124] There it was again: the general's ironclad certainty that the American public was blind and unprepared for the hidden "internal enemy" of communists behind the scenes. Walker advanced some bizarre fantasies: The Kremlin was compiling a dossier on him, starting with his deployment to Little Rock. The unseen puppeteers of the control apparatus were then behind his deployment to Augsburg, where he would be an easy communist target. Walker called it "entrapment" before the skeptical Senate panel.[125]

War in the Fourth Dimension

Some of these conspirators, he charged, were working inside McNamara's Defense Department. Pentagon public information officers, led in Washington by Arthur Sylvester, intimidated officers from taking a harder line on communism in their troop education programs. Walker quoted an air force major who said that after making several appearances to talk about the nature of communism, "the ax fell" and he was under Defense Department investigation.[126] With no basis in fact, Walker said public information officers in the Pentagon are "subservient to the power, influence, and propaganda of the national mass media." He even recommended that the system of public information in the military should be scrapped altogether.[127]

Like Joseph McCarthy a decade earlier, Walker singled out the State Department as a deeply embedded nest of traitors. Walker's theories again ran well beyond the edge of believability. In the Walker fantasy, the control apparatus secretly running the State Department was responsible for giving the communist conspirators open access to every American institution, even the classroom. An ordinarily sympathetic Senator Stennis asked incredulously, "You mean there is a direct connection between the State Department and high schools?" Walker's answer confounded the Senate panel as he revealed a hidden campaign of psychological warfare—or as he put it, fourth-dimensional warfare—against the entire American public. With words that sounded more appropriate for science fiction or an episode of the TV series *The Twilight Zone,* he intoned, "Every man alive is in the fourth dimension. Nobody can get out of the fourth dimension, and this is the dimension the communists are operating in."[128]

When he was asked to explain what he meant by the "real control apparatus," Walker said it was made up of sinister men in power willing to sell the country out. Who were these men behind the control apparatus? Evasive at first, Walker said he was not ready to name names, but senators pushed the general further. It was a step too far, even for his friends in the committee room, as Walker said that he questioned Secretary of State Dean Rusk's commitment "to our sovereignty, security, independence."[129] General James A. Van Fleet, the former commander of ground forces in Korea, thought Walker was completely out of line.[130]

The Kennedy men at the State Department, especially Dean Rusk and Walt W. Rostow, were favorite targets of the ultra Right. They were, in historian David Halberstam's estimation, the "best and the brightest" of the Kennedy White House, but in Walker's mind they were professorial eggheads and appeasers of international communism. The armed forces, Walker said, were being "purged to conform to the no-win plan of W. W. Rostow."[131] Walker told members of Congress that Secretary of State Rusk and Rostow, the Yale-educated chair of the State Department Policy Planning Council, were party to policies that led to the transfer of large areas of the world to the Soviet Union. "This is the hidden State Department policy being implemented by Mr. Rusk and being withheld from public view." When asked about Walker's accusations, Rusk simply said it was not worth commenting.[132]

Walker claimed that the control apparatus embedded in the State Department was intentionally driving the CIA to underestimate Soviet military strength. Behind this deception was Rostow, who had taught economic history at MIT before joining the Kennedy team as a foreign policy adviser.[133] Academics, "the sadistic Harvard associates of the Kennedy brothers," were particularly suspect in Walker's mind. He stated further that Rostow was secretly on the CIA payroll while teaching at MIT, giving him the opportunity to betray his country in some unspecified manner. Officials at MIT called Walker's allegations nonsense, and Rostow himself did not feel it was necessary to respond.[134]

When he was asked if he had someone in the Department of Defense in mind as part of this treasonous cabal, Walker was quick to name McNamara aide Adam Yarmolinsky. "I question [him] one hundred percent," he said.[135] Yarmolinsky, who held the title Special Assistant to the Secretary of Defense, was already suspect in the eyes of the ultra Right. He was a New Yorker, Jewish, educated at Harvard, and in sync with the Ivy Leaguers of the Kennedy White House. He also pushed for locating military assets near desegregated communities, a position that raised the ire of southern politicians.

At a time when innocent adolescent curiosity about communism could land a person in trouble years later, McNamara was put in the position of defending Yarmolinsky—which he did. Yarmolinsky admitted that at the age of fifteen he and a friend went to a meeting of the Young Communist League. It was 1937, a time when many young people became curious about the political party that was packing Madison Square Garden during the worst years of the Depression.[136] Pentagon officials said that while Yarmolinsky was working closely with McNamara, he was not involved in making decisions regarding military policy, nor was he involved in the decision to discipline Walker.[137]

Nonetheless, Walker broadened his attack on Yarmolinsky, accusing Yarmolinsky's mother, a celebrated poet and professor at Columbia University, of being an active member of the Communist Party. Yarmolinsky, said Walker, "is known throughout the Defense Department as an operator . . . and his activities have aided communism."[138] McNamara issued a short response to the accusations, underscoring that he had full trust and confidence in Yarmolinsky, who was instrumental in reorganizing and modernizing the management of the Pentagon.[139]

As a result of Yarmolinsky's support for civil rights legislation, his appointment as the deputy administrator of the War on Poverty program in 1964 was nixed. President Lyndon Johnson needed southern support to pass the legislation, drafted largely by Yarmolinsky. The price for votes in Congress from a bloc of southern Democrats was to dump Adam Yarmolinsky. In the opinion of newspaper columnists Rowland Evans and Robert Novak, "the Yarmolinsky sacrifice" was aided by the "constant vilification from Edwin Walker, John Birch zealots, and the fright peddlers."[140]

The term *fright peddler* might well have been applied to Walker's bizarrely constructed writings, distributed widely to extremist groups. Yet, to some observers, after two days of testimony, Walker appeared to be more pathetic than sinister. Missouri senator Stuart Symington found it "rather sad in some ways that we are having this hearing."[141] Washington reporters covering Walker's testimony concluded that these intricate conspiracies of an invisible apparatus existed only in "Walker's overwrought imagination." It was good, the editors of the *Washington Post* wrote, that his ideas and state of mind were there for the country to see. "He stands today not merely unmuzzled but undone."[142]

Some were relieved to see that Walker's appearance before the Senate would sideline any chance of him winning as a candidate for political office.[143] Washington columnist Mary McGrory, who called Walker "the muzzled martyr," said his answers lacked logic, including his "lightning-quick non-sequiturs." Even Strom Thurmond and John Tower would later regret giving Walker a platform.[144]

The hearings were not without drama. Periodically, Senator Stennis had to ask Walker's supporters in the crowded committee room to quiet down. George Lincoln Rockwell, leader of the American Nazi Party, with its headquarters in nearby Arlington, Virginia, paid a visit to the hearing room. He said he was there to applaud the general, but he was swiftly escorted out for not removing a swastika pin on his lapel.[145]

Some asked whether it was all just political theater. Even weeks before Walker stepped under the bright lights of the Senate committee room, the military correspondent for the *Detroit News* asked whether Walker's actions would justify a "convulsion in Washington."[146] The Walker case was not political theater, however, to those who saw a deeper threat to the nation's democratic values and civilian control of the military. Edwin Walker was not the only man in uniform who some said posed a danger. As the country further examined the extremist ideologies in barracks and officers' clubs, they realized that Walker was only the most prominent member in an underworld of fright peddlers.

3

Military Men on the Fringe

The case of General Edwin A. Walker pitted two powerful southern senators against each other—J. William Fulbright of Arkansas and South Carolina's Strom Thurmond. Was the military voice being censored by overzealous bureaucrats in the State and Defense Departments, as Thurmond claimed, or was Walker, as in Fulbright's opinion, just one of several in uniform undermining US policy with talk about deep state communist sympathizers.

In January 1962, Admiral Arleigh Burke and Lieutenant General Arthur Trudeau were called to Capitol Hill. Burke was asked if he believed military officers were being "muzzled," a term Thurmond used. While he did not believe that was the case, Burke said his own speeches were edited too liberally, "and very peculiarly at times." Burke, who retired in August 1961 as chief of naval operations, defended Walker and his fellow officers: "Who else knows as much about military affairs? Officers are not blind and dumb and stupid. American security is their business."[1]

Burke, who saw action in the Solomon Islands in World War II, pushed back on Defense Secretary McNamara, who defended censoring one of the admiral's particularly hard-line speeches. McNamara was clear that it was not appropriate for men in uniform to offer their opinions on foreign policy. Burke said that while he agreed with McNamara's policy, he objected to a public rebuke of not only him but also any officer who might step out of line.[2] Washington columnist Drew Pearson, who credited Burke with greater mental stability than Walker's, said the admiral "suffer[s] the failings of some combat officers. He forgets the Constitution and seems to think that foreign policy is in the hands of the military."[3]

Republican critics of Kennedy's arms control efforts, like Senator Karl

Mundt of South Dakota, saw the issue as a battle between the politics of diplomacy and taking a tough stance with Nikita Khrushchev. Was McNamara keen on editing harsh anticommunist language from speeches and programs like Walker's Pro-Blue so the administration could continue negotiating with Khrushchev on a nuclear test ban treaty? The defense secretary responded to the administration's critics, saying officers needed to use better judgment, adjusting, for example, their comments before a delicate two-power summit or arms treaty talks. It was a way to ensure the generals were on the same page as the policy makers in the White House. It was critical, in the tensest years of the Cold War, to avoid confusion on the part of allies and adversaries about America's foreign policy objectives.[4]

In one example, McNamara said blunt criticism of the Soviet Union was deleted from a 1961 speech by General Trudeau, the army's chief of research and development. The editing was made because of negotiations with the Kremlin in early January of that year over the release of the two surviving crewmembers of a downed RB-47 spy plane over Russian territory. McNamara said the deletions were done in a way to preserve the substance and sense of the speech but that "certain potentially provocative language was removed."[5] With negotiations concluded, he might not make as many deletions, "but tomorrow or six months from now, my answer might be different."[6]

It was Thurmond, one of Walker's most vigorous defenders in Congress, who pressed the hardest against McNamara. He told McNamara that while his concern over censorship went back to the Truman and Eisenhower years, he saw tighter restrictions on speech in the first few months of the Kennedy administration. Censors in the Defense Department, he said, were carrying it too far in removing references to the Kremlin's stated goals of victory over the West.[7]

McNamara refused Thurmond's repeated demand to release the names of those who removed critical comments about Soviet policy. Thurmond asked whether they failed to fully grasp the threat of communism. Was there a pattern of omitting the worst facts about the Soviet regime? With an air of condescension, he asked whether "some civilian assistant in the Pentagon" was best qualified to educate the American people about the dangers of communism.[8] Senator Richard Russell of Georgia went so far as to ask whether those in the

Defense Department who reviewed and edited speeches were properly cleared to weed out any who might be disloyal or, even worse, Soviet agents. McNamara assured the senator that the FBI conducted a thorough background check on anyone taking a job in the Pentagon.[9]

Critics of New Frontier liberals in the Kennedy administration, like David Lawrence, the *New York Herald Tribune*'s military reporter, compared the editing of officers' speeches to censorship behind the Iron Curtain.[10] Not to be outdone, the Scripps-Howard military writer called those who reviewed speeches for statements that ran counter to administration policy "political commissars."[11] Even one of the Roosevelts got involved. Edith Kermit Roosevelt, writing in the *Augusta* (Georgia) *Chronicle-Herald,* said the Communist Party was cheering any effort to silence military officers. Suspecting a conspiracy, this granddaughter of Theodore Roosevelt urged Thurmond "to find out who in high government places is seeking to discredit our distinguished American leaders."[12]

One of those leaders she had in mind was General Trudeau, who said that some revisions to his speeches clearly came from the State Department. However, others could not be identified, which he said gave him "cause for wonder" about their motivation. Like Walker, Trudeau viewed the Cold War as a life-and-death struggle with a global communism intent on enslaving the world. Trudeau also agreed with Walker about the deep state, warning ominously that communist "dangers lie within our borders."[13]

Defense Department rules about what could or could not be said were ambiguous, in the opinion of syndicated columnist George Sokolsky, who was a friend and defender of Joe McCarthy. Although McNamara said officers were just instructed to use good judgment and restraint during a period of international tension, Sokolsky asked how it would be possible for a military man to address the threat of communism without saying something negative about Soviet Russia or China.[14]

With generals and admirals speaking out of turn, McNamara recognized he had to clarify Pentagon policy. It seemed that the Defense Department had little control over the public pronouncements of military officers, who made as many as eight hundred speeches between mid-January and September 1961.[15] Whether in uniform or not, McNamara said that anyone serving the nation's defense should confine themselves to military matters in their public appearances.[16] Any speech with foreign policy implications would be automatically submitted to the State Department for review and recommended changes. McNamara would not back down on charges that the revisions to an officer's speech could be capricious or politically biased. Both State and Defense Department reviewers, he said, apply "reasonable standards" when making deletions.[17]

The Communist Cell Next Door

The case of Edwin Walker generated another debate in Congress and the nation's press: what to do with troop education programs that went rogue. Senator Fulbright found that Walker's Pro-Blue was not the only example of military indoctrination that reflected an outsized and largely false Cold War hysteria. Seminars were presented under the names of Project Action, Freedom Forum, Project Patriot, Strategy for Survival, and Fourth-Dimensional Warfare. Fulbright said that while these seminars might appeal to the prevailing views of many in the armed services, they presented a potential threat to civilian authority and to American democracy itself.[18]

The efforts of two navy admirals, Robert Goldthwaite and Walter Schindler, were particularly worrisome to Fulbright. Their Project Alert struck an ultra Right chord, rejecting negotiation with the Soviet Union in favor of relying exclusively on military strength. Started in 1959, Project Alert seminars also encouraged military personnel and their families to identify elected officials who were soft on communism and to "demand [they have] a more patriotic attitude." Like Walker's Pro-Blue, they tied drug use, crime, and lax public morals to communist influence in the schools.[19] A Project Alert leaflet carried the foreboding message, "In all probability there is a communist cell operating in your community."[20]

Project Alert reached considerably more personnel than Pro-Blue, with seminars at naval air stations in several states, and in some cases attendance was required. Like Pro-Blue, Project Alert took its John Birch Society message to local PTAs and extended its reach even further by joining forces with veterans' groups. Just as he defended Walker, Thurmond was equally supportive of Admiral Goldthwaite, saying he was unafraid to tell Americans that it was not enough to confront the external adversary in Moscow or Havana; it also had to be done on the home front. Goldthwaite was the victim of a "smear campaign for so-called far right extremism," Thurmond said.[21] But it was not "so-called" extremism to the seventy-seven-year-old patriarch of the Left, Norman Thomas, who considered Goldthwaite "as militant as Walker, if not more so."[22]

That militancy was frighteningly evident when World War I flying ace Eddie Rickenbacker shocked even some conservatives attending one of Goldthwaite's Project Alert events by calling for a preventive war against the Soviet Union.[23] Eisenhower and Kennedy were careful not to stoke the embers of the Cold War into flames, so the bellicose statements of a prominent war hero like Rickenbacker were particularly troubling. Someone with Rickenbacker's stature was bound to influence public opinion that war with the Soviet Union was an option. Walker, who was a Project Alert guest speaker in December 1961, also saw military victory as a strategy, even at the risk of nuclear war. "Our objective is not peace, but freedom," he said. In resigning from the armed forces, moreover, Walker quoted his idol Douglas MacArthur, who said, "There can be no compromise with atheistic communism. It must be all or nothing."[24]

Walker was fond of quoting another general who crossed the line in political pronouncements, Major General Orvil Anderson. In 1950, Anderson was removed as commandant of the Air War College after also making the case for a nuclear first strike against the Soviet Union. Walker repeated Anderson's troubling assertion that he could command a bomber aircraft to destroy the Soviet atomic weapons program and that when he came before God, "I think I could explain to Him that I had saved civilization."[25] Walker even suggested that the decision to push the nuclear button should be in the hands of the generals, not the president. As for a nuclear holocaust, Walker seemed blithely unafraid; after all, he said, the appeasers in the government have "magnified radiation hazards and the fear of nuclear weapons."[26]

Columnist Drew Pearson, who was unsparing when it came to Walker, said loose talk of hitting the Soviet Union preemptively or leaving it up to men like Walker to decide when to launch nuclear weapons was no different than forces inside the Kremlin pushing Khrushchev to take a more belligerent approach to the West. "We have the equivalent of Moscow's 'war is inevitable' faction in Washington . . . Right wingers in the USA breathing down

Kennedy's neck and Right wingers in Russia breathing down Khrushchev's neck make it harder to negotiate for peace," Pearson said.[27] One prominent labor leader and Kennedy ally agreed, saying moderate factions in the Kremlin would have an advantage in knowing that the administration opposed the views of US war hawks.[28] As Cold War anxieties ran high in Berlin and Cuba in 1961, the last problem McNamara wanted to face was Soviet jitters about rogue generals who might contemplate starting World War III. Some of the wild and dangerous ideas proposed in Admiral Goldthwaite's forums prompted McNamara to refer to Project Alert as one of those "cookie-doodle seminars."[29]

Another troop education program that got the "cookie-doodle" label was the *Fourth-Dimensional Warfare* forum. Admiral Chester Ward was a featured speaker, telling about three hundred attendees that State Department policies are "a wonderful way of accelerating surrender." Then there was the *Strategy for Survival* forum that particularly troubled Fulbright, headlining speakers from the John Birch Society. In typical John Birch fashion, one speaker accused the local congressman of voting the Communist party line. The event, held at Fort Smith in Arkansas, was enthusiastically supported by high-ranking officers of the state's National Guard. Fulbright said the forum was advertised to give the false impression that it had the approval of the United States Army; this was the kind of subterfuge that undermined the civilian leadership of the Defense Department.[30] As Cabell Phillips of the *New York Times* concluded in the summer of 1961, "the Pentagon is having its troubles with right-wingers in uniform."[31]

To Walker's friends in the armed forces, the presence of traitors in a federal government office or at CBS headquarters was not a mirage. As they saw it, the New Frontier was dead set on stifling anticommunist rhetoric that ran afoul of the official policy of "appeasement," and it had made Edwin Walker the fall guy. Forcing Walker to resign after Pro-Blue was revealed, they said, sent a clear message: no more mavericks and no more criticism from the front lines that Washington was soft on communism.[32] Walker said the official Pentagon-approved education program, which focused on democracy versus communism, citizenship, and the military code of conduct, was not enough. So he wrote his own script, ignoring those who told him that he was treading on thin ice.

During several days of arduous hearings on Capitol Hill, Thurmond sparred with McNamara over the efficacy of the Pentagon-approved curriculum. Was it anticommunist enough? Was Walker, in Thurmond's colorful expression, "crucified for his patriotism and devotion to the best interests of the country?"[33] The South Carolina senator and secretary of defense wrestled over questions of semantics. Did one film, approved for troop education, only refer to the danger of communist aggression, not to communism per se? "A very namby-pamby film," said Thurmond.[34]

To McNamara, the film and the rest of the material was all sufficiently anticommunist and fair to a range of political opinion. Armed Forces Radio and Television was even-handed, broadcasting an interview with Robert Welch on *Meet the Press.* However, some particularly hard-line materials were taken off the list, such as the film *Communism on the Map,* which was described by Defense Department reviewers as "leaving one with a feeling of defeatism."[35] The film also reflected the deep state conspiracy, referring to a fifth column wielding power in Congress, labor unions, and the media. Among the outrageous claims: Communists dominated the governments of America's closest allies, even Canada. Walker said that taking the film off the shelf demonstrated that troop education in the armed forces is not neutral, but "neutered." Uniformed officers were being silenced, Walker said, "by a class of men who believe in One World."[36]

McNamara was adamant that he was as much a dedicated cold warrior as Strom Thurmond, Walker, and the Birchers. He tried to assure hard-liners in Congress that there were no illusions in the Kennedy administration about Moscow's intentions. "Soviet communism seeks to wipe out the cherished traditions and institutions of the free world," he told senators. "These are not new convictions for me. I have held them for many years."[37] Barry Goldwater, who was already preparing to challenge Kennedy for the presidency, was not convinced that the men of the New Frontier had the stomach to confront the communist threat; instead, he said, they were choosing to "hide behind their squaws' skirts."[38] It was classic Goldwater-speak.

As McNamara derided the "cookie-doodle" seminars, Fulbright raised the more serious specter of a military dictator—an image that brought to mind strongmen waiting in the wings, ready to save America from the communists within. It was a vision of Mussolini's March on Rome or Franco's rule in Spain. One Project Alert speaker reportedly suggested that Supreme Court Chief Justice Earl Warren deserved more than impeachment, as the John Birch Society advocated, but actually merited execution by hanging.[39]

Serving in the Senate for thirty years, J. William Fulbright was best known for his chairmanship of the Foreign Relations Committee, where he was a leading opponent of the Vietnam War. As a Rhodes Scholar and the University of Arkansas president, Fulbright had a reputation among his adversaries as a liberal elitist. As a vocal critic of Senator Joseph McCarthy, it was not surprising he took a prominent role in investigating the issue of troop indoctrination in the armed forces.

In June 1961, just two months after the revelations about Pro-Blue, Fulbright sent McNamara a twenty-two-page memorandum, "Propaganda Activities of Military Personnel Directed at the Public." The efforts of men such as Walker "involve considerable danger," he wrote, and he noted the urgency of maintaining the "strong tradition in this country" of civilian leadership of the nation's defense. Fulbright also expressed concern about what he called "silent speaking"—cases of military officers who give their tacit support just by attending meetings of extremist political groups.[40]

Fulbright said Far Right ideology in the upper ranks of the military went beyond discussions of the Soviet Union; they equated liberalism with socialism, and socialism with communism.[41] If the military is "infected with the virus of right-wing radicalism," he wrote, it could threaten America's democracy. Treating Walker and similar cases as a disciplinary action could arouse sympathy for the individual or the cause he espoused. Fulbright wanted to avoid making men like Walker or Goldthwaite into martyrs.[42]

All this talk in Congress and the press of a potential military coup, Walker said, "is patently preposterous."[43] Walker did not hold back in his attacks on Fulbright, whom he called a "professional intellectual" and enemy of the American military. At his most vitriolic, Walker suggested the Arkansas senator "should be sent to Cuba to take Castro's place." The Fulbright memo, with its warning of a virus of right-wing extremism, was really part of Kennedy's blueprint for a "secret scheme," Walker said.[44] Citing the army's counterinsurgency training, Walker came to a conclusion that would rival any deep state intrigue hatched by Joseph McCarthy. Through counterinsurgency, the Kennedy administration was preparing to crush all opposition to the government. "Counterinsurgency will train the military to crack down on the people," Walker said. Weaving this outlandish fantasy even tighter, Walker told an audience in Dallas that this grand strategy not only was behind the Defense Department's repudiation of his Pro-Blue program but also was designed to block his assignment to lead the VIII Reserve Corps in Austin, a center for counterinsurgency training.[45]

The Revolt of the Generals

In the wake of talk like that, Fulbright was among those who drew a comparison of the Walker case with the revolt of French generals and an attempted coup against the government of Charles de Gaulle in April 1961. In that case, French military officers believed they were not given the support from the government they needed to win the war against Algerian independence. It was a charge that sounded familiar to Walker, who felt the Truman administration had led the country to a no-win stalemate in Korea.[46]

Military officers, French or American, have some common characteristics arising from their profession, Fulbright wrote, and there are numerous "military fingers on the trigger throughout the world."[47] Washington political journalist Alan Barth asked whether the recent events in France made one "feel comfortable about military officers who denounce civilian leaders as treasonable and who work hand-in-hand with Rightist groups which have rejected democracy." And the most formidable among these groups, Barth wrote, was the John Birch Society, whose leader, Robert Welch, had repeatedly sown doubt about the necessity of a democratic form of government.[48]

Among Welch's close advisers was Hilaire Du Berrier, an American-born soldier of fortune. Du Berrier, too, compared Walker with the French generals who felt betrayed by De Gaulle's Algeria policy.[49] However, in the John Birch Society reading of history, those plotting the coup in Paris sought to prevent Algeria from turning into a Soviet satellite. In a letter to Fulbright, Du Berrier said accusations that Walker was a threat, published in the Paris daily *L'Express,* were playing into the hands of French communists seeking to remove "every Army officer likely to oppose a putsch from the Left."[50]

Connecticut congressman Frank Kowalski, who spoke passionately about Soviet rule in Lithuania, also wondered whether America could be vulnerable to the military coups threatening other parts of the world. "We want no military czars in this country. We want no men on horseback." A West Point graduate who served in the army for more than thirty years, Kowalski agreed with the Defense Department's concern about those who have "never truly accepted civilian control."[51] The *Christian Century* also called on McNamara "to keep the armed forces out of the hands of divisive and potentially tyrannical elements" that could send America headlong into dictatorship.[52]

To some, this was the stuff of movies, as demonstrated by *Dr. Strangelove* and *Seven Days in May*, both released in 1964. In each movie, America's democracy is threatened by a power-hungry general. *Dr. Strangelove* is clearly a farce, with its General Jack D. Ripper going over the president's head to launch a nuclear strike against the Soviet Union—a not so far-fetched scenario, given Eddie Rickenbacker's suggestion of a preventive war. In *Seven Days in May*, written by Fletcher Knebel and published as novel in 1962, Walker was the model for would-be dictator General James Mattoon Scott, who accuses the president of treason for signing an arms control agreement with Moscow. His attempt to overthrow the government is derailed by his aide, played by Kirk Douglas.

Although the possibility of a military takeover was mentioned only in the most guarded of conversations in the Kennedy administration, the president recognized the danger that Walker and others in the highest echelons of the military posed to the country.[53] In the memoir of his years in the White House, historian Arthur Schlesinger said Kennedy had Walker in mind when he was asked about the possibility of a military coup. "It's possible. It could happen in this country," JFK said. "But it won't happen on my watch." To Schlesinger, Walker was "in a sense the heir to Major General George Van Horn Moseley," who had been the choice of American fascists, under the Christian Front, to lead a coup against Franklin Roosevelt.[54]

Having read an advance copy of *Seven Days in May*, Kennedy suggested to director John Frankenheimer that a movie version would be a good way to warn Americans of the potential threat of high-ranking officers peddling dangerous ideas that cast doubt on the patriotism of their elected leaders. Kennedy even told Frankenheimer that if he wanted to shoot scenes in the White House, the president would conveniently go to Hyannis Port for the weekend.

According to Schlesinger, however, the idea of putting *Seven Days in May* on the screen was not well accepted inside the Pentagon.[55]

Although Fulbright, like Kennedy, viewed a military coup as a remote possibility, he asked the Defense Department to appoint a civilian committee to assess whether troop education activities were necessary, and if so, how they should be restructured. The 1958 National Security Directive that inaugurated indoctrination programs in the armed forces came out of President Eisenhower's belief that winning the Cold War required all the resources of the military, including books, films, and seminars.[56] The directive gave commanders wide latitude, and most of them veered away from conspiracy theories. If these efforts were still needed, Fulbright wrote in his detailed memo to McNamara, they should be put under strict civilian control, because military personnel lacked the background to appreciate the broader policy issues.[57] Fulbright's call for new rules that would guarantee greater oversight over troop indoctrination prompted Rickenbacker, then chairman of Eastern Air Lines, to call foul on censorship from "the office boy through the chain of command."[58]

Conservative colleagues in Congress also condemned Fulbright's approach. Barry Goldwater accused Fulbright of trying to keep the truth from troops and the American people. Regarding Fulbright's fear of unchecked militarism, the Arizona senator responded that the safeguards were adequate: "They have never been overridden."[59] Arkansas congressman Dale Alford said Fulbright was attempting to "stifle military men . . . in their fight against communism." For Alford, Pro-Blue was far more than anti-Red. "We're for the preservation of our civilization."[60]

Thurmond claimed that Fulbright's memo and the army's campaign against Walker were playing right into the hands of the Kremlin. He pointed to one article published in the Soviet Ministry of Defense daily that referred to a "Pentagon teeming with generals and admirals who openly profess fascism and are attempting to unleash the third world war." As for General Walker, the official Soviet military newspaper said he had "hoped to turn the 24th Infantry Division into a band of headhunters and bandits, spreading the Nazi ravings of [Robert] Welch among the troops."[61]

In Thurmond's view, it was not just the Soviet officers who saw an opening with the Walker case. He was insistent that Walker's admonishment emboldened the American Communist Party to wage a campaign to undermine the military. In Thurmond's home state of South Carolina, the *Greenville News* agreed, telling its readers there was conclusive evidence "that such Red organs as the *Daily Worker* and [US] communist organizations are making the most of the situation."[62] It was quite a stretch, in 1961, to say the Communist Party was behind silencing men like Walker. However, for Thurmond, when it came to exposing the communist master plan, there was only one position to take—the extreme position.[63]

The Communist Party was politically insignificant by the early 1960s, fully discredited after the crimes of the Stalin years were made public and in the wake of the 1956 Soviet invasion of Hungary. Party rolls had reached their height in 1939, during the depths of the Great Depression, with 100,000 members. The number had shrunk to a tiny fraction of that, at most three thousand card-carrying Communists, by the time Walker and the John Birch Society took to the stage to alert America of an insidious threat.[64] Referring to the strength of the American Communists, McNamara called them "well-nigh ineffective."[65] Assurances that the Communist Party was a shell of its former self, however, were not enough to dissuade Walker's defenders on the editorial board of the *New York Daily News* from declaring that the Kennedy team was obscuring the fact that the United States was engaged in a two-front war against the Soviets, or from alleging a "criminal communist conspiracy—strong, devious and determined—in our own country."[66]

For Edwin Walker this two-front war would be won with more than aircraft and tanks. Psychological warfare was part of the arsenal. The experience of the Korean War justified a rigorous effort, like Pro-Blue, to indoctrinate the often naive young men sent into combat.[67] Walker often cited a 1956 army report that said some American soldiers captured during the Korean War had been easily brainwashed by enemy propaganda because they lacked sufficient understanding of communism and the values of their own country. The deficiencies in troop education were not lost on McNamara, who said he "heard with amazement" about prisoners who had "cracked" and cooperated with their captors to the point of voicing support for the North Korean regime.[68]

Confronted with the Soviet adversary in Europe, Walker said Pro-Blue was necessary to train a tougher, more ideologically committed infantryman.

America was too complacent, and its youth were "soft," but groups like the John Birch Society were perfect for officers who set out to train their soldiers in a muscular anticommunism. The East–West standoff now was, in his words, "warfare with respect to man's mind," and the fight for the American mind was "an unlimited battleground involving the entire civilian population and the military."[69] Walker said a major component of Pro-Blue was "to make each a master of the art" of psychological warfare. Learning to fight in this fourth dimension was imperative to prevail against communism, something the civilian bureaucrats in Washington would never understand.[70]

In early October 1961, a month after grueling questioning on Capitol Hill, Secretary McNamara short-circuited Rightist indoctrination efforts in the armed forces with strict new rules. The Defense Department now prohibited military education programs that expressed views contrary to national policy. Civilian and uniformed Defense Department personnel were not permitted to make partisan statements at outside symposia or lectures, and those organizations must be "nonpartisan in character."[71] McNamara was confident that these guidelines would keep military men from overstepping their bounds, but for Walker this was a restraint on those courageous officers who had evidence of a secret Washington–Moscow axis.[72] "Is the New Frontier a new form of government; when will a new form of government be announced?" Walker asked.[73]

An Infection in the Armed Forces

Two months after McNamara set new rules to rein in politically inspired generals, one of the leading labor organizers in America sent a plea to the Justice Department to remain watchful over the rising tide of right-wing radicalism. Victor Reuther, a top official of the United Auto Workers, urged McNamara to continue his investigation of officers "who have lost confidence in democracy." Like Senator Fulbright, Reuther said the revolt of the generals in Paris during the Algerian war proved that even a country as grounded in the Western democratic tradition as France could be threatened by a military coup.[74]

Reuther warned that despite Walker's admonishment and the Defense Department's official repudiation of conspiracy theories, Walker's ideas still represented the opinions of a significant part of the officer corps. It was now time, Reuther said, to "determine how widely the infection is spread in the armed forces." The army should have accepted Walker's resignation in 1959, after he made allegations that Eisenhower's enforcement of the Supreme Court's desegregation decision at Little Rock was the work of a mysterious "fifth column." Reuther claimed that either his superiors in the army agreed with Walker or they simply were not shocked by his views. In either case, the failure to accept his resignation constituted a dangerous tolerance of the extreme Right inside the military.[75]

Appeasing these radicals would not work, Reuther said. The Kennedy administration was reactive—the army did not take any action regarding the Pro-Blue program until it was revealed in the press, which "forced the Pentagon's hand." Reuther called for a shift from a defensive posture to an offensive one when it came to ensuring the separation of military personnel from partisan politics. If it meant the dismissal or resignation of some of these top military officers, so be it, he said. "It would be in the national interest."[76] Reuther's fear of "an infection," like Fulbright's use of the word *virus,* only reinforced the point that radical Right partisan politics in the armed forces was a mortal danger to the health of American democracy.

With this renewed scrutiny of troop indoctrination and calls for tougher penalties for officers who defied Pentagon policy, Walker asked, who in the armed forces would be willing "to stick their necks out now?"[77] Yet there were a number of former officers out of uniform who were courting the most extreme and racist elements of the Right. A few even rose to national prominence, as with Air Force General Curtis LeMay, who, three years after retirement, ran to be George Wallace's vice president, in 1968.

Among the most extreme was Rear Admiral John G. Crommelin, a perennial candidate for office in Alabama after his retirement from the navy. He was a virulent racist, saying the United Nations was intent on enslaving the white race.[78] After graduating from the US Naval Academy, Crommelin participated in some of the major naval engagements in the South Pacific during World War II. After the war, Crommelin became an outspoken critic of Defense Department policies, complaining that naval air power was being shortchanged in a struggle among the services.[79]

While Walker was reluctantly leading troops at Central High School in Little Rock, Crommelin was enlisting the support of the Ku Klux Klan to oppose desegregation. Eisenhower's use of troops at Little Rock was, to Crommelin, an act of war by the federal government. *Brown v. Board of Education,* he said, was a "threat to Western civilization."[80]

Crommelin aligned with the predecessors of armed antigovernment militia groups, and among his collaborators was retired Marine Corps General Pedro Augusto del Valle. Del Valle was born in Puerto Rico, and his family came to the United States when he was just seven. During the 1930s he served as an assistant naval attaché at the American embassy in Rome, becoming an admirer of Mussolini. After distinguished service in the Pacific theater during World War II, del Valle retired. In 1953, he joined Crommelin and other retired officers, including General Clyde Watts, Walker's longtime associate and lawyer, to organize the Defenders of the American Constitution. Del Valle said both Republicans and Democrats were under the spell of an "invisible government" of international Jewish bankers.[81]

In 1964, the FBI was watching Crommelin, del Valle, and Colonel William Potter Gale, who may have been planning a coup to overthrow the government. Drew Pearson regarded del Valle as one of the most dangerous men in uniform, coming close to urging armed insurrection. Del Valle's approach was to vote the traitors out, but if that failed, he advocated "a powerful armed resistance force."[82] Gale, a retired army colonel who had served with MacArthur in the Pacific, later headed the paramilitary Posse Comitatus and the neo-Nazi Identity Church.

Men in uniform or retired from the armed services were only part of the radical Right equation in the early 1960s. Fundamentalist preachers, mostly in the southern Bible Belt, followed much of the John Birch Society line, but with an emphasis on taking up the righteous sword against "godless communism." Billy James Hargis made Walker a featured speaker at his Christian Crusade convention in Oklahoma City, and as one journalist noted, audiences were convinced that the only true patriots left today in America were the Birchers, the Christian Crusade, and "the mushrooming organized Friends of Walker."[83] Support for officers like Walker was strong in the southern states at a time when resistance to integration was at its height. They were an important political asset to segregationists and fundamentalists because of the prestige that their military rank commanded in a region with a martial tradition. With that martial culture came a sense that they were the defenders of the "real" America.

As Edwin Walker took to the lecture circuit, he was encouraged to enter the political arena. Among those making that case was the husband-and-wife team of Kent and Phoebe Courtney of New Orleans. A steadfast supporter of Joe McCarthy, Kent Courtney studied and later taught at Tulane. As for Phoebe, Kent once said, she is "so far Right, the only thing beyond is outer space."[84] The Courtneys' pamphlet, *The Case of General Edwin A. Walker*, sold fifteen thousand copies at two dollars each and was part of the "Friends of Walker" effort to support his speaking engagements. Edwin Walker, they promised, would challenge those who "deride patriotism—the intellectual mafia." In the bizarre and breathless language of the Birchers, the Courtneys warned, "If the Kennedy dynasty is to remain in power, they must get Walker—and quick." As for the American people? They are "slumbering in front of their TV sets."[85]

As Walker considered a run for political office in Texas, he was clear about his obsessions. The sinister forces directing the CIA, State Department, and the local PTA would awaken those who are the "truly militant voice." They would be heard, he said, and "from their fury, constitutional power will prevail."[86] By the spring of 1962, in the heart of the former states of the Confederacy, Walker was unleashing some of the darkest forces of the American Right.

4

Thunder on the Right

Resigning from the armed forces after thirty years and two wars, Edwin Walker declared himself "free from the power of little men" sitting in the halls of Congress and the Pentagon. Trading his army uniform for a dark suit and his signature white Stetson hat, Walker dived into Texas state politics. It was an embarrassing performance.

Only days after his resignation on November 2, 1961, Walker was gaining support to run for office. Noting that the right-wing lecture circuit was enjoying its greatest heyday in decades, *Washington Post* political writer James Clayton asked, "Is Major General Edwin Walker the new man on horseback for America's far political right?"[1]

Walker's hopes were buoyed by rallies in December, including one at the Dallas Memorial Auditorium that attracted more than five thousand enthusiastic Texas voters. Walker spoke for an hour and received a standing ovation when he finished. Referring to his resignation from the army, Walker compared himself to the biblical Daniel, who refused to bow down to the king. "I would say to you, stand up beside Daniel and be counted."[2]

On February 3, 1962, Walker entered the race for Texas governor in the Democratic party primary. He was one of six candidates, including three-term governor Price Daniel and the Kennedy administration's choice, John Connally, who had resigned as navy secretary to run for the statehouse. They were all "professional liberals," Walker said, and as for incumbent Daniel, Walker used the phrase "entrenched mediocrity."[3] Walker was an uncompromising segregationist, and his decision to run as a Democrat was certainly embarrassing to the party of John F. Kennedy's New Frontier, which would challenge southern governors to open the doors of their state universities to African Americans.[4]

With Walker and the incumbent governor in the mix, it looked more like a horse race, even though Connally was seen as the favorite. Announcing his candidacy to the Capitol press corps in Austin, Walker proclaimed that a "thunder on the Right" would elect him governor, and he dismissed Connally and Governor Daniel as "the devious feelers of machine politics."[5] Sidestepping the issues most candidates for state office might address, Walker said his mission was to defend the United States against international communism. America, he said, was a "nation in dire peril . . . [but] stronger than the thunder on the Left would have us believe."[6]

For political observers in Washington and Austin, Walker, unleashed in the political arena, promised to "bring spark to a primary fight that is already a brawl."[7] Governor Daniel was described as "a gray-haired man with a winsome smile, not the image of the flamboyant Texas politician." As for Walker, *Time* magazine noted that despite his flat, stumbling platform style, he "could probably talk in sign language and still draw some right-wing votes." One thing was for certain now: this primary campaign would be "a real old-style Texas shootin' match."[8]

This Texas shootout, however, seemed more like Walker's audition for the national stage. Already, there were those on the Far Right who were talking about a Walker candidacy for president. Only six days after announcing his run for governor, he was the featured speaker at a Citizens Committee for General Walker rally in Chicago before an audience of almost five thousand. Like a latter-day Caesar, Walker appeared with a large gilded eagle suspended behind him. As many as thirty undercover police officers were stationed around the auditorium, anticipating protesters, several of whom were ushered out.[9] The Texas primary, said one journalist, would be a measure of the radical Right's "political pulling power—a good clue to the volume of that thunder."[10]

Again taking a page out of the John Birch Society playbook, Walker warned of a master plan to rob America of its sovereignty, with help, of course, from communists in Moscow and inside the US government. Returning to his recent experience in Augsburg, Walker expressed his well-worn theme of betrayal, claiming that "the greatest soldiers in the world, with the greatest industry behind them, could fail to survive only if they were sold out."[11]

A significant part of his campaign rhetoric involved what he termed the "flaccid policies" regarding Cuba and the threat of communist revolution in Latin America. Walker told his followers in Chicago that the defense of the United States "pivots on Texas."[12] To Walker, Texas and its governor had an outsized significance; in the Cold War, he said, "there are no more important posts than the governorships."[13]

Living in a state with a border on the Rio Grande and major military assets, Texans had to be more vigilant than others. With Havana in Moscow's orbit and restive states in Latin America, Walker said, Texas was a prime target of Soviet attention. Raising fears about a Castro-style revolution in Mexico, Walker charged that former Mexican president Lazaro Cárdenas was arming pro-Marxist guerrillas with the goal of turning Mexico into the next Cuba—"an iron curtain across the Rio Grande." Catering to Lone Star mythology, Walker called on the "traditions of the Alamo [as] a bulwark against communism."[14]

With all this emphasis on foreign intrigue, subversion, and tales of the Alamo, Walker's campaign looked like a farce. The question was whether Walker could emerge as a political force to be reckoned with and whether he would be the Right's successor to the late Joe McCarthy. Observers saw nothing surprising in Walker's campaign style, and like his erratic performance on the lecture circuit, it raised doubts about his fitness to serve as governor. He was the "arrogant, shouting General," in the words of one Texas daily. "A surly, uncontrolled bully used to having 'yes sir' men around him is no figure to place in public office."[15]

Walker's closest allies, Dallas congressman Bruce Alger, Strom Thurmond, and Texas senator John Tower, advised him to forego what would most likely be an unsuccessful political career. Typically, Walker ignored the counsel of his friends on Capitol Hill.[16]

The Washington press corps, which ordinarily would pass over a state primary campaign, could hardly dismiss Walker's growing popularity. They described him as lacking political savvy, and he was often misinformed. Walker advised Texans not to buy United Nations bonds, not realizing that they are available only to governments, nonprofit trusts, and other institutions.[17] While Walker's main appeal to conservatives was his call for ousting Fidel Castro, syndicated columnist Doris Fleeson said the general was unaware that "American voters have still to elect a governor for foreign policy reasons." Walker's political theatrics also posed a problem for an emerging youthful conservative movement. Fleeson noted that moderates on the Right were concerned that Walker's reckless comments and abysmal speaking style would paint the conservative movement as just another group of crackpots.[18]

That conservative movement, a New Right, found its voice among the contributors to William F. Buckley's *National Review.* In May 1961, two weeks after Walker's demotion at Heidelberg, Buckley leapt to his defense, printing a letter in *National Review* from an officer who had served in Augsburg. In Buckley's opinion, he gave another view of army life under the "recently humiliated" Walker. The unsigned letter asked the magazine's readers, "What will you do to help keep General Walker from being thrown to the wolves?"[19] By November, following Walker's resignation, Buckley had the answer: standing with the general "to fight at his side when . . . he next joins battle with the enemy." Walker was not to be treated as a martyr, Buckley said, but as a hero for having the "personal courage to carry his case to the country." *National Review* publisher William Rusher also praised Walker at a Dallas rally of conservatives that same month. Yet Buckley recognized that Walker could be his own worst enemy, "not being the best formulator" of ideas. He found Walker's reference to the "little men in the Pentagon" to be an indication that Walker would not qualify as the spokesman for the New Right.[20]

Despite his reservations, Buckley agreed with Walker and the John Birch Society's Robert Welch on the broader issue of anticommunism. In step with the Birchers, Buckley and L. Brent Bozell, in their book *McCarthy and his Enemies,* praised the Wisconsin senator as one who had "tried to alert the nation to the communist threat."[21] Buckley, like Welch, opposed Eisenhower's nomination in 1952, favoring the conservative flank's Robert Taft, and declared the GOP platform to be "essentially one of measured socialism." John Huntington, in his *Far-Right Vanguard,* said Buckley's socialism-in-both-parties rhetoric bore a strong resemblance to some of the more radical conspiratorial language.[22] Additionally, *National Review,* which made its debut in 1955, had benefitted from Welch's financial support of $2,000 in its first two years.[23]

Welch, Walker, and the Mainstream Right

In 1960, Buckley was among the founders of Young Americans for Freedom, so that the academic Left was not the only voice leading the conversation about America's future. It was the same year that Barry Goldwater's *Conscience of a Conservative* laid out a blueprint for capturing the White House. By 1962, as Walker campaigned through Texas, Buckley's conservative intellectuals became more disenchanted with the general turned political candidate, as well as with some of the Birchers' more outlandish views.

Goldwater and Buckley were worried that the Birchers could tarnish the image of the emerging New Right. Yet Buckley's attempt, in 1962, to excommunicate Robert Welch from the conservative movement was not entirely successful. As Edward Miller notes in his biography of Welch, "the argument that Buckley successfully drummed Welch out of the conservative movement, that Buckley promoted for decades, has been greatly exaggerated." In addition, Miller writes, Buckley and many historians underestimated the support for the John Birch Society among the conservative mainstream.[24] Indeed, mainstream conservatives did not fully turn away from Far Right ideas. In fact, ultraconservatives molded many of the themes of the New Right, including a rejection of government as an agent of social change, whether that meant school integration or Medicare.[25]

While Buckley tried to unhook the ultras from the moderate Right, the familial ties would be difficult to untangle. Medford Evans, one of Walker's closest advisers, was a regular on Citizens' Council radio and a member of the editorial board of Welch's *American Opinion.* Yet Evans was a welcome contributor to *National Review.* William Schlamm, who spoke of a "preventive war" against the Soviet Union, was also on *American Opinion*'s editorial board and served as a *National Review* editor. Miller notes that the John Birch Society's national council was "filled with folks" closely associated with *National Review* including Clarence Manion and, in the magazine's early years, classics professor Revilo Oliver. Oliver also wrote for the explicitly pro-fascist *American Mercury,* a once-respected journal that was later bought by a group of Texas investors, including Edwin Walker.[26]

As the Texas race made headlines, Barry Goldwater's supporters were beginning to see Walker as a distraction and a liability they could not afford. Goldwater was preparing for his 1964 run for the presidency and he had to appeal to a wider range of voters, but at the same time he could not ignore a part of his base that included the Birchers. In the estimation of one newspaper columnist, even if Goldwater did not shake hands with them, neither could he wave them away.[27] Staking out a respectable distance from the John Birch Society, Goldwater said Welch made accusations without evidence. "I disagree with Earl Warren, but I see no reason to impeach him."[28]

When Goldwater was scheduled to speak at a Young Americans for Freedom rally in Madison Square Garden on March 7, 1962, both the Arizona senator and John Tower asked that Walker be taken off the program. At first, the conservative student organization resisted, but when Goldwater said he could not share a stage with the general, the Young Americans for Freedom advised Walker that his appearance might be perceived as an endorsement in the Texas governor's race. The rally itself was a story of two American right wings. As Goldwater spoke inside, several of Walker's followers began to protest and were escorted out by police. Outside, on the streets of New York, members of the American Nazi Party carried leaflets emblazoned with "the Jew Goldwater."[29]

The national Democratic Party, touting a youthful and forward-looking image, also found itself in an uncomfortable position with Walker's entrance into the primary race. Despite his visceral dislike of the Kennedys, Walker chose to run as a Democrat, believing that Kennedy liberalism could be routed in Texas and the rest of the South. *New York Daily News* columnist Ted Lewis, in his "Capital Circus," wrote that "Democratic party eggheads who tried to convince voters that the GOP was in cahoots with the John Birch Society now had to revise this strategy."[30]

Even Texas congressman Bruce Alger, who labeled Lyndon Johnson a sellout to "Yankee socialists," thought Walker would do more harm than good. "I now no longer consider him an effective conservative."[31] Walker's Bircher affiliation was enough for the Pecos, Texas, newspaper to call him unfit to be governor. Walker, in the opinion of the *Pecos Daily News*, was "vindictive, vicious and vituperative—the hallmark of Robert Welch's John Birch Society."[32]

Despite the optimism among national Democrats that Walker would find little support outside his die-hard base, he had been bringing in donations from across the country since his well-publicized resignation from the army. In a letter to contributors, Walker boasted of a grassroots campaign from "my friends in 49 other states."[33] In response to rumors that his run for office was underwritten by H. L. Hunt and the John Birch Society, Walker was adamant: "I am financed by no one individual or group of individuals."[34]

Political journalists in Washington were watching closely for the national implications of an outside chance of a Walker win or a runoff that would knock out John Connally, a close friend of fellow Texan Lyndon Johnson. Some saw the race as a test of Johnson's continued influence in the state. As for Walker, he was banking on a six-way split, which would favor him for a spot in the runoff.[35] The editor of the *Lubbock Sun* promised a political upset, saying that while the Republican candidate's support appeared lukewarm, at best, Walker was packing in cheering crowds in Houston. Texans, he said, would back a man who stood up to the appeasers in Washington. And if Walker were to lose, the reason would be simple: the liberal press, which conspired to ignore his campaign.[36]

Texas would be a perfect state for the ultra Right to score a political success, and even if Walker were to lose, a good showing against an incumbent governor and a former navy secretary would hold national significance. John Birch Society membership was greatest in two states, California and Texas. California had the most Birch chapters. Southern California, in particular, was a center of extreme Rightist politics during the early 1960s; the Christian Anti-Communism Crusade could pack twelve thousand into the Hollywood Bowl in 1961.[37] And California had elected two Birchers to Congress, John Rousselot and Edgar Hiestand, who were facing strong challengers for reelection at the time of Walker's primary campaign. The John Birch Society hoped that if Walker did well in Texas, it might mean a last-minute, all-out effort in California. Both Birchers failed to win reelection that year.

As for Texas, one Washington observer described the state as a "hotbed of extremists, and Walker is [their] hero."[38] Indeed, Walker was confident that voters would make their state "a patriotic stronghold from which to expand."[39] Texas was home to dozens of John Birch chapters, which prompted Robert Welch to boast that, unlike other states, they didn't have to worry about communists in their midst.[40]

With a wealthy and politically powerful conservative base, the city of Dallas was fertile ground for a Walker movement. Edward Musgrove Dealey, publisher of the *Dallas Morning News,* was a prominent voice for the Texas Right. With a circulation of 250,000 by the early 1960s, the *Dallas Morning News* was the biggest-selling paper in Texas. Although it had endorsed the New Deal under Dealey's father, George, the paper made a sharp Right turn under Edward. With views similar to those of the John Birch Society, the newspaper's editorial policy included opposition to the United Nations, foreign aid, welfare programs, and "virtually anything except the Dallas Zoo," said Stanley Marcus of the Dallas department store Nieman Marcus.[41] Dealey loathed the Kennedys, and according to a report in the *Washington Post,* he poked fun at Kennedy for riding little Caroline's tricycle, saying the country needed a man on horseback.[42] The newspaper defended Joseph McCarthy's anticommunist witch hunts and referred to the Supreme Court as the "judicial Kremlin."

Chinese Troops Poised on the Rio Grande

Walker could count on the segregationist vote when he voiced support for the state's poll tax. In an interview at the height of the campaign, Walker called the poll tax a necessary protection against voter fraud, but in reality it was a not-too-subtle method of voter suppression.[43] The Warren Court was particularly villainized for ruling that segregation was unconstitutional. For Walker, maintaining segregated schools was a matter of states' rights. The states of the Union are not provinces, Walker said, in a pamphlet he titled "The American Eagle Is Not a Dead Duck." Reflecting the position of the Citizens' Councils that international communists were behind racial integration, Walker said, "The obliteration of state lines is high on the agenda of communists." The ultimate goal of Moscow and their fellow travelers in the civil rights movement, he imagined, is "race-mixing."[44]

Calling Walker the Sam Houston of '62, the ad hoc Texas Voters for Enforcing the Constitution was representative of Walker's base, drawn to staggering fantasies of Chinese troops preparing to invade the United States. They envisioned foreign forces "pouring into Mexico," ready to cross the Rio Grande and take Texas. Kennedy and his "gang of socialists" were determined to enslave American citizens under a one-world government enforced by legions of Asian soldiers. As for Governor Price Daniel, he was "part and parcel of this secret conspiracy."[45]

And who better than a decorated army officer of two wars to stop the treasonous disarmament of the United States? As the Texas Voters for Enforcing the Constitution promised, "Elect General Walker and remain free men and women."[46] Walker was praised by his admirers for saying that as governor he would take full command of the Texas National Guard to prevent its troops and weapons from being federalized to enforce an integration order from Washington, as had occurred during the Little Rock crisis. Walker told a campaign rally in Dallas that his command of the National Guard also would prevent a takeover by those UN forces poised at the border. In a letter written in July 1962, Walker urged state governors to resist any attempt by President Kennedy to federalize their National Guard units. JFK, after all, was in on the UN plot.[47]

Walker had grandiose ideas about the Lone Star State and his own place in history. In his mind, the "sovereign state of Texas" was still the Republic of Texas, and in campaign literature, he traced his lineage to Confederate war heroes as well as to Charles Cotesworth Pinckney, one of the signers of the Constitution.[48]

Saying his campaign was about preserving Texas traditions and heritage, Walker saw himself in mortal combat against the politicians on the Potomac. With his predictable attacks on Washington, he said the Texas farmer and the oil industry would benefit from fewer restrictions at the national level. Texas, he said, was "built on the blood of our heroes of San Jacinto and the Alamo . . . We should never prove ourselves unworthy heirs."[49] To Walker's defenders, here was an authentic American, and in Walker's mind an authentic American rejects compromise. "You have been taught to be broad-minded, that you must be tolerant. Men in the Alamo were tolerant of nothing but their own rights as free men."[50]

And who was storming the modern-day Alamo to crush American sovereignty and Walker's hopes for political office? The Communist Party, of course. An appeal for money from campaign headquarters boasted that the *Daily Worker* had devoted two pages to Walker's run for governor. "No other candidate—Democrat or Republican—holds that distinction."[51] Walker spent little time on issues that mattered to average Texans, but occasionally he would advance a commonsense proposal like greater oversight of state bureaus and commissions. He advocated for better pay for teachers, "to retain the self-respect they so well deserve," and for granting more power to local school boards.[52]

It was the issue of school textbooks—a communist Trojan horse at the gates—that particularly concerned candidate Walker. Textbooks, he said, written by "a cult of American intellectual sophisticates" and Ivy League Marxists, were pushing an agenda that questioned Christianity, morality, American traditions, and the military.[53] The threat of subversive textbooks tainting the minds of impressionable school children was nothing new in the radical Right subculture. Referring to his command of soldiers in Augsburg, Walker employed his usual gift for fanciful exaggeration, saying he had educated "thousands of American boys whose church attendance was the highest of any army in the world."[54]

Walker opposed any restrictions on gun ownership. The dark hand of the United Nations, Walker told Texans, was behind a strategy to disarm Americans in preparation for surrender. It was a view wholly consistent with that of the Birchers and the well-armed Minutemen.[55] There would be no victory by any of his imagined enemies as long as Americans were armed; this was "the greatest assurance of liberty—next to the grace of God," he said.[56] Consistent with antitax conservatism, Walker opposed the 2 percent state sales tax enacted by the legislature in 1961. Although Governor Daniel did not support the tax, it had to be passed to prevent the state from going broke. Despite that, Walker and many voters put the blame on Daniel, saying he was a tax-and-spend liberal with "irresponsible and extravagant fiscal policies."[57]

Typically, Walker's answers to questions on the campaign trail did not inspire much confidence. When he was asked whether elected officials should reveal their personal finances, Walker's reply was that Texans should only put trustworthy people into office in the first place.[58] His speeches were no better. Sounding like a Texas preacher at a revival, Walker warned of the imminent struggle between the forces of Christian righteousness and godless communism. Sometimes he would begin by leading his audience in "Onward, Christian Soldiers" and then declare that he would "stand firm in the Gospel of Christ."

Finally, he would pose a question to his audience: "Who can be against us except Satan and the atheistic communist conspiracy allied with him?"[59] These were words that evoked a holy war, surely resonating with the Christian Right.

In a letter to donors, Walker again framed his campaign for governor in apocalyptic terms, saying he was in the race to stem "the destruction of the individual and his God." Predictably, those in government—presidents from Roosevelt to Kennedy—had subjected the American people to the "most fatal brainwashing in the history of this nation."[60]

Despite Walker's vocal appeal to the Divine, his campaign was in a free fall by early April as the "responsible Right" steered clear. Walker's call to voters to counter "Left-wing efforts to censor the Thunder" also fell flat.[61] Far from a "thunder on the Right," Edwin Walker's foray into politics was more of a "blunder on the Right," in the opinion of the editors of the *Washington Post*.[62]

Living in a Nightmare World

Washington insiders, like Texans John Tower in the Senate and Bruce Alger in the House, recognized that the militant Walker base was too small to carry a statewide election. Winning in Texas required the votes of mainstream conservatives—and keeping a safe distance from an unstable reactionary. While Tower said he did not question the sincerity of extremists like the John Birch Society, and quietly welcomed their support, he insisted that he rejected conspiracy theories.[63]

Walker's political aspirations were also derailed by his testimony before a Senate committee only a month before election day. Just two days on Capitol Hill were enough to convince most observers that Walker was indeed detached from reality. To the editors of the *Washington Post*, Walker "seems to be living in a nightmare world . . . of demons and hobgoblins."[64] Some correctly assumed that Walker would blame a defeat on the work of the control apparatus, those anti-American traitors of the deep state. As a conservative with presidential ambitions, Goldwater was among those who looked forward to a quick denouement to Walker's political career.

The results were indeed career-ending for Walker, who came in last in the field of six on election day, May 5, 1962. Any hope of running for president dissolved. Out of 1.4 million votes cast, Walker received 138,000.[65] Although Walker's defeat was not surprising, it was significant that he was able to garner almost 10 percent of the total. That was more than earlier estimates, which had placed Walker's vote at a maximum of 88,000. Additional votes may have come from some Republicans who were attracted to Walker's ideology.

Connally won the Democratic nomination after a runoff against Houston lawyer Donald Yarborough, and subsequently the election as governor. Connally's win was predictable, given his strong business ties and political allies, including the vice president. Connally, with a sizeable campaign fund, also made a pitch to women, and while other candidates traveled the state with their families, Walker took to the campaign trail with his mother. When he was asked whether women should be allowed to buy and sell stocks without their husband's permission, Walker thought for a moment before telling the political editor of the *Dallas Morning News* that not being married, he was unfamiliar with the issue.[66] The *Dallas Morning News,* like many observers of the primary race, felt that Walker put a nail in his political coffin every time he opened his mouth. Overall, his last-place showing in Texas did demonstrate the weakness of the radical Right's power at the ballot. As one Dallas Republican put it, Walker, far from being their white knight, was the "dud of the year."[67] With Walker out of the race, it was very likely that almost all his voters went to the Republican candidate Jack Cox, a conservative who opposed civil rights legislation.[68]

Following Walker's defeat, there were those who again raised questions about his mental stability. Some of his friends found that he became lonely and bitter. He believed that his campaign had been snubbed by the Dallas power structure, including the conservative Texas oil barons. His speech and demeanor became increasingly odd as he spent his days writing open letters to the president and granting interviews. Some said his house looked run-down and seedy. There was a hole in the dining room ceiling, and Walker had converted the hallway into a makeshift command center.[69]

In fact, anyone visiting Walker at his spacious stucco Turtle Creek Boulevard home could see clearly his various political hobbyhorses, even before entering the front door. Aside from the American and state of Texas flags, his three flagpoles might have the Confederate battle flag, the South Vietnamese, or the Rhodesian flag. Tellingly, his adversity to the federal government was clear, as the Texas and the United States flags flew on separate but equal staffs.

Fresh from his rejection by the voters of Texas, Walker remained determined to tilt at the windmills of communist one-world conspiracies. His obsession next led him to the campus of the University of Mississippi, where he again took center stage in one of the most important events of the modern civil rights movement.

5

Insurrection at Ole Miss

It would be the last year the University of Mississippi was a university for whites only. The 1961–1962 yearbook, in the voice of its mascot, Johnny Reb, described the campus as a place of "spreading magnolia and ante-bellum columns . . . as the darkies sing softly in the moonlight."[1]

Situated in Oxford, the home of that authentically southern writer William Faulkner, the University of Mississippi campus reflects its heritage in its Georgian and Greek Revival buildings. In his exaggerated accent, Johnny Reb reminded incoming students, in the opening pages of the yearbook, "Incidentally, suh, [this] is the one hundredth anniversary of the founding of our glorious confederacy." That "glorious" Confederacy was no Lost Cause to Ole Miss students a century later, where fraternity parties usually had the Confederate battle flag prominently displayed.

Edwin Walker, now out of uniform and a celebrity of the ultra Right, saw the desegregation of the University of Mississippi as a line in the sand. First on the airwaves and later on the university campus itself, Walker would lead the charge as hundreds converged for two days of rioting that left two dead and Ole Miss smoldering. To Walker, as well as the Birchers and Citizens' Councils, admitting African American students to Ole Miss was the work of communists to rob the states of their "sovereignty."

The story of how Ole Miss opened its gates to its first Black student starts with the man who did everything he could to preserve racial segregation in Mississippi, Governor Ross Barnett. His picture was featured in that 1961–1962 yearbook, which called him a "loyal son of Ole Miss" who "clings with uncompromising determination to the principles for which the South has always fought."[2]

Barnett was, to use a stereotype, a country lawyer born in 1898 in rural Leake County. In the summer, to pay for college expenses, Barnett worked as a janitor and a barber. After graduating from the University of Mississippi School of Law in 1926, he built up one of the most profitable law firms in the state, specializing in personal injury cases.[3]

As the grandson of a Confederate soldier, Barnett was steeped in the mythology of the Lost Cause. Like any politician who hoped to get elected in Mississippi, Barnett let it be known that he marched in lockstep with white supremacist ideology. "I believe the Good Lord was the original segregationist. Mixing the races leads inevitably to the production of an inferior mongrel," he said, leaving no doubt where he would stand if a Black student tried to enter the gates of Ole Miss. In 1959, Barnett was elected governor, but he served only one tumultuous term.[4]

Segregationists like Barnett knew time was running out. The 1954 *Brown v. Board of Education* decision would eventually catch up with Jim Crow throughout the South, but men like Barnett tried to hold back the inevitable for as long as they could. In 1956, the Mississippi legislature declared *Brown* invalid and enacted a resolution of interposition, hearkening back to John Calhoun's nullification of federal laws in the name of states' rights. Mississippi also established its Sovereignty Commission, a network of informants and bullying tactics designed for political oppression and voter suppression.

At the time, Mississippi was the poorest state and had the third-highest illiteracy rate in the country. While the state had the nation's largest proportion of Black citizens in 1960, approximately 43 percent of the population, there were no Black sheriffs, state highway patrolmen, or National Guard members. The 22,000 Black voters in 1952 were whittled down to just 8,000 by 1958, thanks to the Citizens' Councils, the Sovereignty Commission, and, of course, the Klan.[5] Segregation created a stark inequality in education that was reflected in the numbers. In 1959–1960, whites-only schools received $81.86 per child as opposed to $21.77 for each Black child.[6]

The state imposed an official racial orthodoxy that every citizen was expected to follow. A 1963 report to the United States Commission on Civil Rights was blunt in its assessment: "A pattern exists in our state that leads to the denial of constitutional rights, and in some instances, to brutality and terror . . . [Black] citizens of this state must either accept an inferior station in life and an attitude of servility or endanger themselves and their families by protesting."[7]

One of Governor Barnett's closest advisers on race was Bill Simmons, the head of the Citizens' Councils in Mississippi. With their national headquarters just two blocks from the Mississippi statehouse in Jackson, the Citizens' Councils were adept at flexing their political muscle and mobilizing voters. In Jackson, the Citizens' Council could boast six thousand members, and with Barnett in power, they began receiving state funds.[8]

In the estimation of historian James W. Silver, Mississippi was a closed society. Silver, who joined the Ole Miss faculty in 1936 and served as chair of the history department from 1946 to 1957, chronicled the events that led to the school's racial integration. The Citizens' Council and the Sovereignty Commission kept a watchful eye on every governmental body, from the local police to the legislature, making Mississippi, in Silver's words, "as near to approximating a police state as anything we have yet seen in America."[9]

Educators were under particular scrutiny in this closed society. In 1955, the University of Mississippi Board of Trustees required a screening for all speakers brought to campus. A clergyman was turned away when it became known that he had contributed to the NAACP. The incoming president of the Southern Historical Association was barred from delivering a lecture after the disclosure that his wife had written in the *Saturday Evening Post* of her teaching experience with African American students in Atlanta.[10]

In January 1962, as the showdown over integration at Ole Miss was taking shape in the courts, Barnett was preparing to defend the walls that kept his state shut off from the rest of the country. He asked the legislature to outlaw the Communist Party, to pass an enforceable sedition act, and to compel state employees to take an oath of allegiance to the state of Mississippi.[11]

The governor could appeal to the hard-core segregationists, using the strongest language possible. "Nobody wants violence, but red-blooded southerners should not turn aside from a fight when such important principles are involved—a fight to preserve what we know to be right," he said.[12] The battle Barnett promised to wage ended with a nation awakened to the lengths to which segregationists would go to deny Black Americans the right to an education equal to that of its white citizens. It also ended Ross Barnett's tenure in the only elected office he ever held.

At the center of the maelstrom was James Howard Meredith, the first Black student to be admitted to Ole Miss. Meredith was not the first Black Mississippian to try. That distinction goes to Clennon King, who arrived in Oxford, accompanied by news reporters, to register for classes in 1958. The act was so audacious that Governor James Coleman assumed King was insane, committing him to twelve days in the state mental hospital.

It took another three years before someone again dared to pry open the university's doors for Black students. In January 1961, Meredith began the application process with words that started the chain of events that reached its climax more than a year later: "I sincerely hope that your attitude toward me as a potential member of your student body . . . will not change upon learning that I am not a white applicant . . . I am an American-Mississippi-Negro citizen."[13]

Meredith, who was twenty-nine at the time, was clearly the right person to test the waters. He was an Air Force veteran with a spotless record and he was ready for college-level courses. There would be no reason to deny his application except on the grounds that he was Black, but that is exactly what happened. He received a response from the university one month later, with the terse warning, "We advise you not to appear for registration."[14]

James Meredith, the grandson of a slave, was born in the heart of central Mississippi in the town of Kosciusko, named for a Polish freedom fighter who fought in the American Revolution. Meredith is not the only hometown celebrity; Kosciusko can also claim Oprah Winfrey.

As the armed forces became the first truly integrated institution in America, James Meredith saw a way out of small-town Mississippi by joining the Air Force right out of high school in 1951. From his post in Japan, Meredith saw events unfold in Little Rock, saying years later, "When Eisenhower, who had been the biggest general in our history, committed the troops to support the right of citizenship, that was what my objective was in the whole Mississippi scheme."[15] In July 1960, Meredith was honorably discharged and returned home, registering for the fall semester at Jackson State College. His course of study was political science.

Reasoning That Defies History and Common Knowledge

Meredith expected the university to reject his application, and he had a strategy in place that included calls to the Civil Rights Division in Robert Kennedy's Justice Department and to the NAACP's Medgar Evers. He also took his case to the US District Court. In December 1961, Judge Sidney Mize ruled that Meredith had not been denied on racial grounds, and in February 1962, Mize ruled again, this time that the University of Mississippi was not a segregated institution. After all, the university did admit students from Asia and other parts of the world.[16]

Meredith pursued his case through the courts, and on June 25, 1962, the Fifth Circuit Court of Appeals in New Orleans ordered that Meredith should be admitted. Judge John Minor Wisdom disagreed with the university's and Mize's opinion that Ole Miss was not motivated by race when denying Meredith's application. That was reasoning that "defies history and common knowledge," Wisdom said. "We find that James Meredith's application for transfer to the University of Mississippi was turned down solely because he was a Negro." He also noted that the university "engaged in a carefully calculated campaign of delay, harassment and masterly inactivity."[17]

That summer and through September, the university's board of trustees and Barnett continued to stand in the way of progress. On September 10, 1962, the US Supreme Court upheld Meredith's right to enrollment.[18] As Silver writes in his recounting of the events at Ole Miss, Meredith now had "an absolute legal right to enter the university," but a Supreme Court ruling was not enough to convince Barnett that the case against Meredith was another Lost Cause.[19]

Just three days after the Supreme Court ruling, Barnett, in a statewide radio and television address, said the federal government was using "naked and arbitrary power . . . to deny self-determination." In his strongest language yet, the governor said he was prepared for a fight. "They now seek to break us physically with the power of force." Barnett vowed to go to jail rather than submit to the court's order. Calling the crisis at Ole Miss the greatest since the war between the states, Barnett used the familiar trope of Leftist agitators—integration was the work of "a motley array of un-American pressure groups."[20] With the headline "United We Stand," the state's major newspaper, the *Jack-*

son Clarion-Ledger, applauded Barnett and called for resistance to "federal encroachment."[21]

A week later, on September 20, the day the university registered new students, Meredith left a safe house in Memphis under the protection of federal marshals. Barnett was waiting, and now, as self-appointed registrar, rejected Meredith's registration.[22] On September 24, the board of trustees appeared before the Fifth Circuit Court; they must register Meredith the next day or be held in contempt. Undeterred, Barnett continued his desperate struggle against the tide of history.[23]

Frightening images, employed for more than a century, were resurrected. On September 27, the *Clarion-Ledger* warned of a possible gun battle at the university. In Washington, Mississippi senator James Eastland spoke of "a judicial tyranny as black and hideous as any in the history of the United States."[24] With an echo of the Civil War, one Mississippi legislator proposed that the state sever relations with the federal government.[25]

As President Kennedy was preoccupied with the Cold War, he put his brother, Attorney General Robert Kennedy, to work behind the scenes to persuade southern governors to comply with the law. Robert Kennedy and Deputy Attorney General Nicholas Katzenbach were committed to opening the closed society not only in Mississippi but also in Alabama, as they witnessed a more assertive phase of the civil rights movement. Throughout the South in 1961, all forms of segregation were challenged, from lunch counters to bus terminals. The Freedom Riders endured attacks in Birmingham and Montgomery, Alabama, bus terminals as they tested the Supreme Court ruling that prohibited segregation in interstate travel. President Kennedy wanted to avoid these violent confrontations on the University of Mississippi campus at all costs.

Among the tactics discussed at the White House was a proposed meeting between the president and Barnett, similar to the one Eisenhower had with Governor Faubus during the Little Rock crisis. Kennedy also considered having Vice President Lyndon Johnson escort Meredith to the registrar's office. After all, Johnson was a southerner.

If he had to intervene, Kennedy preferred to use the ninety-four US marshals and more than three hundred deputies at his disposal. White House adviser Theodore Sorensen said sending federalized National Guard or regular army troops would be an option only if "all other avenues of action are at a dead end." Comparing the University of Mississippi case to Little Rock, Sorensen told the president to consider "the many graduated steps" between inaction and calling out troops.[26]

Although the US Marshals Service was far from an elite fighting force, it had successfully repelled a mob attacking a meeting of civil rights activists, including Martin Luther King, in Montgomery in May 1961. As for Barnett, he had a small army of 220 highway patrolmen and 250 armed fish and game wardens.[27]

On September 25 and 26, federal authorities, including John Doar of the Justice Department Civil Rights Division, tried unsuccessfully to get Meredith registered. Doar informed Barnett on the morning of September 25 that he was in contempt of court, but to no avail, as Barnett read a proclamation drawn from his breast pocket: "I hereby finally deny you admission to the University of Mississippi."[28]

On September 26, Meredith and his escort were blocked by the state highway patrol, headed by Colonel Thomas Birdsong. Birdsong told Chief US Marshal James McShane that his orders were to escort the marshals and Meredith as far as the campus entrance and no farther. This time Doar came face to face with Lieutenant Governor Paul Johnson, who held his ground even as Doar tried to push past him. Again, for the third time, the marshals retreated as Johnson promised that "force will be met with force" if federal authorities tried to bring Meredith past the gates of the university.[29]

By the next day, September 27, the streets of Oxford and the campus were beginning to fill with angry crowds, many of them armed with guns, knives, and bricks. Snipers were rumored to be in place to assassinate Meredith. Alabama governor John Patterson cabled the president with a warning that sending troops to Oxford "would brand the federal government as a dictatorship of the foulest sort. It will mark the end of our existence as a democratic republic." Resurrecting Walker's command at Little Rock, Patterson referred falsely to "American paratroopers bayonetting American civilians."[30] Fearing a bloody confrontation, the fourth attempt to get Meredith on campus failed. Only twenty miles from Oxford, Meredith's convoy was ordered to return to Memphis.[31]

On September 28, the Fifth Circuit Court of Appeals ruled that Barnett had until October 2 to register Meredith or face a $10,000-a-day fine and be subject to arrest.[32] This was just as the Mississippi Senate approved a statement condemning the federal government's "police state and gestapo methods." The Sovereignty Commission had six thousand postcards printed, addressed to President Kennedy, denouncing the "warfare" against Mississippi.[33]

Sensing that Barnett had no intention of giving in and that the college town of Oxford was becoming a magnet for the most radical factions of segregationists, Kennedy started to prepare for military action. On September 29, after failing to get any assurance from the governor that would allow Meredith to register for classes peacefully, Kennedy ordered the Mississippi National Guard federalized.[34] Secretary of the Army Cyrus Vance and Major General Creighton Abrams established Memphis Naval Air Station, about seventy-five miles from Oxford, as the staging area. In addition, the number of marshals deployed to Memphis increased from 140 to 500.[35]

Along with the marshals, the army was prepared to send in its elite antiriot squad, along with tear gas specialists, ambulances, and even a light helicopter company. This would be a small portion of the approximately twelve thousand army and three thousand federalized Guard troops committed to the Oxford area by October 2. It was the largest deployment for a single domestic crisis in the nation's history.[36]

A Defiant Governor Looks for a Way Out

For Kennedy, Meredith's admission was not negotiable, but he was hesitant about sending a force more threatening than the marshals. The sight of US soldiers would inflame southern sensibilities even more. One sensitive issue faced by the army was the presence of African American soldiers, which could result in an even more volatile situation. It was agreed that while Black soldiers would be deployed to Oxford, they should be kept away from any confrontation with protesters. It was a lesson learned from Little Rock, when Walker ordered that the more than one hundred Black soldiers of the 101st remain hidden from view.[37]

Kennedy attempted to work out an agreement with Barnett that would allow Meredith to register quietly on October 1. Barnett could save face by saying the federal authorities acted behind his back. For public consumption, Barnett dug his heels in deeper, but at this point he knew the game was over. He was ready to cooperate if he could still appear to be the defiant governor standing up to the power of the federal government.

On Sunday, September 30, with the Mississippi National Guard fully under federal control, Meredith was flown from New Orleans to Memphis, finally arriving on campus about 6:00 in the evening. He was escorted by a Mississippi Highway Patrol car through a side entrance of the campus and into Baxter Hall, one of four men's dormitories built after World War II. The university chancellor believed a face-saving deal with Barnett was sealed; however, word got out that Meredith was secreted in the empty dormitory under federal protection, igniting violence.[38]

Between 5:00 and 6:00 p.m., a combination of students and outsiders converged on the center of the campus as US marshals took their position around the Lyceum, which housed administration offices. Soon a crowd of about five hundred threatened the marshals, and by dark there were more than a thousand throwing bricks, bottles, and in some cases Molotov cocktails. As more agitators poured onto campus, surrounding the Lyceum, some started to puncture the tires and smash the windows of government trucks. At one point, the crowd surged and was pushed back. For a second time, they surged toward the building, and again they were pushed back, by marshals using three-foot riot batons.[39]

At 7:30, Barnett went on the air to announce that he had been informed by the attorney general that Meredith was on campus. Once again, Barnett tried to play both sides, saying that the campus was "surrounded by the armed forces and oppressive power of the United States of America . . . but we must at all odds preserve the peace and avoid bloodshed."[40] Attorney General Kennedy accused Barnett of double-dealing, saying that he had gone back on his word to maintain order on campus and to allow Meredith to register quietly behind the scenes.[41]

About a half hour later, when a two-foot piece of pipe struck one of the marshals, James McShane gave the order to fire tear gas. The crowd was forced back to a thirty-foot Confederate monument near the Lyceum. "From then on, for quite a while, [it] was a fairly tough evening," said attorney general press aide Ed Guthman.[42] Local radio stations were broadcasting bulletins of the "federal takeover." By 9:00, a number of Mississippi highway patrolmen, obligated to enforce the law, stood back, and in some cases they were aiding the protesters in their ugly confrontation with the marshals.

With the highway patrol abandoning its positions, carloads of men streamed through the gates. It appeared to Attorney General Kennedy that the state police officers withdrew at a crucial time, leading to an escalation of the violence. "Those bastards just walked off and left us," said one Justice Department official.[43] Deputy Attorney General Katzenbach pleaded in vain with Colonel Birdsong to order his officers back as the number of protesters on campus grew to close to two thousand.

Edwin Walker was prepared for just this moment. As early as December 1961, as Meredith's case was running its course through the courts, Walker took his self-described Truth Crusade to Jackson. It was his third public appearance since resigning from the army. Walker was already a local celebrity, greeted at the airport by more than fifty admirers, including Barnett and Congressman John Bell Williams.[44]

That evening, before more than 3,500 packed into the Jackson city auditorium, Walker called for preserving segregation in Mississippi, saying he was there "to take my stand, to live and die for Dixie." Walker dug deep into history, recalling "the federal tyranny of Reconstruction." For ninety minutes he was cheered as he used words that sounded like a call for violent insurrection if the segregationists didn't get their way in the courts. The state's "resolute determination to defend its sovereignty," Walker said, was "due to the fact that few states have as high a percentage of men and women who know how to use firearms."[45]

He praised the Citizens' Council as patriots prepared to "die in the assault." The battle, Walker told his adoring followers, was between the state of Mississippi and unnamed communists. "I came here to meet the communists on their battlefield right here in Mississippi. We are at war. Man your weapons and attack."

In the months leading to the explosive events at the Ole Miss campus, Walker fantasized about a well-orchestrated master plan by the Kremlin and the invisible deep state inside the Kennedy administration to integrate southern schools, opening the way for race mixing. The "anti-Christ conspirators in the Supreme Court" were behind James Meredith's attempt to attend classes at the University of Mississippi. It was "a conspiracy from within."[46] Walker said newspapers and broadcasters had defamed the good people of Mississippi. Magazines like *Time, Newsweek,* and *Look* were "un-American." Among Walker's media enemies was one journalist he called out by name, Washington columnist Drew Pearson.[47]

Just two days before the riot that left the campus smoldering, Walker was on the radio, riding on his popularity among the hard Right as the muzzled army general. In an interview with WNOE of New Orleans, Walker compared the coming showdown at Ole Miss with his command of troops at Little Rock five years earlier. "It was unconstitutional [and] I knew it was unconstitutional. My principles have not changed, but now out of uniform I am on the other side and this time on the right side." Fighting over integration, he said, diverted our attention from Nikita Khrushchev, "who has established that he intends to bury us."[48]

"We Will Move with the Punches"

Walker claimed he had been overwhelmed with offers of assistance to block Meredith's admission.[49] In call-in radio programs in Shreveport and Dallas, Walker urged extremists to mobilize "ten thousand strong" to converge on Oxford. "It is time to make a move . . . It's time to rise, to make a stand beside Governor Ross Barnett." Walker seemed to be preparing for a long showdown with the federal government with his call to "rally to the cause of freedom . . . Bring your flag, your tent, and your skillet."[50] When he was asked whether volunteers should come to Oxford armed, Walker was careful in his words, but the dog whistle was clear: "I have stated that whatever is necessary to oppose [Meredith's entry to the campus] should be done." For Walker there was no ambiguity—if troops were deployed to Ole Miss, "we will move with the punches."[51] With threats like that, the FBI was taking notice that Walker's call for volunteers was striking a chord with some of the more dangerous elements.

As the day for campus registration moved closer, Attorney General Kennedy was ready to cite Walker for contempt of a federal court order if he made good on his promise to block Meredith's entrance to the university.[52] Dwight Eisenhower, looking back at Little Rock, supported Kennedy's firm stand at Oxford. The former president also distanced himself from Walker. "I don't think I know the gentleman but I'll tell you this: Don't ever believe that this federal government can afford to evade its responsibility of enforcing the law."[53]

Walker arrived in Oxford on Saturday, September 29, as the streets of the quiet college town were beginning to fill with an angry mob spoiling for a fight. Walker acted as if he were still in uniform, commanding what he believed would be "thousands, possibly tens of thousands, of people on their way to Mississippi from across the nation." Again, his language betrayed more than just delusions about the number of his supporters. In a statement to NBC later that day, he compared the use of federal troops to enforce the law to the crucifixion of Christ.[54] Even Citizens' Council chief Bill Simmons thought Walker was too extreme.[55]

One person who repeatedly tried to talk Walker out of going to the Ole Miss campus was his lawyer, Clyde Watts. Watts called Walker in Oxford on September 29, saying that he had been alerted by friends in Washington that Walker could be charged with sedition. Watts urged him to stay in his hotel room, but as usual, Walker refused to listen even as he was under surveillance.[56]

FBI field offices in several states were receiving calls, most lacking credibility, about the number of men on their way to Oxford. The Houston office received a highly exaggerated tip about thousands en route to Mississippi. The FBI also tracked reports that as many as six hundred Klansmen from Alabama were on their way. The Alabama Klan's imperial wizard, Robert Shelton, had already staged a rally and cross burning in Tuscaloosa. Shelton said he was prepared to come to the assistance of Barnett and "any official who will defy President Kennedy."[57]

Aside from the Klan, agents were concerned about Robert DePugh's Minutemen, a small but dangerous group of domestic terrorists. One twenty-two-year-old member of the Minutemen on his way to Oxford was arrested by Dallas police, who discovered an arsenal in the car's trunk, including four pistols, a rifle, and up to three thousand rounds of ammunition. He told police he was inspired by Walker's call to action and that he knew Walker personally.[58] In one instance, FBI informants warned that if Meredith was admitted, "Walker's followers will go underground" to wage war against the federal government.[59]

On the afternoon of September 30—just hours before the outbreak of violence—Walker held yet another press conference, at the Ole Miss Motel. Detached from reality, Walker told reporters "the movement is national. Thousands are moving in and the roads are blocked from every direction." Typical of his odd behavior, Walker insisted that reporters stand in front of him and not photograph him from the side.[60] With Walker clearly identified as a threat, Secretary of the Army Vance ordered General Abrams to seize Walker if necessary.[61] That evening, as Walker was getting dinner at a downtown restaurant, hundreds of students were in open conflict with the armed marshals at the Lyceum.

President Kennedy tried repeatedly to convince Barnett to end the crisis, even as the governor told an exasperated president that the students were not the problem. "There are thousands of outsiders that will be there . . . There are men in there with trucks and shotguns and all such as that."[62] After three separate telephone conversations with Barnett and no settlement in sight, the president addressed the nation, saying that Americans were free to disagree with the law but not to disobey it. "No mob, however unruly or boisterous, is entitled to defy a court of law." Kennedy then announced that the National Guard would be deployed to restore order. Kennedy closed his address by saying it was regrettable that the stalemate with Ross Barnett had come to this but that "all other avenues and alternatives . . . have been tried and exhausted."[63]

Walker's "Ghostly Glow in the Gloom"

"Nauseating," Walker reportedly said, as he listened to the president's speech over dinner. He was a local hero, and one patron offered to pick up his tab. Dinner over, Walker was on his way to join the battle.[64] Walker's earlier attempt to enter the campus by car had failed, so he now made his way on foot, arriving between 8:45 and 9:00.[65] By this time the marshals were backed into a defensive position against rioters armed with pipes and bricks. The first casualty in what had become a full-blown riot was a member of the press. Around 9:00, the body of Paul Guihard was found, shot in the back with a .38-caliber revolver. Guihard was a thirty-year-old New York–based reporter for Agence France-Presse. His killer was never identified.[66]

Walker took his position at the Confederate monument on a circle opposite the Lyceum. As one correspondent poetically recalled, Walker's "dark suit and white western hat gave off a ghostly glow in the gloom."[67] Now, the very center of the campus became a rallying point for those looking for a fight, some hailing Walker as the leader of the insurrection. Those surrounding Walker took his word that thousands of armed volunteers were on their way—a pure fantasy.[68]

From there, the chain of events becomes murky as various witnesses gave accounts of the night of September 30 and the morning hours of October 1. Standing at the base of the towering monument, Walker began urging a crowd of about two hundred to keep up the confrontation with the marshals to force them to "drop their badges and just turn around and desert." The numbers at the monument grew by several hundred more over the next hour as carloads of mostly young men entered the campus. The occasional sound of gunfire could be heard in the darkness.[69]

A reporter for the *St. Louis Post-Dispatch* wrote, "When word of [Walker's] identity spread, people moved toward him as if attracted by a magnet. It was as if he played some magic music on a flute, so eager were these people to see him."[70] Easily recognizable under his Stetson hat, it seemed to some observers that Walker had command over about a dozen men who appeared to be coordinating some parts of the riot. Newspaper reporters also approached Walker for interviews, which he turned down. According to Deputy Sheriff Talmadge Witt, Walker asked to be deputized, a request that was quickly rejected.[71]

At one point, Walker led the mob, now swelled to close to eight hundred, from the monument toward the Lyceum, but they were repelled by a volley of tear gas. Witnesses recalled that Walker told those huddled around him that Thomas Birdsong, the chief of the state highway patrol, had sold them out by allowing federal marshals on campus. However, highway patrolmen were already abandoning their positions.[72]

Although Walker declared that he had done nothing to encourage violence, later court proceedings painted a different picture. Some witnesses said Walker instructed the crowd to charge the federal marshals, shouting, "Any bloodshed here tonight is on the hands of the federal government . . . Don't let up now . . . You will win in the end." As students reported injuries, Walker pushed them to continue their assault. "You are getting news all over the country. Now you've got casualties."[73] According to some accounts, Walker told one group at the base of the monument, which was described as his command post, "You must be prepared for possible death. If you're not willing to pay the price, go home now . . . Show them what you're made of."[74] Conservative commentator James J. Kilpatrick of the *Richmond News Leader*, who called the riot "the gravest state-federal conflict since the Civil War," described Walker as "one of the strangest characters in this drama . . . flashing messianic fire from cold, fanatic eyes."[75]

As the fighting intensified through the night, Walker got into a nasty exchange with Reverend Duncan Gray, rector of Oxford's St. Peter's Episcopal Church. Only three months earlier, Gray had presided over the burial of William Faulkner, and in the days leading up to the crisis he served as a conduit between the Justice Department Civil Rights Division and the university chancellor.[76] Calling on the crowd to leave the campus in peace, Gray started to clear away some of the bricks and bottles used as weapons. Recognizing that Walker had the ear of the rioters, Gray asked him to intervene; the town he loved was being destroyed.[77]

Walker responded by saying he was not interested in halting the riot, and that even if he wanted to, it was a spontaneous protest that was unstoppable. He then turned to the reverend and said, "You're the kind of Episcopal minister that makes me ashamed to be an Episcopalian."[78] Gray's second appeal to Walker ended in what some said was a threat against the pastor, as Walker told those around him, "There is an Episcopal priest here who wants you to go home." Gray was pulled off the base of the monument and pinned to the ground, but within seconds he was shielded by friends and escorted to the YMCA building not far from the Lyceum.[79]

Most witnesses and journalists agreed that Walker was acting in the role of a military commander, orchestrating the course of the riot and giving orders to charge the Lyceum or to retreat. He directed students to break into the power plant to shut off lights on the campus and urged them to attack a fire truck. To shouts of "Give 'em hell, General," Walker responded, "I sure will."[80]

Sometime around 10:30, Walker gave another order for the entire crowd of several hundred to advance at once from the statue to the Lyceum, with the words, "Stand by your governor. Charge!" Walker encouraged them to hurl rocks and other debris at the marshals, until they were again repulsed by tear gas.[81] When Walker was pressed about the arrival of the thousands of volunteers he had promised, he replied, "They'll be here tomorrow all right . . . Don't let the communists get you down."[82]

Later that night, Walker became more cautious, knowing that federal authorities were watching, as he dissuaded one man from using his army sharpshooter skills to shoot the lights out of the marshals' vehicles. He told the marksman the government should be the first to fire. By 11:00, Walker saw the riot reaching a critical point and told those surrounding him at the monument that he was ready to broadcast to the world. "As soon as I get on the radio, I'll tell them what's going on here."[83] Informed of Walker's role in the crisis, President Kennedy replied, "General Walker, imagine that son of a bitch having been commander of a division up until last year. And the Army promoting him."[84]

As the situation became more dire for the embattled federal marshals, and as cars on campus went up in flames, Katzenbach instructed General Charles Billingslea, the top army officer for the operation, to send federalized Mississippi National Guard troops to the campus. Arriving at about 11:30, a small unit of guardsmen endured bricks, Molotov cocktails, and gunfire on their way from the campus entrance to the Lyceum. A dozen of the guardsmen were injured and one jeep had six bullet holes.[85] About a half hour later, the rioters commandeered vehicles, including a fire truck and a bulldozer, to charge the marshals, but each time they were repelled by tear gas.[86] One deputy marshal told Katzenbach that the fighting had turned into an armed insurrection against the United States, especially as a large number of agitators, including contingents of Klansmen, continued to converge on Oxford.[87]

The president again called on Barnett to get the highway patrolmen back on the job. Barnett and Kennedy also talked about the possibility of evacuating Meredith by helicopter, as the president knew that more troops were needed to rescue the overwhelmed marshals.[88] Aside from Paul Guihard, the other casualty in the Oxford battle was a twenty-three-year-old jukebox repairman named Ray Gunter who went to the campus that night to simply observe. He was felled by gunfire, shot in the forehead with a .38-caliber round. It was never determined who fired the gun.[89]

Although Kennedy feared that the young Mississippi guardsmen might not obey a federal order, historian James Silver said there were no incidents of any of them refusing to serve. These were men who may have shared the prejudices of their fellow Mississippians, but they were first and foremost soldiers of the United States, summoned by the president to enforce the law.[90]

By midnight, many of the students had returned to their dorms and the outsiders took over. Barnett again was on the radio, still defiant. "I will never yield a single inch . . . I call upon every Mississippian to keep his faith and his courage. We will never surrender."[91] In the early morning hours of October 1, more than three thousand regular army soldiers and guardsmen were restoring order on campus. Ironically, among them were paratroopers from the 101st Airborne Division, the very soldiers Walker had led at Little Rock five years earlier.

By 5:00 a.m., the university was under federal control. Meredith would be registered at 8:00. A squad of marshals, Chief US Marshal James McShane, and the Justice Department's John Doar accompanied Meredith to the Lyceum as the first African American student at the University of Mississippi. Segregation at one of the most impenetrable bastions of white supremacy was ending. As one journalist wrote, "A second American civil war was fought on the campus of the University of Mississippi."[92]

Barnett ordered the Mississippi flag flown at half-mast and accused "trigger-happy" US marshals of igniting the violence. For Attorney General Kennedy, Barnett was guilty of letting loose a mob by not demanding that state police officers return to their posts and stop convoys of outsiders entering the campus.[93]

The Justice Department Orders Walker's Arrest

With the university returning to some semblance of normalcy, the toll and scope of the insurrection was revealing itself. In addition to the two civilian deaths, 166 US marshals were injured, twenty-nine of them with gunshot wounds.[94] The army reported that forty-eight soldiers sustained injuries and up to seventy people were treated in the university infirmary. Estimates of total nonfatal injuries on campus and in town topped three hundred.[95]

Within hours of the riot's end, as many as fifty FBI agents from field offices in Dallas, Memphis, New Orleans, and St. Louis were rushed to Oxford to interview witnesses and detainees. At the same time, the Justice Department was making its case against Walker, identifying him as a leader in the insurrection. Deputy Attorney General Katzenbach issued an order to arrest the former army general.

The Justice Department was particularly concerned about Walker's activities at about 2:00 on the morning of October 1, when he apparently drove with a companion to a Gulf gas station near the university's west entrance. There, he met with several other men, who grabbed a twenty-four-bottle case of empty soft drink bottles, filled a five-gallon can with gasoline, and drove off in a Chevrolet station wagon toward campus.[96] Walker then returned to the Mansel Motel on Highway 6 West, having checked in earlier under the assumed name of John Waters. The motel was under FBI surveillance, and Walker's phone had been tapped.[97]

Although the rioting on campus was over after daybreak on October 1, a volatile situation remained at Oxford's Courthouse Square. As many as five hundred soldiers, armed with bayonets, blocked off the square as they faced young men hurling bottles and rocks. Tear gas canisters exploded, sending them back several times.[98] Emerging from his hotel at about 9:00, dressed in a dark blue suit and white Stetson, Walker took a commanding position at the square. He was encouraging several large groups of young men who periodically showered passing cars and trucks with bricks and bottles. Some were calling for a violent march into the town's Black neighborhood.[99]

A squad of infantrymen approached Walker with bayonets, but they were unaware that he was a wanted man. From there, he made his way across the square to his car, amid about one hundred supporters.[100] "The crowd cheered him like a baseball hero after the home run that won the game . . . They followed him out of the square like the Pied Piper," according to Army Lieutenant Charles Shockley, an African American soldier.[101]

At about 9:30, Walker proceeded to a pharmacy near campus and read a statement over the phone to the Memphis radio station WREC, blaming the violence on the marshals and the Kennedys. Walker claimed that several people were beaten after being handcuffed. The South, he said, was not ready to yield to modernity. "They don't understand in Washington that most of the students come from homes favoring segregation."[102]

Walker, along with his close friend Robert Surrey, started to drive out of town toward Jackson sometime after 10:00 a.m. Before they got more than three miles on Highway 7, their car was stopped at an army roadblock. The soldiers radioed senior officers back at Courthouse Square, and after about an hour Walker was returned to the Lyceum under an army escort.[103] From there he was brought to the Federal Building downtown, where he was formally charged with seditious conspiracy—opposing by force the laws of the United States. He also was charged with impeding federal officers and inciting and engaging "in an insurrection against the authority of the United States." Bail was set at $100,000. If convicted of all charges, Walker could face thirty-nine years in prison and fines of up to $40,000.[104]

US Attorney H. M. Ray said federal officials felt a sense of urgency in apprehending Walker, viewing him as a serious danger to the rule of law. At the time, said Ray, "nobody had any idea whether we were going to have [a] kind of Coxey's army in Oxford," referring to an 1894 march on Washington by hundreds of unemployed workers.[105]

General Edwin A. Walker was among about two hundred people arrested between September 30 and October 2, with the majority coming from outside Oxford. Now in US custody, he told reporters, "They don't have a thing on me." Walker said he was just an observer. "I never locked hands with anybody . . . The whole thing was a campus affair."[106]

In Washington, Attorney General Kennedy held an impromptu press conference outside his office, the first since the violence began, to inform reporters of Walker's arrest. Beyond that, the White House was saying little.[107] After two questions about Walker's status with the army, White House press secretary Pierre Salinger let out an exasperated, "He is out. He resigned. He quit the service. He is a civilian."[108] Walker received no sympathy from former colleagues in the Pentagon. General Maxwell Taylor, chairman of the Joint Chiefs of Staff, made it clear that Walker no longer wore the uniform of the US Army and should stand trial.[109]

Outside the Deep South, the press largely applauded Walker's arrest. The *St. Louis Post-Dispatch* called for Walker to be "quite unceremoniously clapped into jail. He was entitled to make all the incoherent speeches he cared to about the Mississippi situation, but when he incites to violence he becomes an ordinary criminal and should be dealt with as such."[110] Philadelphia's major daily asked why the Justice Department did not act earlier and remove Walker from the campus before the outbreak of violence.[111]

Not surprisingly, Walker had his defenders in the segregationist press. Columnist Tom Ethridge of the *Jackson Clarion-Ledger* saw the Kennedy White House and the Supreme Court as dead set on the "enslavement of the American people by a Washington dictatorship." The dictatorship allusion went to even more bizarre lengths in rural Texas, where one newspaper's headline read "Heinrich Himmler Reincarnation Shown in General Walker's Arrest."[112]

"America's First Political Prisoner"

Columnist James J. Kilpatrick of the *Richmond News Leader,* who had earlier described Walker as one of the strangest characters in the Ole Miss riot, objected to the way Walker was treated during his arrest by "five husky deputies."[113] In the summer of 1963, as Alabama's segregated schools were challenged, the editors of the Richmond daily again waved the banner of states' rights, warning that Kennedy was ready to use the army to enforce school desegregation in yet another southern state. "It has been an eventful year full of surprises. We doubt that Mr. Walker was surprised."[114]

Some editorial writers in the South deplored the attempt to deny James Meredith his right to attend a public university. The *Charlotte Observer* poetically noted that Governor Barnett and his followers had reaped the whirlwind, and the equally poetic editors of the *Louisville Courier-Journal* referred to Walker as "the pinup boy of the Birchers."[115] But Walker was no pinup boy to his lawyer, Clyde Watts. In his view, Watts's client and longtime friend was America's first political prisoner; there was no proof that Walker had advocated anything more than peaceful protest. He went to Mississippi "fully cognizant he was a target of the federal government."[116] Friends in the Far Right ecosystem offered their counsel, seeing a host of conspiracies behind Walker's arrest. For some, the conspirators were the newspapers, infiltrated by communists.[117] Others saw Walker's arrest as part of a government scheme to discredit him—he was "being railroaded." Walker's bail, said one member of Congress, was more than was required for "hardened criminals."[118]

In response, Burke Marshall, the head of the Justice Department Civil Rights Division, said that given the seriousness of the charges, "armed conspiracy against the United States," the bail was "entirely reasonable." Marshall concluded that a large number of confiscated weapons—"and very dangerous weapons"—came from those heeding Walker's call for insurrection.[119]

Walker waived a preliminary hearing, believing he could post bail immediately. He scrambled to try to raise the money, calling his brother, George, figuring he could come up with the sum from family property and investments.[120]

Meanwhile, US Commissioner Omar Craig directed that Walker be confined to a jail in the Northern District of Mississippi. But that changed rapidly as the director of the Federal Bureau of Prisons in Washington concluded that there was no facility suitable to hold Walker in Mississippi and that he should be sent to the Medical Center for Federal Prisoners in Springfield, Missouri.[121]

In a matter of about four hours after he was formally charged, Walker was in a Border Patrol aircraft flying to the federal medical center, where he was held in the psychiatric wing. Clyde Watts objected to the spiriting of his client to Missouri without a reasonable time to make bond, and without counsel or a hearing, but US Attorney Ray said the jails in Oxford and nearby counties were not built or staffed to hold a high-profile inmate like Walker. Ray also was concerned that asking local sheriffs to hold Walker would "put them on the spot" and might even have aided in his escape, given that they likely would have been supportive of Walker's segregationist stance.[122]

Burke Marshall defended the government's actions and said that Walker was fully accorded all his rights, even as he waived counsel and a preliminary hearing.[123] Watts sniffed a scheme planned by Robert Kennedy's Justice Department to get Walker far from Oxford as soon as possible. Watts was certain Kennedy wanted Walker out of the way so he could not "tell the true story" until after the news media spread its version of events at Ole Miss.[124]

Walker would undergo a psychiatric examination to determine if he was competent to stand trial. His sanity came under question from a number of quarters. Duncan Gray, the minister who confronted Walker at the Confederate statue, described him as having "a wild, dazed look in his eyes." One US senator labeled Walker a psychopath, and another, Oregon senator Wayne Morse, thought Walker might be insane, and "if he is, he ought to be committed."[125] Walker's sanity was even questioned in the international press, with one Rio de Janeiro headline on his arrest reading succinctly, "Racist Jailed: Crazy."[126]

Walker's brief incarceration not only fed radical Right conspiracy theories about psychiatry and mental health treatment but also contributed to a national debate about the rights of politically prominent figures suspected of being mentally unstable.

American Nazi Party leader George Lincoln Rockwell had fulsome praise for Edwin Walker and attempted to recruit him. Although Walker expressed many of the same racist views as Rockwell, he declined the invitation to join the Nazis. (Library of Congress, Prints and Photographs Division, Washington, DC)

Marina Oswald told FBI agents that it was her husband, Lee Harvey Oswald, who had attempted to kill Walker as he sat by a window in his Dallas home. It was just six months before Lee Oswald assassinated President John F. Kennedy. (Library of Congress, Prints and Photographs Division, Washington, DC)

Arkansas senator William Fulbright (*left*) said General Walker and other extremists in the armed forces were a potential threat to democracy. Senator Wayne Morse of Oregon (*right*) was more blunt in his assessment of Walker. If Walker was insane, Morse said, "he ought to be committed." (Library of Congress, Prints and Photographs Division, Washington, DC)

Arizona senator and 1964 presidential candidate Barry Goldwater said he would much rather have a tough-talking anticommunist like Edwin Walker as a commanding officer than have a "bunch of namby-pambies as our generals." (Library of Congress, Prints and Photographs Division, Washington, DC)

On September 25, 1957, General Walker (*left*), with Colonel William Kuhn (*right*), led federal troops to ensure that nine Black students could safely enter Central High School in Little Rock, Arkansas. Although Walker was an unrepentant racist, he carried out President Dwight Eisenhower's orders with military efficiency. (Library of Congress, Prints and Photographs Division, NYWT&S Collection, LC-USZ62-135290)

The bayonet became a potent symbol for the Citizens' Council and for segregationists throughout the South as soldiers under General Walker protected the Little Rock Nine from a violent mob. One southern senator went so far as to compare Walker's tactics with Hitler's storm troopers. (*Citizens' Council* 3, no. 2 [November 1957])

Fundamentalist preacher Billy James Hargis, shown here in a publicity photo, made Edwin Walker a headliner at his Christian Crusade conventions. In 1963, the pair took a twenty-seven-city tour to sound the alarm about a conspiracy at work in the United Nations and the Kremlin to create a one-world dictatorship. (Special Collections, University of Arkansas Libraries)

Edwin Walker told five thousand enthusiastic supporters at a Dallas rally in December 1961 that he was free from the power of the "little men" in Washington who had forced him out of the army. Two months later he would launch an unsuccessful campaign for Texas governor. (Shel Hershorn Photographic Archive, Dolph Briscoe Center for American History, University of Texas at Austin)

General Walker's defenders claimed he had been "muzzled" by career diplomats in the State Department who were more interested in arms control deals with Moscow than the imminent threat of a communist conspiracy to enslave America. (Edwin A. Walker Papers, Dolph Briscoe Center for American History, University of Texas at Austin)

6

"Standing on the Brink of the Pit of Hell"

It was a humiliating sight as Edwin Walker, who had led troops in World War II and Korea, was now escorted by armed US marshals to a prison for psychiatric patients. The morning after he was checked into the US Medical Center for Federal Prisoners, Walker's legal team got to work, calling for his immediate release.

Ruling from Oxford, Mississippi, Federal District Judge Claude Clayton ordered that Walker be committed for sixty to ninety days to undergo psychiatric examinations. Did Walker understand the charges against him, and could he accurately recollect his actions the night of September 30 and the morning of October 1?[1] Clyde Watts said he was unaware that his client had been flown to Missouri until after the plane had landed, calling Walker's detention illegal and a violation of his constitutional rights. Walker would not become eligible to be released on bail until after his psychiatric examination. Watts objected to Judge Clayton ordering Walker to a psychiatric hospital without him being present in the courtroom; the judge was unable to see for himself Walker's "absolute mental clarity."[2] Watts advised his client to only give his name, rank, and serial number—"the same as any American soldier who has been captured."[3]

Confined to a room by himself with the door locked only at night, Walker was among one thousand other inmates at the facility, the only one of its kind housing federal prisoners with psychiatric problems. Walker was held in the jail part of the complex, not the psychiatric hospital, and by all accounts he appeared calm and lucid on his first day.[4]

On October 3, Watts requested the federal district court in Springfield to grant either a writ of habeas corpus, to contest his confinement, or an injunction against any medical treatment without the presence of a physician or psychiatrist approved by Walker's lawyers. Watts insisted that his client was innocent of charges that he incited the violence, and in fact had tried to prevent it.[5] The "laudable efforts" to admit James Meredith to Ole Miss, said Watts, had also led to denying the constitutional rights of one of the country's most "devoted, selfless, and patriotic ex-soldiers."[6]

That same day, on the floor of the House of Representatives, fellow Texan congressman Bruce Alger referred to "sinister overtones" in the Justice Department's handling of Walker's arrest. Alger had received a frantic call from Walker's mother, Charlotte, he said, "appealing to me to protect her son from what appears to be a deliberate conspiracy."[7]

Joining Walker's legal team was Robert Morris, the former president of the University of Dallas and a key figure in ultra Right politics in Texas. Morris, who had served as a lawyer for the House Un-American Activities Committee, called on Mississippi senator James Eastland to convene an investigation into Walker's incarceration. "One would think we're in Havana or Budapest the way General Walker has been treated," Morris said in a telegram to Eastland. It was done, Morris said, "in the face of overwhelming evidence that he is in full possession of his faculties."[8] The argument that Walker's confinement was a violation of his civil rights found support in a few places outside his team of lawyers. The editorial writers of the *Washington Star,* falling short of labeling Walker a political prisoner, said "there is strong support his legal rights have been violated."[9] To the editors of the *Wall Street Journal,* if due process of law was suspended in one case, "then no man can be safe from the scowl of the Attorney General."[10]

While it condemned Walker's appeal to the most racist and violent elements of society, the American Civil Liberties Union questioned whether Walker was being treated fairly. Agreeing with Clyde Watts, ACLU chairman Ernest Angell said that he also objected to the fact that neither Walker nor his lawyers were present at the court hearing that ordered Walker's confinement. He added that holding Walker for sixty to ninety days was unusually long. "We urge the examination be completed as expeditiously as possible to avoid even the impression that he is being detained to deny him bail or a speedy trial."[11]

Outside the federal prison, a few of Walker's supporters gathered, handing out a single-page flier warning that his case was "grim evidence of what can happen to a patriot who dares speak out against a vindictive administration."[12] The Justice Department was explicit that given Walker's status as a former military officer "who had served his country for 30 years," he was treated with respect during his stay in Springfield.[13] Saying that Walker's arrest and commitment were fully in accordance with the law, the Justice Department also felt it was necessary to settle any doubt about his competence to stand trial.[14]

The court's decision to order a psychiatric examination was based on a government physician's assessment of Walker's mental health. Dr. Charles E. Smith, chief psychiatrist for the Federal Bureau of Prisons, said that Walker's behavior included "unpredictable and seemingly bizarre outbursts of the type often observed in individuals suffering with paranoid mental disorder." Smith did not meet with Walker but evaluated his army medical records and news accounts of his actions at the University of Mississippi as well as his appearance before Congress. In particular, during the April 1962 Senate hearing, Walker had told of a government fifth column—the so-called control apparatus. For Smith, this pointed to a deep-seated paranoia. In addition, at the time of the hearings, Walker had assaulted a news reporter. Looking at the full picture of Walker's actions and words, Smith concluded that "his recent behavior has been out of keeping with that of a person of his station, background, and training, and it may be indicative of an underlying mental disorder."[15]

US Attorney H. M. Ray defended the decision to commit Walker based not just on news reports and congressional testimony but also on eyewitness accounts of his behavior at the Confederate monument. Walker clearly was a leader of the insurrection as it moved from the university to downtown Oxford.[16] To Ray, someone of Walker's stature in the armed forces who is charged with sedition could well be insane, or certainly not competent to stand trial.[17] One attorney was a bit more blunt, saying that "it is one thing for rednecks" to be involved in a mob, but quite another for a man who had attained the rank of general.[18]

Morris questioned whether an accurate diagnosis of Walker's mental state could be made from afar without interviewing the patient. Morris called for Smith's firing, and in language that could only be described as reprehensible by today's standards, Morris went further, saying, "For Dr. Smith to conclude on the basis of news reports that General Walker is mentally disturbed and paranoid is one more shred of evidence that General Walker is being lynched not by a rope but by a psychiatric examination."[19] The American Medical Association received as many as 2,500 letters from physicians questioning whether Smith's failure to conduct a personal examination before reaching his conclusions was a breach of medical ethics. Some of the letters also claimed that making public statements regarding Walker's mental health was a violation of physician–patient confidentiality.[20]

The more conservative Texas Medical Association commended the AMA for looking into the matter, but in the final analysis, the AMA, along with the American Psychiatric Association, ruled that Dr. Smith had not violated medical ethics in recommending Walker for psychiatric evaluation.[21] Technically, Dr. Smith had not made a medical diagnosis. In fact, the AMA concluded that "physicians are frequently called upon by attorneys or courts to render a professional opinion." Then it is the court's responsibility to assess that opinion.[22] Nonetheless, Walker's defense team held that Smith had made a diagnosis, and they pointed to a government brief that referred to Smith's conclusions as a "psychiatric diagnosis."[23]

Walker's lawyers were moving quickly to free their client, but there would be strings attached. US District Judge John Oliver ordered the federal government to show cause why Walker should not be released upon posting bail, and on October 6 his bail was reduced from $100,000 to $50,000. Walker's family put up the money and he was released that night. When he was met by his mother, who arrived from her home in San Antonio, Edwin Walker reportedly said, "You surprised me. Where did you get all that money?"[24]

Attorney Watts made the questionable claim that the government was prepared to negotiate Walker's release in the face of public pressure. "The government, although they had not seen the light, was beginning to feel the heat," and the Justice Department could not ignore the "cries of outraged citizens."[25] Justice Department lawyers said that Walker's release on a reduced bond refuted Watts's position that Walker was a political prisoner.[26]

In return for his freedom, Walker agreed to report to the Southwestern Medical Center in Dallas, within five days, for a preliminary evaluation. Dr. Robert Stubblefield, the center's chief psychiatrist, along with an additional psychiatrist named by the government, would examine Walker. Following that, he would report for a full battery of psychiatric tests.[27]

Walker swiftly returned to Dallas by private plane, telling about two hundred followers gathered at Love Field that he had been on a "short trip to Mississippi that was extended to Missouri."[28] When local reporters asked about the insurrection at Ole Miss, lawyers intervened. Even so, Walker made the hardly believable statement that he was on campus for a peaceful protest. As for his sanity, Walker told the press, "That is what we are trying to determine." Referring to his failed campaign for governor, he added, "I am sorry to put 140,000 voters into the position that my sanity is being questioned." Quickly hustled off by lawyers Morris and Watts, with his mother close behind, Walker exited to the singing of "For He's a Jolly Good Fellow."[29]

Indicating no rush to comply with the court order, Walker's attorneys dragged their feet, waiting until just before the five-day deadline to check him into Southwestern Medical Center for a twenty-minute consultation. Morris called it "inconceivable" that the psychiatrists would not find that Walker met the minimal standards of mental competency set by law.[30] Morris also objected to Dr. Winfred Overholser, the government psychiatrist who was to work alongside Dr. Stubblefield. Morris called Overholser, the retired superintendent of St. Elizabeth's Hospital in Washington, DC, "a man who presses for commitments to mental institutions." The court upheld Morris's complaint and Overholser was withdrawn from the case.[31]

The Department of Justice remained confident in Stubblefield's ability to examine Walker fairly and he was permitted to appoint his own medical team. Stubblefield chose Dr. Andrew Watson, a member of both the medical and law faculties of the University of Michigan, Charles Webster of the Southern Methodist University School of Law, and Dr. Titus Harris from the University of Texas Medical School. Stubblefield told the court the team would be open about the methods used to judge Walker's competence, anticipating that Morris and Watts would challenge their findings if they concluded that Walker was mentally unstable. In particular, they wanted to determine whether he could understand the charges against him and could accurately remember the incidents leading to his arrest. Just as significantly, Stubblefield told the court—and this was underlined for emphasis—he wanted to ensure that Walker could consult with his lawyers "with a reasonable degree of *rational* understanding and whether he had a *rational* as well as factual understanding of the proceedings."[32]

"Some Worrisome Behaviors"

Finally, on November 8, Walker entered Parkland Hospital in Dallas for two days of comprehensive physical and psychiatric exams. Physically, the fifty-three-year-old Walker seemed healthy, with just a slight hearing loss in one ear and poor eyesight, evident by his thick glasses. As for his psychological state, Stubblefield found Walker "functioning at the superior level of intelligence" and described him as "friendly, alert, and cooperative." The conclusion was that Walker was competent to stand trial. Yet Walker did exhibit certain behaviors that were worrisome. He was quick to anger and harbored conspiratorial beliefs that were far outside the mainstream. What was left open to question was not his sanity but why he believed what he did, Stubblefield said. That would take a much more penetrating exploration.[33]

The FBI, which had closely followed Walker's activities at Ole Miss, offered its own, less scientific assessment of Walker's mental state. Though he was competent to stand trial, Walker, in the opinion of one informant, "appears to have a strong unconscious resentment toward the United States." In what may sound like a bit of armchair psychology, the FBI source saw in Walker "a mama's boy—that is, he is dominated by his mother." The FBI report concluded that Walker "operates better when he believes he is being persecuted." When Walker feels he is being ignored, "he is liable to do something to attract attention."[34]

On November 20 and 21, Walker was back in Oxford, facing Federal District Judge Claude Clayton, for a lengthy pretrial hearing. Clayton rejected a request to strike from the record Dr. Charles Smith's assessment that Walker suffered from paranoia.[35] In strong language that challenged Smith's evaluation of Walker's sanity, Clyde Watts said Smith's statements were "libelous, scandalous, and scurrilous." Smith's diagnosis, Watts said, should not be allowed to "pollute the records of this court." Clayton disagreed, saying the government was justified in taking into account Smith's report.[36]

US Attorney H. M. Ray pressed Smith about the general's medical condition when he commanded the 24th Infantry Division at Augsburg. Smith indicated that many of Walker's various physical complaints were likely psychosomatic. Smith noted that Walker had been treated for severe headaches, chronic backache, insomnia, and stomach problems, all of which "were found to be without apparent organic basis."[37]

Walker's lawyers asked why some medical records were not taken into account. For instance, in September 1961, the chief surgeon at army headquarters in Europe had found Walker mentally sound. Watts also asked why Smith only referred to an Associated Press report that described Walker urging the crowd to charge the US marshals, while not mentioning a United Press report that indicated Walker was holding the students back.[38] Watts, who often attached the label "Leftist" to the media, said newspaper reports leave the reader with an image of Walker as "an insurrectionist and perhaps a lunatic."[39]

In a testy cross-examination, Watts asked Smith if he believed that only a "lunatic" would be apprehensive about communist infiltration of the US government. Watts, no stranger to deep state conspiracy theories, also asked whether Smith would change his evaluation if it was proven that Walker was the victim of a "secret apparatus" running the army. But Smith was not having it, replying that until this secret apparatus was revealed, Walker was harboring "abnormal suspicions."[40] The chief of the campus police testified that he had heard Walker order the rioters to charge the marshals but that Walker, who was unarmed, stayed behind as the mob surged forward. He also told the court that the riot was in full force even before Walker gave the order to charge.[41]

Although Judge Clayton accepted the assessment that Walker was mentally competent and could be brought to trial, Walker was never tried. An all-white federal grand jury in Oxford adjourned without an indictment, and on January 21, 1963, Judge Clayton dismissed the charges against Walker and six others who also had been arrested. Walker's lawyers said it was a "vindication from charges of crime and lunacy." They also called for an end to compulsory pretrial psychiatric examinations, especially when it came to political cases like Walker's.[42] It was "an aberration of justice," Morris said, that "government psychiatrists had complete control over Walker's destiny without due process."[43] Of course, the liberal media, Watts said, gave more coverage to Walker's arrest than to the decision by the grand jury.[44]

Civil rights groups called the failure to indict outrageous. The *Mississippi Free Press,* a prominent voice of the NAACP, said that while Walker helped incite a mob to violence and had been freed, civil rights worker Clyde Kennard "languishes in prison." Kennard, who attempted three times to register at an all-white college, was falsely accused of burglary in 1960 and sentenced to prison, where he died at the age of thirty-six.[45]

Edwin Walker was now free, but the question of his sanity still lingered. Was he a deranged and possibly threatening political figure who commanded a following among some of the most violent and extremist groups in America? In a speech before segregationists in Mississippi, Walker made the incredible claim that unnamed communists were "trying to destroy me. They haven't succeeded yet." Some asked how a man with obvious paranoid fantasies could rise to be a two-star general.[46]

Inside the armed forces, those who knew Walker said he was sincere in his zealous but simplistic belief that every problem in America was somehow related to a communist plot. The situation in Walker's mind was so urgent that any action, no matter how extreme, was justified. Views this far outside the norm made Walker unfit to continue serving in the top echelons of the armed services. Most disturbing to some in the Defense Department was Walker's disregard for the law, a perilous course of action for a former army officer. Had Walker expressed some of these views earlier, he never would have made it through the ranks to major general.[47]

Some who recalled his service on the battlefields of World War II and Korea noted that Walker's personality had changed after he returned from Korea, as he became restless and impatient. "He is not at all the man he was when he was a combat officer," one of Walker's colleagues told the *New York Times*. Walker had asked to be relieved from a 1957 Pentagon staff assignment and was subsequently sent to command the Arkansas Military District, a "safe" post where little happens. After he led the troops at Little Rock, Walker's personality took an even sharper turn.[48] A psychiatrist testifying at Walker's pretrial hearing told the court "there is a real possibility that there has been a deterioration in the mental processes . . . in the past year or two."[49]

His friends in the military searched for reasons for Walker's increasingly abnormal behavior. Maybe it was the stress of rising through the ranks; career officers are under constant scrutiny in a system that demands conformity. But it was surprising to some that Walker would buckle under such stress. One longtime friend said that in war, Walker "always sought the toughest assignments—paratrooper, ranger, Special Service Force."[50]

Arkansas journalist Harry Ashmore recalled conversations with Walker during the crisis at Little Rock. The general had opened up about his personal troubles, telling Ashmore that his slow and steady climb up the military chain of command after Korea was sidelined. Maybe it was due to his political views, but being sent to Arkansas would have been more appropriate for an officer of a lower rank. Unseen forces, and possibly communists in the control apparatus, were at work against him even as far back as his days at West Point.[51]

Walker's Incoherent Speaking Style

Of all of Walker's eccentricities, it was his inability to express himself that was most noticeable. During Senate hearings in April 1962, the press was able to observe behavior that was markedly strange for a high-ranking officer. Washington columnist Mary McGrory said his answers to questions were repetitious and incoherent. "In the world of Mr. Walker, sentences have no beginnings, no endings, no verbs."[52]

Chalmers Roberts of the *Washington Post* said the hearings regarding Walker's troop indoctrination program revealed little except that Walker was inarticulate. "His speech was fumbling, his thoughts ran wild, he could not seem to answer a question." Roberts, like many in the press gallery, noticed that Walker's hands shook and that he nervously smoked cigarettes as he answered questions. Many of his answers took five to ten minutes and were rambling. Clyde Watts and Medford Evans sat at his elbows, trying desperately to coach him.[53] The military analyst for the *Detroit News,* General Samuel Marshall, described Walker as "an odd one. When he opens his mouth, his emotions run away with his judgment." Marshall, who had served as the chief historian of the European theater in World War II, said that Walker's swan song to Congress, when resigning from the army, was "maudlin, inaccurate, and peculiarly unmilitary in its self-pitying tone."[54]

The FBI, which was carefully monitoring Walker's public statements, filed a copy of an interview Walker had given to a radio call-in show in Shreveport, Louisiana, as tensions rose at the University of Mississippi. In the interview, Walker referred cryptically to "the invisible government" as part of an enormous international network. He then read a statement addressed to President Kennedy. In a jumble of words that hardly made sense, Walker revealed much about his confused and unsteady grasp of reality. Desegregating Ole Miss, he said, was the work of a "demagogic power being used by the federal law enforcement agencies in Mississippi as an internal policy which is corroborating and reciprocating in purpose with the enthronement and the escalation of Moscow's Castro."[55]

Walker's considerable ego was also revealed here when he told the radio audience that he had sent one thousand copies of this statement to the press. He urged listeners to check their local newspapers to see which members of the press had failed to print his letter, a sure sign that the media was controlled by the dark forces of the invisible government. Finally, his mood became more ominous. "I would like to warn your listeners further that it's time to make a move . . . We have listened and we have been pushed around far too much by the anti-Christ Supreme Court."[56] Walker's reference to anti-Christian forces operating inside the government was typical of what was often an apocalyptic tone. Even in a Christmas card to his troops at Augsburg, Walker had written, "We are standing on the brink of the pit of hell."[57]

An FBI informant attending one of Billy James Hargis's Christian Crusade conventions in Oklahoma City observed that Walker appeared distraught in the presence of reporters and photographers. A reporter for a local newspaper attending that same event, in August 1963, remarked that Walker, "twitching and bleary-eyed," was angrily defensive when television cameras approached. One of Walker's aides explained that flashbulbs and strobe lights "drive him crazy."

Even so, Walker, who said he "glories in his experience at Oxford," clearly enjoyed the times he was greeted by adoring followers.[58] Speaking to that enthusiastic crowd of Christian fundamentalists in Oklahoma City, he answered the applause of his audience by asking, "What am I doing? I'm propagandizing and agitating. Do you like it?" The question was answered with calls of "Walker for president."[59]

Dr. Manfred Guttmacher, a Baltimore psychiatrist who testified at Walker's hearing before Judge Clayton, said Walker had grandiose delusions of his power to mobilize thousands at Ole Miss.[60] It also seemed to Guttmacher that Walker was strangely misinformed for an army general, citing as examples his belief that cosmonaut Yuri Gagarin's flight into space on April 12, 1961, was a hoax, or that Kennedy had been considering sending foreign troops to quell the riot at Ole Miss.[61]

Walker could be uncomfortable and awkward in public, and some observers recalled that he sometimes would pause for several seconds, halfway through a sentence, staring blankly into space before finishing his thoughts. To Guttmacher, he often appeared confused.[62] At the end of the Senate hearings, McGrory concluded that Walker was living in an alternate universe "where only he identifies the enemy. Things are seldom what they seem in the world of Mr. Walker." Cecil Holland, McGrory's colleague at the *Washington Star*, wondered whether Walker was the "American General who could go haywire and start a nuclear war." Holland had hope that Walker was "so imbued with the military chain of command that he would never fire a shot unless ordered."[63]

Watching Walker under scrutiny on Capitol Hill was enough to convince Holland and many others in the press and in the armed services that he should never return to a position to command troops.[64] Nationally syndicated columnist Doris Fleeson was so amused with Walker's performance that she came to the conclusion that he was harmless and in no position to mobilize any movement of the militant Right. "Walker is not a menace . . . He wants to talk at length, not be a figurehead."[65]

Walker's erratic behavior could also become violent, and on several occasions he assaulted news reporters he felt were asking probing questions or were photographing him at the wrong angle. Tom Kelly of the Scripps-Howard newspapers was greeted with a right hand to the eye after approaching Walker with a question during hearings on Capitol Hill in April 1962. Kelly wanted to know whether Walker would disavow praise from Nazi leader George Lincoln Rockwell. After Walker struck Kelly, Watts quickly whisked Walker away. A few moments later, Kelly was further assaulted by a small group of women who had loudly voiced their support for Walker in the committee room. Seeing Kelly struck, one of them ran up and spat in his face as another attempted to grab his arm. Kelly's story the next day carried the headline "The General Led from the Right."[66]

For Kelly, the punch from "a confused man is not significant." It was the political mental health of the nation that was most troubling.[67] George Dixon, whose column for King Features appeared in hundreds of newspapers, noted "an ominous number of newsmen socked" recently, including three news photographers. As for the women who spat at Kelly, Dixon commented, "I can't imagine where those females came from, and I surely hope it's not my neighborhood."[68]

Walker's jab to Kelly's face would not be the last time he would strike out at a journalist. The following year, at the Public Affairs Luncheon Club in Dallas that featured Alabama Governor George Wallace as guest speaker, Walker objected to being photographed and shoved the cameraman for KRLD-TV to the ground. News director Eddie Barker filed a complaint with the FBI.[69] The press, to Walker, was the enemy—a coconspirator with the control apparatus. During speeches, Walker would often ask his audience to identify newspapers and radio and television stations that had been "infiltrated" by communists.[70]

Unsurprisingly, some of Walker's admirers also trafficked in ridiculous fantasies. The FBI took note of letters addressed to field offices, such as the one written after Walker was taken into custody following the riot at Ole Miss. The two-page letter alerted FBI Director Hoover that Walker's captors might be "tampering with his mind and body" and possibly subjecting him to a lobotomy or brainwashing him with drugs.[71] As it became clear that Walker was often unhinged, even prominent Birchers distanced themselves from the man they once believed was a potential leader of the American Right. California congressman John Rousselot, who came to Walker's defense during the debate over anticommunist troop indoctrination, began to see him as a political liability, saying that if Walker did incite violence at Ole Miss he should be expelled from the John Birch Society.[72]

Visions of an American Gulag

Edwin Walker's brief incarceration sparked a national debate about the government's power to commit a public figure to a psychiatric hospital. Walker's lawyer Robert Morris condemned pretrial psychiatric examinations for being biased by a psychiatrist who might very well be a communist.[73] On the political Right and among civil libertarians, Walker's incarceration was a dangerous precedent that reminded some of the forced treatment of dissidents in the Soviet Union. Walker's confinement was retaliation for opposing the Kennedys,

Morris said, and now anyone who raised their voice in protest could be rushed off to a psychiatric ward.[74]

Although the American Medical Association concluded it was permissible for Dr. Charles Smith to make an evaluation based on medical records and news reports, there was concern that a physician's opinion could be used to quash dissent. The AMA found that situations could arise when "a physician might be subject to political control . . . or be used as a tool for political purposes." The AMA urged doctors "to be alert to such possibilities" and to refuse to give medical opinions that might be used politically.[75] As one executive of the AMA noted, "An opportunity exists for abuse of authority."[76]

Clyde Watts agreed that the power to hold a defendant indefinitely without bond could be a weapon against dissidents—"a sword for the persecution" of someone out of favor with the government.[77] Watts recalled watching his close friend suffer "six gruesome and dismal days and nights in a federal hospital for the criminally insane."[78]

Several months after his confinement, Walker painted a picture of those "gruesome days and nights" to which his lawyer alluded. It is difficult to know how much of his account was true or fabricated, but Walker was obviously eager to tell his side of the story and sat down for several hours with a sympathetic reporter from an Amarillo newspaper. He told of being locked in a cell alone and periodically strip-searched. "Each time my mother visited me, I was stripped naked and searched . . . They took me from my cell into another room . . . and they searched me from the top of my head to the bottom of my feet."[79] In Walker's mind, this treatment was an attempt by the government to brainwash him into accepting racial integration. In another interview, he said, "I had Bobby Kennedy's indoctrination course in six days, and it didn't take."[80] Elsewhere he described his arrest as a way for the president "to get rid of me. He showed me how far we have gone down the police dictatorship line."[81]

Walker's allies on the Far Right saw his experience as proof that the government was about to build an American version of the Soviet gulag. Navy admiral John Crommelin believed that Americans soon would be herded into psychiatric facilities in Alaska to "reeducate" them into accepting racial integration.[82] Mainstream conservatives such as William F. Buckley Jr. and Russell Kirk of *National Review* rejected these ultra Right fantasies. Kirk, one of the leading conservative intellectuals, joked that Robert Welch was insane and ought to be put away. "Put away in Alaska?" Buckley asked.[83]

Yet for conspiracy theorists of the radical Right, it was no joking matter. Committing Walker to a series of psychiatric examinations was proof of federal tyranny. The John Birch Society envisioned a secret scheme to "dominate the psychiatric profession and use mental health laws as a means of gaining coercive control over those who oppose communism." Among the goals of the communists, as listed by the John Birch Society, was the ability to treat all behavioral problems as psychiatric disorders for political purposes.[84]

In the ultra Right worldview of the 1960s, the majority of psychiatrists were committed to secularism and socialism, and they were adept at mind control. But psychiatrists were not the only ones planting subversive and godless ideas into American thoughts; brainwashing came from every direction. Evangelists with Billy James Hargis's Christian Crusade saw a secret communist plot to flood American teens with immoral lyrics through the songs of the Beatles. The Fab Four were "invad[ing] the minds of our children to render them mentally incompetent and neurotic."[85] Walker told the five hundred guests of Hargis's Christian Crusade convention in Oklahoma City that he had been committed by secular government psychiatrists who "make heroes out of beatniks undermining military discipline." It was a master plan, of course, of psychiatrists trying to silence the voice of patriots in the armed forces.[86]

The John Birch Society found brainwashing and psychiatric treatment at the root of the United Nations strategy for a one-world government, and Walker's case was a prelude to what the communists had in store for the American people, especially those who opposed membership in the UN. Like fluoride in the water, psychiatry and mental health programs were suspected of weakening the minds and bodies of the American people, making them susceptible to Marxist doctrine.[87] Robert Morris said government psychiatrists were quick to call Walker delusional but this was not surprising. "Communists are moving into the [psychiatric] field to seize some of this power over human beings."[88]

A conspiracy of psychiatrists to control the thoughts of a vulnerable American public was nothing new in the ultra Right's alternate reality. Six years before Walker's incarceration, Birch Society leaders Kent and Phoebe

Courtney saw the threat of subversive psychiatrists behind the Alaska Mental Health Enabling Act. It was one of those innocuous-sounding Trojan horses wheeled onto the nation's shores by the Kremlin, the United Nations, and their deep state allies. The legislation provided mental health services, including hospitalization, to Alaskans who previously would have been treated at a Portland, Oregon, hospital. With the growth in population after World War II, Alaska needed facilities much closer to home to care for the mentally ill. In 1949, Dr. Winfred Overholser led a team of mental health experts to towns across Alaska, concluding that a state as large and in many ways as isolated as Alaska needed a more humane way to address its mental health patients. Overholser, who would later emerge as the government psychiatrist Walker's lawyers rejected, proposed a 350-bed hospital in central Alaska.[89]

It sounded like a simple and nonpolitical proposal to build mental health facilities, but to those on the fringes of political discourse, it was part of a sinister plan. Only days after the bill was passed by the House of Representatives, in February 1956, an unsigned advertisement, "Siberia USA," ran in a California newspaper. In part, the ad stated, "This legislation will place every resident of the United States at the mercy . . . of any person with whom they might have a disagreement . . . with immediate deportation to SIBERIA USA." Conservatives were at particular risk; anyone espousing Christian principles at the local PTA was liable to be shipped off to the American gulag. Sounding like scenes from a 1950s science fiction film, the ad warned of psychiatry's "power tearing human minds to pieces and putting them together again in new shapes."[90]

The right-wing conspiracy mill spread rumors of Arctic labor camps financed by Moscow pulling the strings at the United Nations. Dr. Overholser was called an agent of the United Nations based simply on his membership in the World Federation for Mental Health, which consults with the UN's World Health Organization. It was enough to brand Overholser a conspirator in the UN's scheme for world domination.[91] In the words of the extremist *American Mercury,* "Psychiatrists are to take the lead in WHO's crash program of brainwashing the world."[92]

In hearings on Capitol Hill, senators heard from eighty-two-year-old Leigh Burkeland of Van Nuys, California, the author of "Siberia USA." Like critics in the later debate over Walker's court-ordered psychiatric examination, Burkeland charged that the government had the power to declare anyone mentally ill and ship them off to a hospital against their will. "How far a political group could go with this kind of legislation is too terrific to contemplate," she said.[93]

Opponents of the Alaska mental health bill raised the specter of mind-altering drugs used on those held incommunicado. In what was one of the more bizarre conclusions, the Texas branch of Women for Constitutional Government claimed that the legislation fit into the UN's plan for "a world brain, a world mind, a world culture . . . the basis of a world government." Behind mental health measures was a "secret government," hiding in the offices of UNESCO, leading America down the path of slavery.[94] Six years later, Clyde Watts resurrected the image of an Alaskan gulag for dissidents, saying that had Walker been transported to Alaska rather than Missouri, he would have been more easily deprived of his rights, isolated far from the mainland of the United States.[95] In some of the most paranoid musings, Dan Smoot saw the wide-open spaces of Alaska as room enough for anyone the government might find inconvenient.[96] Taking this line of thinking to the outer limits of believability, Walker asked whether secretly built American gulags might even come under Russian control. "What will the US do concerning the Soviet intent to take Alaska?"[97]

One of Walker's most prominent, and controversial, allies in the debate over the uses of psychiatric evaluations in criminal cases was Thomas Szasz, a professor of psychiatry at the State University of New York. An outlier in the profession, Szasz argued that there is no generally accepted standard of what constitutes mental health. Because psychiatrists control the definition of mental health, they can conveniently come up with a diagnosis against those who "violate certain political norms." This weaponized psychiatry, Szasz said, was used especially against those stigmatized as right-wing extremists, like the poet Ezra Pound, who was committed to St. Elizabeth's Hospital in Washington for more than a decade after World War II for his vocal support of the Axis powers.[98]

Now the government and its psychiatrists had targeted General Walker. It was a move that offered "unlimited possibilities for tyranny." If it could happen to a public figure like Walker, Szasz said, then ordinary Americans who found themselves in a similar situation might suffer an even worse fate.[99]

Unconventional views like this convinced Robert Morris to enlist Szasz's help soon after Walker was flown to Springfield, Missouri. Morris wanted Szasz to examine Walker and certify that he was perfectly sane and should not be subject to a psychiatric examination. Szasz declined, telling Morris that with his Hungarian name and accent, he would not be the best witness in an American courtroom.[100]

Szasz said the general—and by extension Szasz himself—were vindicated when Walker was declared mentally fit to stand trial. However, it would take another forty years before the law was amended to ensure that a defendant will be a full participant in the court's determination of their mental competence.[101]

A psychiatrist's ability to render an opinion about an individual's mental state without an examination was also challenged during the campaign of Barry Goldwater, during which Szasz accused psychiatrists with a liberal agenda of trying to paint Goldwater as mentally unstable.[102] A month before the 1964 election, *Fact* magazine noted a poll of more than 1,100 psychiatrists who declared—without benefit of examination—that Goldwater was psychologically unfit to be president. The Arizona senator was described by some as paranoid. Goldwater successfully sued *Fact* for defamation.

As a result of the *Fact* magazine poll, in 1973 the American Psychiatric Association established the Goldwater Rule in its code of ethics. Reflecting the cases of Goldwater and Walker, psychiatrists were advised that they should not offer a professional opinion unless they had conducted an examination with the individual. The Goldwater Rule reemerged during the Trump presidency, when some psychiatrists weighed in on his mental state. Dr. Bandy Lee, a professor of psychiatry at Yale School of Medicine, said in 2017 that in the case of Donald Trump, maybe the Goldwater Rule should be reconsidered.[103]

With the dismissal of the charges against him on January 21, 1963, Walker went on the offense. His target was the Associated Press and several newspapers that had reported on the insurrection at Ole Miss. The subsequent US Supreme Court battle between Walker and the Associated Press became a landmark case in the annals of First Amendment law.

7

Into the Vortex

In Edwin A. Walker's conspiratorial imagination, the media was a willing partner of the control apparatus. Broadcast journalists and newspaper columnists like Drew Pearson were pushing Moscow's agenda to an unsuspecting American public. "I have little doubt," Walker said, "that a knowing public will see through their propaganda."[1]

Even the satirical *Mad* magazine was a Walker target in 1959. Although *Mad* was unsparing in its satire of Nikita Khrushchev, the Far Right viewed the magazine and many of its Jewish contributors as subversive. Walker contacted the FBI to encourage its agents to investigate. Each article, he said, had a hidden meaning, and even the ads made disparaging remarks about the military and American institutions. The FBI apparently did not take Walker's concerns seriously.[2]

Walker's attack on *Mad* may have been an amusing sideshow, but his demand for $33 million in compensatory and punitive damages from the Associated Press and fifteen other news organizations was center stage in courtrooms from Fort Worth to the chambers of the United States Supreme Court. It would end with a landmark decision in libel law.

Walker claimed he was falsely accused of leading the Ole Miss riot. It was malicious, the suit said, intending to "harm his reputation and blacken his good name." Among those named were newspapers from Atlanta, Fort Worth, Louisville, and New Orleans. Additionally, Walker sued the Mississippi *Delta Democrat-Times* and editor Hodding Carter Jr. for $2 million.[3]

The John Birch Society and others among the radical Right encouraged Walker to sue every newspaper that published defamatory articles about his role at the University of Mississippi. Kent and Phoebe Courtney's *Indepen-*

dent American said that if men like Walker "slapped a couple of well-founded $1 million lawsuits for libel . . . the brainwashing of the American people by the Left-wing establishment would be seriously hampered." We might see, the Courtneys naively predicted, "an immediate reversal in editorial policy."[4] *National Review* publisher William Rusher also found the press biased against American conservatives, pointing to *Newsweek*'s cover story that featured Walker's picture and the headline "Thunder on the Right." Rusher said neither *Newsweek* nor *Time* distinguished "extremist elements in the conservative movement from its responsible core." And Walter Cronkite of CBS had dutifully led Dwight Eisenhower, in a November 1961 interview, to condemn military leaders like Walker for expressing opinions on political matters. To Rusher, journalists rarely acknowledge that conservatives "might have something constructive to contribute."[5]

Walker began his three-year courtroom odyssey in June 1964 with a suit against the *Fort Worth Star-Telegram,* WBAP radio and television stations, and the Associated Press. All of the defendants except the AP were dismissed because, as subscribers to the national wire service, they relied solely on what the AP reported. For the editors of the Fort Worth newspaper, the decision to publish the wire service dispatches from Oxford was based on the belief that they were true and written without the intention to defame.[6] The *Star-Telegram* went so far as to issue an apology that satisfied Walker.

The Associated Press reports from Ole Miss were written by twenty one year-old reporter Van Savell. It was his first big story, and he was determined to do it justice. "I dressed as any college student would and easily milled among the rioters on the University of Mississippi campus," he wrote to the wire service subscribers.[7] At issue was his reporting, which stated, "Walker assumed command of the crowd which I estimated at 1,000." Savell further reported that Walker led the charge of students against federal marshals.[8] In his deposition, Savell recalled that when a group of rioters retreated to the university's Confederate monument after the first surge against the marshals, he heard Walker say, "We'll get together and charge again." Savell also described Walker as giving the rioters technical advice on combating the effects of tear gas. At about that point, Savell said, he ran to telephone his office in Atlanta.[9]

Walker said Savell's version of events was far different than what was reported by the rival wire service, United Press International. That was, in Walker's mind, proof that the Associated Press was part of the control apparatus plan to silence and discredit him. Reaching deep into his imagination, Walker said Van Savell was not the real author of the news reports; they were written inside the White House. "I am convinced the AP's report was written in Washington and not by a twenty-one-year-old on the campus grounds."[10]

In the Fort Worth district court, Clyde Watts testified that Walker did not lead the charge against federal marshals. Rather, he turned down several requests to do so, and pleaded with students to keep the protest peaceful. Watts pointed to the wording of the United Press account: "During a lull in the rioting, General Walker mounted a Confederate statue . . . and begged the students to cease their violence . . . His plea was greeted with one massive jeer."[11] The AP, Watts said, "knowingly and falsely [accused] Walker of crimes against the penal code of the United States." Why did Walker go to the campus of Ole Miss? Watts told the jury of eight men and four women that he was there simply to object to the use of federal forces on US soil. Furthermore, Watts insisted that Walker was concerned that the diversion of soldiers to Oxford would leave the country vulnerable to attack from Cuba.[12]

Among the witnesses Watts called was a twenty-year-old prelaw student who said that all Walker did was tell the students that they had the right to protest. When asked who the students sought as a leader, he replied, "They didn't look to anyone."[13] Another witness called the events at Ole Miss that day "just a bunch of college boys blowing off steam, having a good time."[14] Associated Press lawyer J. A. Gooch used Walker's own words to prove he was in charge of at least some of the rioters when he urged his followers to come to Oxford with "your flag, your tent, and your skillet." Gooch called Walker "a great man when he was in the Army—until he started meddling with things he had no business to meddle in." The former general, Gooch said, had "injected himself" into the turmoil at Oxford.[15]

Gooch, a native Texan who practiced law in Fort Worth, recognized that the all-white jury was likely sympathetic to the segregationist cause, and he made it clear that "we are not trying a segregation or integration case." The dispatches by the AP on that day, Gooch said, "were true and are true in fact and substance." He also warned that an award to Walker would set a precedent of restraint on the freedom of the press.[16]

Among Gooch's witnesses over the two weeks of testimony were other journalists who had reported on the events at the University of Mississippi. Craig Ellis, a reporter for the *Nashville Banner* at the time, testified that he heard Walker tell students, "There is no stopping point . . . many people from out of state are coming to Oxford." John King, a radio newscaster, also testified, saying he heard Walker urge students, "Riot, riot. You are getting news all over the country. Now you've got casualties."[17] It seemed to Tom Gregory, a reporter for the *Meridian Star,* that a group of about two hundred at the base of the Confederate monument was following Walker's command.[18]

In closing arguments, Walker's attorneys took aim at Savell by accusing journalists of aspiring to be writers without respect for the truth. The AP is "fighting for the right to lie," Watts said. As for Walker, Watts told the jurors, he is a man "whose concepts of duty, honor, country reach a sublime plane of selfless devotion." Watts, like others of the ultra Right, saw the trial as they saw most other political issues. It was a battle between the forces of good and evil. This was not just about libel, Watts told the jurors; it involved the "absolute survival of this country."[19] One of the problems for Gooch was that the AP could produce no witness who heard Walker speak the exact words that Savell attributed to him, although testimony seemed to corroborate the overall picture of events.[20]

After about two hours of deliberation, the jury awarded Walker $800,000 in damages. Punitive damages made up $300,000 of the award. The men and women of the Fort Worth jury concluded that Savell's reporting was false and did not constitute fair comment. Walker's mother was in the courtroom, telling her son, "They cleared your name." During the trial, Walker remained quiet, probably following good advice from his lawyers, who were accustomed to their client's poor speaking skills. He also refused to take any questions from the press. However, upon leaving the courthouse, Walker told reporters that the jury reflected "the attitude of the entire country with respect to false and one-sided reporting of the news."[21]

Despite his victory in Fort Worth, Edwin Walker's war with the press was far from over. Associated Press general manager Wes Gallagher was confident the verdict would not be upheld on appeal.[22] When he heard that the AP would appeal, Clyde Watts said, "They have as much chance of reversing this case as I have of flying out that window around the First National [Bank]

Building and back." Watts also predicted the Fort Worth verdict would help his old friend's stalled political career, put on hold since his loss in the 1962 gubernatorial primary.[23]

Watts offered his legal services to Walker free of charge, as the friendship between the two went back to prep school days, when they played varsity polo at the New Mexico Military Institute. Watts and Walker shared a love of polo, and while Watts was captain of the University of Oklahoma polo team and was narrowly defeated for the national championship in 1929, he called Walker one of the greatest polo players he had known.[24] Watts went on to the University of Oklahoma College of Law, with the bulk of his practice involved in settling personal injury cases. Walker and Watts both built a career in the armed services and both rose to the rank of US Army general. Watts was in China during World War II, in command of a regiment of Chinese soldiers, and he served for a time as an adviser to Nationalist leader Chiang Kai-shek. Though he was not a member of the John Birch Society, he was a strident anticommunist and saw Walker as an embattled soldier on the new front lines, fighting the traitors of the control apparatus. "I believe Ted Walker is the most mistreated individual in the history of this country," he said.[25]

Days after the decision to award Walker damages, Jack Moseley of the *Fort Worth Press* went searching for answers from the jury. Were they influenced by politics? He spoke with six of the jurors and found they were concerned that Savell did not take the witness stand and so they had to depend only on his written deposition. The jurors also said that at no time did they discuss their views of the Kennedy administration, civil rights, or Walker's association with the John Birch Society. One of the jurors told Moseley that while she did not agree with Walker's politics, she believed he deserved compensation. Another said he did not regard the libel award "to be an attack on the American press."[26]

Attorneys for the Associated Press, however, did see the award of punitive damages as a frontal assault on press freedom, and just a month after the jury's verdict they requested Judge Charles Murray to set aside the award. Judge Murray cut his summer vacation short to hear the AP's case. Gooch said that witnesses did confirm that Walker had led rioters toward the marshals. Evidence conflicted only as to the number of rioters who followed Walker. Watts countered, insisting the award was fair and that the AP's request was only another example of "arrogance and tyranny" in the news media. Watts further said that Walker, on the basis of false news reports, had been forced to spend six days and nights in a "prison nut house."[27]

Taking the Case to the Supreme Court

Judge Murray threw out the award for punitive damages, reducing the amount to compensatory damages of $500,000. Although the jury had concluded that Savell's reporting treated Walker unfairly, Murray disagreed, saying that statements in the AP story that Walker led the charge were not written with malice.[28] Lawyers for the AP, now seeking to overturn Walker's $500,000 award, claimed there was plenty of evidence that some of the jurors made statements that indicated a prejudice against the news media. One juror was rumored to have said that the award to Walker should have been $1 million because the Associated Press had plenty of money and would never miss it.[29] While the jurors may have made such statements, Murray maintained there was no indication they affected the outcome of the case.[30]

The Associated Press then took its case to the Court of Civil Appeals and the Texas Supreme Court, which affirmed the district court ruling that the AP must pay Walker his $500,000 award. However, Walker's Texas victories would be short-lived. The next stop would be the US Supreme Court led by Chief Justice Earl Warren, the nemesis of the Far Right. Watts would face one of Washington's most prominent lawyers, former attorney general William Rogers. His political career had begun in 1938, and as assistant district attorney in New York, he took on organized crime. As Eisenhower's deputy attorney general and then attorney general, Rogers had played a critical role as the president navigated the tense days during the crisis at Little Rock. Rogers would later serve as Richard Nixon's first secretary of state.

Rogers was a perfect choice to make the AP's case, having argued on behalf of the *New York Times* in another landmark libel case before the Supreme Court, in 1964. *New York Times v. Sullivan* put limitations on the ability of a public or elected official to recover damages for libel. In overturning a $500,000 libel award to the police commissioner of Montgomery, Alabama,

Supreme Court Justice William Brennan wrote that restraining criticism of government officials is inconsistent with the First Amendment.

A libel judgment would succeed only by proving that the statement was made with "actual malice"—with knowledge that it was false or with "reckless disregard of whether it was false or not." In a commentary on the Supreme Court's decision, the *University of Pennsylvania Law Review* noted that *New York Times v. Sullivan* "left little doubt that the balance should be weighted heavily in favor of unrestricted speech."[31] Now, with the Associated Press case against Walker, the standard applied to public officials would be extended to public figures, meaning those who might be prominent in news events.

The Supreme Court heard *Associated Press v. Walker* with one other, similar case, *Curtis Publishing Co. v. Butts.* University of Georgia athletic director Wallace Butts had sued the *Saturday Evening Post* for a story alleging that he conspired to fix a football game by providing the playbook to the coach of the opposing team, the University of Alabama. Butts maintained that in the *Post*'s zeal to stand out as a muckraking publication, it deliberately printed information that it knew rested on very flimsy evidence.[32]

The Supreme Court upheld Butts's libel award of $460,000, finding that the magazine had engaged in "highly unreasonable conduct" that was "an extreme departure from the standards of responsible journalism." The *Saturday Evening Post* was fighting other libel charges and was deeply in debt at the time. The sizeable award to Butts was a factor in the eventual demise of the publication. Lawyers for the *Saturday Evening Post* made the case that large libel awards had the power to silence a publication by putting it out of business, which would be a restriction on the First Amendment. Justice John Harlan said he could not accept that line of reasoning and that publications had an obligation to act responsibly in their reporting.[33]

In Edwin Walker's case, the court found that during the violence at Ole Miss the Associated Press had operated under very different circumstances than the *Saturday Evening Post* in the Butts case. Reporter Van Savell had filed his story with the Atlanta AP office in the middle of a rapidly changing news event. The battle on the University of Mississippi campus needed to be reported in the public interest, and unlike the Butts case, Savell's coverage "required immediate dissemination."[34]

Although Watts insisted that Savell's account of Walker's activities was fabricated,[35] the court had no reason to doubt that Savell was a competent and unbiased journalist, and there was nothing improper in the writing of his dispatches. The court could find only one small problem in Savell's recounting of the events to his editors at the AP, related to whether Walker had spoken to a group of rioters before or after approaching the federal marshals. "Negligence, it may have been," Harlan said, "malice, it was not."[36] The court could find no malicious intent on Savell's part, which was critical to overturning Walker's award.

As for Edwin Walker, the court found he fit the description of a "politically prominent" figure who had made well-publicized statements that he would oppose the government's order to allow James Meredith to register for classes at the University of Mississippi. *New York Times v. Sullivan* was applicable here, as Walker "thrust himself into the vortex of an important public controversy." The court even made note of Walker's extremist following, the so-called Friends of Walker.

Justice Harlan said Savell's account "would not have seemed unreasonable to one familiar with General Walker's prior public statements on the underlying controversy." Harlan footnoted his opinion with references to Walker's radio interviews and news conferences before the outbreak of violence at Oxford. In one, Harlan said, Walker had called for "violent, vocal protest." In another, during a September 30 press conference, Walker had "again urged defiance of court orders and federal power."[37]

The Supreme Court Affirms Press Freedom

Chief Justice Earl Warren made the point that the distinction between public officials and public figures had become blurred. Warren explained that since the Depression of the 1930s and World War II political power, the power to guide policy was no longer limited to elected officials. This "blending of power," Warren said, applies to not just large corporations but also to individuals. A high-ranking army officer with a substantial following, like Walker, can "shape events in areas of concern to society at large." Someone such as Walker has the same access to mass media as an elected official to influence opinion and counter criticism. The press, Warren said, should not be restrained from reporting on the activities of these "prominent public figures."

The Supreme Court Justices were careful to make note of the delicate competing interests of protecting someone from malicious defamation and not putting undue restrictions on First Amendment freedoms. The fact that the First Amendment right to publish matters of great public concern should be protected does not mean a newspaper publisher is free to "invade the rights and liberties of others."[38]

On June 12, 1967, all nine justices voted to dismiss Walker's suit and reverse the $500,000 judgment he had won in Texas three years earlier. After the verdict, Rogers called the Supreme Court's decision a significant victory for press freedom. The size of the award from the Texas jury would have set a dangerous precedent. Without protection, news organizations would be inhibited from thoroughly covering controversial public figures.[39] With the Supreme Court's decision, individual claims against newspapers that relied on AP reporting were also dismissed. As one journalist noted, the court's decision kept the door wide open for "robust debate about public issues."[40]

Among Walker's other targets for harassment was liberal southern journalist Hodding Carter Jr., editor of the Mississippi *Delta Democrat-Times.* Carter had delivered a speech as part of the University of New Hampshire's Distinguished Lecture Series in October 1962. Addressing a New England audience of about 1,500 students and faculty, Carter explained the southern mind-set during a period of explosive change. Carter, who won a Pulitzer Prize in 1946 for editorials against racism and segregation, said only a minority of students participated in the violence at Ole Miss and that the troublemakers were mostly hoodlums, crackpots, and racists from the outside. And they were led by General Edwin A. Walker, "a seditious psychopath." Walker filed a slander suit against Carter, seeking $2 million in damages, but the judge dismissed the case in December 1967, citing *Associated Press v. Walker.* The judge noted that when Carter made his statements, Walker had been arrested for sedition and had been taken to a federal psychiatric hospital to determine whether he was competent to stand trial. Carter, the judge said, did not act with malice.[41]

Predictably, Walker viewed the Supreme Court's decision as just one more piece in the control apparatus puzzle. *Public figure,* he said, is "a new category of citizenship needed for a *Redder* country, to protect a *Redder* press." As for the AP, Walker said that this "fanatic wire service army" was in on the communist conspiracy to divert attention from the real enemies in Moscow and Havana.[42] As expected, Walker's allies went on the offense against the Warren Court, a perennial right-wing punching bag. Dan Smoot said, "This decision was a gross injustice which was clearly motivated by the judges' animosity." Smoot said that although Walker was not indicted by a grand jury for sedition, the AP report still had branded him "a lunatic and a criminal."[43]

On Capitol Hill, the Supreme Court decision prompted a speech by a Louisiana congressman and leading segregationist. John Rarick called the ruling "a flimflam use of words . . . invented out of fantasyland." To Rarick, who had called Martin Luther King "an errand boy" for international communism, Edwin Walker was "one lone man against the establishment."[44]

In the months following the insurrection at Ole Miss, Walker was certain he was that lone man on a mission to alert Americans about the enemies lurking just below the surface. Coming to Ross Barnett's side against federal power only added to Walker's prestige. The Mississippi House of Representatives gave him a standing ovation when he paid a visit in December 1962.[45] Already celebrated by the John Birch Society for exposing the "invisible government" and undergoing what they labeled Soviet-style psychiatric confinement, the fight against the Associated Press solidified Walker's status as the martyred warrior of the Right. With a sentiment that continues to echo in right-wing circles, Walker said the press was controlled by anti-American editors and reporters. "Read and listen with the view that 90 percent is false or the truth is omitted."[46]

Walker imagined himself a modern-day Paul Revere, and in 1963 he joined one of America's foremost evangelists on a cross-country bus ride with the dire message that it was only a matter of a few years before blue-helmeted troops from Africa and Asia would enforce their one-world government on an unsuspecting nation.

8

Midnight Riders of the Ultra Right

Just days after a federal grand jury in Oxford, Mississippi, declined to indict Walker on conspiracy to incite an insurrection, he received a call from evangelist Billy James Hargis. The two of them, Hargis said, would take a twenty-seven-city road trip to alert the nation about the communists in their midst, the deep state, and most importantly, the evil residing on Manhattan's East Side—the United Nations. They would call it Operation Midnight Ride, for Paul Revere's warning of British invasion.

Hargis, who was no amateur when it came to self-promotion, put on a theatrical traveling medicine show. The elixir was a combination of militant Christianity, anticommunism, and white supremacy. Midnight Ride would feature a stage decked with American flags and speeches, first by Hargis and then Walker. They would sell tickets at the door for a dollar a piece but also pass a bucket through the audience for more cash. The profits would be split between Hargis's Christian Crusade and the somewhat loosely organized Friends of Walker. Of course a table would be set up, stacked with pamphlets, books, and recordings—another source of revenue for both.[1]

With portraits of Hargis and Walker, posters advertising Operation Midnight Ride billed it as "triumphant coast-to-coast rallies." Attend, the poster urged, "so that America may be spared a communist grave."[2] One newspaper noted that Hargis saw himself as an ally of the John Birch Society, Edwin Walker, and Jesus.[3]

Hargis, who took the leading role, said he chose Walker because "no man, except the soldier who lies forgotten in a lonely cemetery on the battlefield, has paid a greater price to preserve freedom than Edwin Walker."[4] They were an unlikely pair: Walker, an Episcopalian and trim, battle-tested veteran of two wars, and Hargis, the overweight ordained minister of the fundamentalist Disciples of Christ. What united them was their fierce anticommunism and equally strong desire for notoriety. They also found common ground in their belief in a grandiose scheme hatched by powerful forces working together in the United Nations and the Kremlin.

To the ultra Right of the 1960s, the teachings of Christ and Kennedy's New Frontier were incompatible. Walker and Hargis presented their audiences with the message that America's independence and the survival of Christianity itself were threatened by a combination of one-world globalists, sex education in the schools, socialism, and racial integration. In this 1960s battle for the soul of America, Walker had a simple answer: "All morality is based upon Christianity, nothing else."[5] It was a tone that prompted the *Christian Century* to comment, "These two men will in effect be crying to the American public, 'the Reds are coming' not by land or by sea but from your schools and colleges, your churches, your textbooks, your libraries, your government . . . The nation will be alerted to a domestic enemy which exists largely in the minds of the radical Right."[6]

Billy James Hargis was born in 1925 in Texarkana, Texas. He was only ten when his mother became seriously ill, and he said he devoted his life to God after praying for her eventual recovery. Hargis attended Ozark Bible College in Bentonville, Arkansas, a town known today as the home of Walmart headquarters. Although he did not finish with a degree, Hargis was ordained as a minister in the Disciples of Christ at just seventeen. In 1950, he resigned from the church to launch his campaign to save America from communism, the Christian Crusade. Starting in 1953, Hargis and the New Jersey fundamentalist Carl McIntire made periodic trips to Central Europe, where they released balloons containing Bible quotations printed on paper strips, hoping the prevailing winds would carry them over the Iron Curtain. Hargis was a vigorous defender of Joseph McCarthy and the House Un-American Activities Committee's commitment to rooting out suspected traitors in the government.

In 1952, the first full year of his Tulsa-based Crusade, Hargis took in more than $70,000 in contributions.[7] He was adept at using radio and his skills as a preacher at the podium to appeal to the religious Right for money. In 1957, after Hargis attacked the National Council of Churches as communist, the Disciples of Christ withdrew his ordination. That did not put a dent in the popularity of the Christian Crusade, which brought in about $1 million in mostly small donations by 1963. In the words of one observer at a three-day Christian Crusade convention in Oklahoma City, Hargis could collect dollar bills "with the skill of a super-auctioneer waving his arms and dispensing a 'God bless you.'" As for those making the donations, it seemed they were mostly middle-aged and without a college degree, but with a "new vocation—to save the United States."[8] In 1962, Hargis opened his Anti-Communist Leadership School in Tulsa and enrolled more than 170 students. By the following year he could boast more than 75,000 subscribers to his *Weekly Crusader* magazine, a daily broadcast on hundreds of radio stations, and a headquarters staff of fifty.[9]

Of all American evangelists during this time, Hargis was the "most zealous and energetic, and perhaps leaves the greatest impact," according to Arnold Forster and Benjamin Epstein in their 1964 study *Danger on the Right.* Forster and Epstein described Hargis as "a pudgy, prosperous evangelist who has turned radical Right propaganda into big business."[10] Yet even as Hargis was attracting donors, he was spending recklessly. Midnight Ride would be another source of new members and revenue, but that would not be enough to keep Hargis's ambitious empire afloat.

His *Weekly Crusader* echoed Walker's conspiratorial message with articles such as "The Communications Media: Aiding the Kremlin," "Mr. Kennedy, Whose Side Are You On?," and "Subversive Forces Influence 1962 Election."[11] Although Hargis advised Walker not to go to Oxford, he came to Walker's immediate defense after the violence at the University of Mississippi. Hargis did little to separate himself from the base racism that resonated with Walker's followers in the South.[12] The first session of Hargis's Anti-Communist Leadership School, for instance, featured a speech by a Georgia lawyer who praised segregation as a way to separate white students from "an inferior race."[13] Walker had found common ground with what he termed "dedicated, patriotic, and militant Christians." With his flair for language at its most frightening and poetic, Walker said an alliance with the Christian Right would be a potent weapon to combat "the destructive force of little and evil men in their seditious conspiracy against mankind."[14]

Edwin Walker and Billy James Hargis began their Midnight Ride on February 27, 1963, and at each stop along the way they wrote up a one-page "Operation Midnight Ride Daily Report" that was sent to subscribers. They were not shy about being controversial. "Controversy fills the auditorium," Walker said in an urgent message to Midnight Ride organizers. "Fill the seats. We mean business. We are coming in loud and clear." Walker even included sample radio ad copy demonstrating that same urgency for organizers. "Call your friends, bring them to hear a Minister and a General . . . The hour is late, the enemy knocks at the gate."[15]

Yet as they began their road show, it quickly became apparent that Hargis had the stage presence, energy, and preacher's rhetorical flourish that Walker severely lacked. Walker could be so tongue-tied and his train of thought so confounding that according to one news reporter, he "could put two and two together and get 666."[16] Despite Walker's wooden performance and his abysmal showing in the Democratic primary in Texas the year before, WALKER FOR PRESIDENT signs sprang up at some Midnight Ride rallies.[17]

The first stop was Miami, drawing about 1,600 to the Dade County Auditorium. Walker and Hargis were viewed with some wariness in a city with a sizeable Jewish community. Writing in the *Miami News*, Will Maslow, executive director of the American Jewish Congress, said Walker's followers were not conservatives. "Their suspicion [and] hatred dissolve the cement that holds America together." Maslow called out Walker and the Birchers for their use of the PTA to indoctrinate people—a tactic, he said, that mirrored the communists. "People of radical Right-wing thinking are so far to the right that they almost join hands with the communists." Maslow also called attention to those who blindly accepted Walker's unsubstantiated accusations of traitors behind his still undefined control apparatus. These Friends of Walker who would like to see him be president "essentially have a basic distrust of the world around them. They live in a world that is a jungle to them."[18]

The next stop was Palm Beach, at the invitation of the Florida Coalition of Patriotic Societies, a group founded in 1959, whose purpose was to alert Americans that the war against communism "is a holy war between the forces of God and power of evil." With support from some conservative members of Congress, the organization made opposition to the United Nations a cornerstone of its efforts.[19]

Arriving in Palm Beach, Hargis and Walker were put up at the winter home of socialite Countess Guardabassi.[20] Born Rosalind Wood, she married into Italian royalty in 1928. Her late husband, Count Francesco Guardabassi, had worked before the war to gain support in the United States for Mussolini's government. For her part, the countess was the inheritor of a Boston fortune from the textile industry, and a generous patron of the arts as well as of Far Right causes.

Hargis and "That Woman in the Front Row"

At their Palm Beach stop, both the Midnight Ride duo and the local press came out swinging. Edith Haynie, who covered the event for the *Palm Beach Post*, provided her readers with a colorful account and asked some tough questions, which raised the ire of both Hargis and Walker.

It started with a press conference, when Haynie asked Walker if he was planning to get involved in the integration fight in Alabama. Recalling Walker's command of troops to integrate Central High School at Little Rock and his arrest for insurrection at Ole Miss, she wanted to know, "if you go to Alabama, which side will you be on this time?" Hargis was visibly uncomfortable as Walker sidestepped the question with his signature set of non sequiturs. "I went to Mississippi because of Cuba . . . If I go to Alabama it will be because of Cuba, and I hope you print that in your paper." And she did.[21]

Then came the rally that night, before a crowd of about one thousand, and what Haynie described as a "finger-jabbing, rip-roaring attack on this reporter and newspapers in general." Hargis, Haynie said, spent thirty-five minutes in a vocal assault on "that woman sitting here in the front row." Hargis, who weighed about 250 pounds, cut an imposing figure as he strode the stage, saying, "I've been mad all day and just waiting for this night." Looking directly at Haynie, Hargis scolded, "For your information, lady, every word I'm saying is being recorded for a permanent record." Hargis compared her question at the press conference to "waving a red flag before a bull." According to Haynie's reporting, the crowd loved it, with shouts of "That's telling her, Billy."

In true Hargis style, he pounded the podium, mopped his brow with a handkerchief, and with arms waving, chastised the press. "They tell how we take up donations and sell books, and pass the ice cream buckets for money, but they don't tell what we say." As for those unpatriotic newspapers, Hargis promised, "Well, we're gonna start our own newspaper. I can tell you that."

As in several of these rallies, the audience could seem threatening. As they rose in a standing ovation at the end of Hargis's remarks, several yelled for Haynie to stand. "What's the matter with that damn reporter? Can't she stand up?" As for the ice cream bucket, Midnight Ride took in close to $3,000 that night.[22]

In one of their daily dispatches, Hargis called the Palm Beach stop a success despite the "loaded question" from Edith Haynie. "If we lose this country," Hargis told subscribers, "it will be due in no small part to the sympathy for socialism and communism so apparent in the liberal press."[23]

From Florida, Midnight Ride took a turn to Alabama, Georgia, and South Carolina—all states where resistance to integration and civil rights legislation was at its height. Walker and Hargis found that hotel ballrooms were in some cases not large enough to accommodate the unexpectedly larger audience. In stops through the Deep South, Midnight Ride received the endorsement of the local segregationist Citizens' Council.[24] Appearing in Montgomery before about one thousand in a downtown auditorium, Walker lent Governor George Wallace his full throated support in what would be a showdown with the federal government over school desegregation in September. As for Attorney General Robert Kennedy, he was the "little stupid brother," a slur that elicited cheers.[25]

In Birmingham, Hargis and Walker were given "the keys to the city" by Mayor Arthur Hanes as they addressed an overflow crowd at the Municipal Auditorium. They were strident in their opposition to integrating restaurants and public accommodations, and among those in the audience was Birmingham's police commissioner, Eugene "Bull" Connor. That spring Connor would become known worldwide for using fire hoses and police dogs in his brutal assault on civil rights marchers while Martin Luther King sat in the city jail. King was "anything but a saint," Hargis said, declaring that communist agitators were behind the movement to allow African Americans to eat at local lunch counters.[26]

Although they were greeted enthusiastically by segregationists at each stop, they also were met by protesters. Appealing to the most vile racism, Hargis said that some of the picketers at the Indianapolis event were "white women with colored men. It is a privilege to be picketed by a group like this." Confronted by signs outside one rally that read "Gen. Walker aided and abetted violence at Oxford, Miss," Hargis defended his fellow Midnight Rider, saying, "Regardless of the facts, the NAACP apparently blames General Walker for every tragedy from the Civil War to the Oxford incident." He reminded them that a grand jury had cleared Walker of all charges, and he asserted that John F. Kennedy had sought to integrate Ole Miss just to attract Black voters for his reelection.[27]

In speeches during the Midnight Ride tour and later that year, Walker would revisit his confrontation with US marshals at Ole Miss, comparing the campus riot to war on a foreign battlefield. Walker said he was impressed with the ingenuity of the students "in finding ways to protest the occupation of their campus by federal troops." Those students, he added, would make good soldiers.[28] When asked if Black Mississippians had been denied their rights, Walker responded in typical fashion with an answer that dodged the issue: "There are places in the United States where white people are denied their rights."[29]

Given the battle over civil rights in South Carolina, Walker and Hargis found many in Greenville eager to hear that the NAACP was a Soviet front. "It has never been for colored people," Hargis said.[30] Hargis and Walker avoided hostile reporters like the *Palm Beach Post*'s Edith Haynie by holding their press conference on the campus of the evangelical Bob Jones University. Bob Jones Jr., the college president and a member of the Christian Crusade board, introduced the Midnight Riders before an enthusiastic crowd of about 1,500, some waving the Confederate battle flag. As the *Greenville News* reported, for three hours it was "another flow of bitter words" against one of their chief targets, the National Council of Churches. "We commit sin when we support the National Council of Churches," Hargis said.[31]

In Tampa, Hargis continued his attack on the radicals "who are leading the Protestant church down the road to hell."[32] For Hargis, liberal theologians strayed away from what he believed to be fundamental religious values, such as a literal reading of the Bible and condemnation of homosexuality and women's rights. John Birch Society founder Robert Welch, who saw the invisible hand of Moscow in very corner of American life, called Protestant clergy "the largest body of communists in America."[33]

Established in 1950, the National Council of Churches stood for civil rights legislation and critiqued laissez-faire capitalism, which led Hargis to declare the council un-American, even though the organization condemned communism as well. Hargis told a Midnight Ride rally in Jacksonville that the affiliated churches were bringing Soviet bloc clergymen to the United States and that they "lie through their teeth when they claim that there is religious freedom in Russia."[34] Hargis and fellow fundamentalist preacher Carl McIntire pushed the FBI to investigate the National Council of Churches, alleging subversive activities, but J. Edgar Hoover showed no interest in these unsubstantiated allegations.[35]

A Midnight Ride event would not be complete without allegations that their voices were being purposely muzzled. In Alabama, Walker declared that treasonous editors were intentionally ignoring his cross-country tour. "Our troops on foreign soil will get no word of this patriotic meeting. The whole free world begs to know where is America?"[36] These anti-Americans in the nation's newspapers were keeping Castro in power and feeding the American people Khrushchev's propaganda "for breakfast, lunch, and dinner."[37] In Greenville, Hargis suggested that his audience learn the truth from the John Birch Society's *American Opinion,* the *Dan Smoot Report,* and of course his own Christian Crusade, instead of reading *Time* magazine, *Life, Look,* or *Newsweek.*[38] Returning to one of his favorite subjects, Walker said the American people had been denied the truth through a mass brainwashing. It was time for citizens to learn the science of psychological warfare to defend themselves against these hidden adversaries in the corporate offices of the *Time–Life* empire. "It could turn this country around in ten minutes flat."[39]

Despite their accusations that reporters came to Midnight Ride rallies to "throw loaded and trick questions at us," Hargis and Walker welcomed any publicity. "We are trying to hold press conferences daily. It is easy to spot our friends and our enemies at these conferences."[40] Even as Hargis complained that his words were often taken out of context or omitted altogether in news reports, he oddly prohibited any recording of his or Walker's speeches.

Along the way, local police encountered few problems during the Midnight Ride road show, but there were some tense moments due to Walker's quick turn to anger. He got into a shoving match with one Columbus, Ohio,

TV reporter who ventured too close while asking Walker for a final comment during a press conference. Police had to respond to a bomb threat in Cincinnati. The caller said one hundred sticks of dynamite were set to explode at Emery Auditorium, where Walker and Hargis were scheduled to speak. Police, who had the auditorium under surveillance anyway, found no explosives.[41]

"The Greatest Living American"

As Hargis and Walker cast doubt on the patriotism of the president in cities across the country, the novel *Seven Days in May* was enjoying considerable popularity. Author Fletcher Knebel modeled his fictional general on Edwin Walker, so it was not surprising that *Seven Days in May* was not on the top of the Midnight Ride reading list. In their daily report, Hargis and Walker told the faithful that Knebel "tries his best to plan [*sic*] a deep suspicion of the military leaders in this country who are outspoken against [those who] run the machinery of government."[42]

It was their last rally, at the Shrine Auditorium in Los Angeles, that drew the largest crowd. Hargis took aim at one of his favorite targets, the NAACP, as more than three hundred protesters gathered outside. One of those picketers was a young city council candidate named Thomas Bradley, who ten years later became the first African American mayor of Los Angeles. Hargis took on liberal California campuses that denied free speech to conservatives. "They are referred to as the stupid set. All I can say is, that thank God I am a stupid pro-American."[43]

For the California ultra Right, Walker was clearly the headliner. Up to six thousand people waited to hear the man the John Birch Society called "the greatest living American." Walker was visibly emotional after a grueling monthlong bus ride, but he amused his audience by telling them that the Supreme Court "has gone to the left so far it has encircled itself three times." He made a pitch for a conservative third party that would have the support of Birchers and segregationists. "Both [Republican and Democrat] parties have given aid and assistance to our enemies."[44]

By the time they finished, on April 3, Midnight Ride had reached as many as forty thousand people.[45] But it was exhausting. Walker told organizers in the various cities not to prepare any other events, including dinners or after-hour receptions. "This coast-to-coast tour is strenuous and extremely difficult for us from a physical point of view," Walker said.[46] Despite the nonstop schedule of events, however, Midnight Ride did little to improve the finances of the Christian Crusade, even as Hargis claimed it had added ten thousand new names to his mailing list.[47] By August 1963, only four months after Midnight Ride, Hargis was making a plea for money. "We need help and we need it desperately," he said, as he cut his staff of fifty in half and sold his Tulsa headquarters.[48]

The Los Angeles finale demonstrated the zeal for Walker's brand of politics in the West, proving that a racial and Far Right message could resonate with those beyond the Deep South. A year before Midnight Ride, Walker addressed a packed Los Angeles Memorial Sports Arena, with chartered buses bringing attendees from outlying towns. Walker spoke for close to two hours amid five standing ovations. Before the rally, dubbed "Make Mine Freedom," Walker was greeted by followers at the airport. He basked in the attention, receiving a bouquet of roses and exchanging his Stetson for a paper Uncle Sam hat.[49] Walker later remarked that the enthusiasm of the Los Angeles crowd was "indicative that southern Californians have a good grasp of world conditions."[50]

A shift to the right in the California GOP concerned former President Eisenhower. Were the Birchers moving the Republican party too far outside the mainstream? In 1963, Wyoming senator Gale McGee said Birch money and organizers were in the state, working to unseat him with a well-coordinated disinformation campaign.[51] In the words of a *Houston Post* editorial, the John Birch Society was a "strange product of a strange time."[52]

Unlike the Republican and Democrat establishments, Walker and the Birchers rejected the internationalist spirit that had guided American foreign policy since the end of World War II. That policy had led to rebuilding Europe, creating the NATO alliance and the financial institutions under the Bretton Woods Agreement. With the rise of the modern conservative movement of the late 1950s and early 1960s, this internationalism came under fire.

Then there was the United Nations—the most visible and tangible symbol of the plot against America. It was a central theme on every stop along the Midnight Ride. For Walker and the John Birch Society, a nefarious UN was an existential threat to America's survival. Walker saw the UN as an anti-American network with the singular goal of establishing a world government dominated by African and Asian countries. To Walker, both parties were equally guilty of subordinating US interests to UN Secretary-General Dag Hammarskjöld. As an example, Walker cited the proxy war in the Congo between factions aligned with the United States and the Soviet Union.

In 1960, civil war erupted as the Republic of the Congo (soon to be Zaire) won its freedom after eighty years of Belgian colonial rule. The newly independent nation, headed by Patrice Lumumba, was riven by competing political factions. One of those factions, led by American ally Moïse Tshombe, seceded from the Congo to form the southern state of Katanga, in a region with the world's richest uranium mine. That mine, called Shinkolobwe, had provided almost all the uranium needed for the bombs dropped on Hiroshima and Nagasaki.[53]

As Lumumba fought for control of the Congo, he appealed to the Soviet Union for help, a serious worry for the United States. The Kremlin quickly deployed advisers and military equipment, including one hundred trucks and ten military aircraft. Walker claimed that Hammarskjöld was behind Lumumba and his chief sponsor, Nikita Khrushchev. "The greatest uranium mines in the world are at stake," Walker said.[54] However, Hammarskjöld was not swayed by Lumumba's pleas for support; the UN would not be used to tip the balance one way or the other, angering Khrushchev.

After a coup in September 1960, Soviet personnel were expelled, and in January 1961 Lumumba was assassinated. Nonetheless, Walker declared that Moscow's interests were being served by the United Nations and the State Department. As the country endured a bloody civil war, Walker said Tshombe was sold out. "No wonder Tshombe has now accused us of having communists in our government. What other explanation is there?"[55] UN Secretary-General U Thant by January 1963 sent troops to put an end to Tshombe's Katanga regime in the interest of unifying the chaotic Congolese state.

The UN's Plan to Subjugate America

Neither Dag Hammarskjöld—the "Red Swede," as Walker called him—nor his successor, U Thant, conceived of the United Nations as a prelude to world government. Rather, they considered it a system of more effective cooperation among member states. In U Thant's vision, the UN provided the most workable method by which nations could keep pace with the changes that made individual states more interdependent. For Walker, this was just a cover for Soviet intentions. In Congress, Bircher John Rousselot called for withdrawing from the world body and booting the headquarters out of the United States. After all, it was filled from top to bottom with spies.[56] The UN is not only a "tool of Russia," Walker said, but "has laid the United States wide open to invasion."[57] It was an outlandish prediction of foreign soldiers, carrying the UN flag, descending in unmarked helicopters and streaming across the Mexican border.

Walker envisioned a "hidden policy" in Washington that was ready to hand over the US armed forces to the United Nations. The federal courts and deep state actors operating subversively from the Council on Foreign Relations were all in on it.[58] Painting a picture of a future worthy of a Hollywood thriller, Walker said the army would be defenseless against an invasion force, "while the government is destroyed and taken over by a communist-inspired mob."[59] Appearing in front of a Senate panel just a month before his losing bid for the Democratic Party nomination for Texas governor, Walker, in a rambling monologue, appeared to construct a web so elaborate as to confound reason.

Claiming to get his information from sources in "high places," Walker said the State Department had begun a program "to take our weapons, the greatest in the world, and physically give them to our enemies, leaving us none for the defense of our country." Soon, Walker predicted, the American soldier, his weapons, and his orders would be under the control of godless UN generals. He went so far as to insist that soldiers under UN commanders would be forced to turn against the American people.[60] Reaching well beyond the bounds of credulity, Walker asked rhetorically, "When will UN currency replace US currency?"[61]

Once again, for Walker, this scheme was made possible by the enemy's adept use of psychological warfare. America's impressionable young men in uniform will be "de-Americanized" and "UN-ized" as they abandon their love of country, he said.[62] Speaking to that overflow crowd at the Los Angeles arena in January 1962, Walker made an emotional appeal intended to stoke fear. "These sons of ours have been taught to forget their allegiance to our country and become a tool of the United Nations."[63]

Walker placed the blame on career State Department diplomats, those Ivy League bureaucrats who were "brainwashing the American public on UN-ism" and internationalist ideas.[64] In Walker's conception of national security, international agreements came at the cost of America's independence. In another departure from reality, Walker said the World Court could order the execution of an American president for fighting the communists in Vietnam. Even the trans-Atlantic NATO alliance was suspected of serving Moscow's interests. NATO, Walker declared, is "so fabulously expensive [and] never permitted to interfere with what the Soviets want."[65]

Walker, of course, saw the UN's pervasive hand in his forced resignation from the army following the report of his Pro-Blue education program at Augsburg. Soldiers under his command, he said, were prevented from learning the truth about communism, with the United Nations pulling the strings in Washington. "I could no longer serve in uniform and be a collaborator," he said.[66] In Walker's overwrought imagination, the United Nations was also the agent behind desegregation. In 1963, he told the leaders of the Citizens' Councils that the court order to admit James Meredith to the University of Mississippi was "the first UN military operation on American soil . . . Unless we oppose the United Nations, there will not be a President of the United States again." So outrageous were these fantasies that he had to assure even this group, "I'm not a fanatic, but I do get angry when the truth can't be told."[67]

Like Walker, Hargis called the UN a "traitorous outfit in New York City." He asked the faithful, "What are you sitting around for—waiting for a tornado? When are you going to do something to bring the truth to the American people?"[68] Walker and Hargis painted the UN as a political threat, but also as a powerful weapon against Christianity. A room for silent meditation in the UN headquarters was proof to Walker that the world body was anti-Christian.[69]

The twin perceptions of the UN as communist and godless dovetailed neatly for Midnight Ride audiences, who were a mix of militant anticommunists and fundamentalist Christians. Fundamentalists viewed Washington and the UN as accomplices in Mao's victory in the Chinese civil war. They had "sold [China's] Christian president Chiang Kai-shek down the river," said one prominent fundamentalist, in the aptly named *The Sword of the Lord*. Truman and the New Deal Democrats had turned China over to the communists "willingly and gladly."[70]

Hargis and other fundamentalists, like Carl McIntire, awaited the return of Christ to inaugurate a thousand years of peace; any attempt to better mankind was doomed to failure, whether it came from the UN or Congress. Man-made ideas are not in Christ's plan. In fact, support for the UN or social legislation would only delay the Second Coming.[71] Hargis saw Christ's struggles against Satan in every conflict, including the apocalyptic battle against the Kremlin. He looked to the book of Revelation for clues to the real, but veiled, intent of the UN. As in any good conspiracy theory, it was up to men like Hargis to pull back the curtain to find the hidden truth. Revelation indicated quite clearly, said Hargis, that the atheistic UN, armed with the atomic bomb and control of the global economy, would be the sole ruler of the world until Christ's return.[72]

Coexistence was impossible either in Walker's secular critique or in Hargis's eschatology, which saw any attempt at peacemaking as futile, given God's ultimate battle against Russia. Normal political discourse was useless in the face of this worldview, where the only thing that is certain is deception. Walker's and Hargis's Christian fundamentalists saw conspiracy as the motive force behind history. In fact, history *is* a conspiracy, set in motion by demonic forces. As one admirer wrote to Walker in 1966, "We are only fighting the skirmishes until that battle at Armageddon."[73]

Hargis also brought up his favorite bogeyman, the National Council of Churches, as a coconspirator in the UN's strategy to subjugate the free world. The sight of a UN flag beside the American flag at the council's founding congress in Cleveland was positive proof that these Protestant churches pledged allegiance to atheist Russia, not Christian America. Support for the UN by liberal clergy, Hargis ominously predicted, will "destroy our religious heritage." Even the Supreme Court ruling in 1962 that prayer in the public schools was unconstitutional was masterminded by the anti-Christian United Nations. Hargis looked no further than UNESCO to find the blueprint for replacing Christianity with a "world church," just as Walker saw the UN's eventual goal to be the establishment of a world government.[74]

Hargis, in his "confidential report" on the United Nations in 1958, said the UN was founded by one of the most notorious Russian agents, Alger Hiss. Hargis charged Hiss with being "the No. 1 man in the State Department on UN planning." It was Hiss, Hargis said, who helped draft the very form and structure of the United Nations under Soviet direction. Although it was presented under the guise of promoting world peace, they were in fact "evil, clever forces destroying our nation."[75]

Hiss, who attended the Yalta Conference in 1945 as an adviser to President Roosevelt, was an organizer of the conferences that laid the foundation of the United Nations. He was also a chief adviser to the US delegation at the first meeting of the General Assembly in 1946. However, Hiss was accused of acting as a Soviet agent while working in the State Department, in the 1930s, and of providing classified documents to Whittaker Chambers, a former Soviet agent in Washington, DC. In January 1950, Hiss was convicted of perjury and served more than three years in prison. He always maintained he was never a Soviet spy.

UNICEF: Pennies for Castro

Walker's and Hargis's attack on the UN tapped into the racism of some of their followers. The UN was racially mixed through its inclusion of postcolonial African states, which Hargis considered only "semi-civilized nations."[76] Walker was convinced that there were torture chambers in the basement of UN headquarters and that the pennies collected by children on Halloween for the United Nations Children's Fund (UNICEF) went straight into the pockets of Fidel Castro.[77] For Hargis, opposition to UNICEF was not just about pennies for Castro but about sending money to the "unsaved masses."[78] In Santa Barbara, California, the political clout of the ultra Right was felt down to the level of the school board, with harassing phone calls to teachers whose lessons might include discussion of the UN as well as attempts by some parents to kill the UNICEF Halloween fund drive.[79]

But the Far Right's campaign against the UN did not stop with late-night phone calls to California teachers. The office of the American Association for the United Nations in Encino was firebombed in early 1963, the result of "outrageously false and inflammatory materials," in the estimation of Arthur Larson, who served in the Eisenhower administration as head of the US Information Agency. Larson spoke in Encino a month after the bombing, voicing concern that extremist language that urged Americans to "put an ax to the root of this evil" would lead to domestic terrorism. Larson, who taught law at Duke University, appealed to conservatives to disavow the Birchers and "restore some modicum of decency to the political dialogue." In particular, Larson called on Barry Goldwater, as the leader of the conservative movement, to "help clean up these excesses."[80]

As Midnight Ride rolled into Louisville in mid-March, Walker made a statement that was typically oblique. Castro's Cuba had put America at risk, he said, and that included risk to President Kennedy himself. Just eight months before the assassination that shook the world, Walker wondered aloud whether Kennedy would survive his first term: "Well, I'd think if he didn't survive his first, he certainly wouldn't survive his second."[81] Just a month later, Walker himself would be drawn into the conspiratorial world surrounding the death of President John F. Kennedy.

9

Edwin Walker: America's "Leading Fascist"

On the evening of April 10, 1963, Edwin Walker was sitting at a desk in his den, working on his taxes. It was about 9:00 and all the lights were on. From his seat by a window, he heard a rifle shot break the silence in this suburban Dallas neighborhood. The bullet passed through the wooden frame of the window and hit the wall just three inches above Walker's head.[1]

Walker's right arm was showered with slivers of the bullet, wood, and pieces of glass. At first, he thought it was a firecracker tossed by neighborhood children. Realizing what had happened, the former general ran upstairs to get a pistol and headed to the back of the house. Seeing no one, he called the police.[2] In the frank opinion of one of the detectives investigating the case, "Whoever shot at the general was playing for keeps. The sniper was shooting to kill."[3] Dallas detectives speculated that Walker must have moved his head just as the trigger was squeezed.[4]

With that shot, Walker was brought back into the dark realm of conspiracy theories. The man behind the rifle was Lee Harvey Oswald, who would assassinate President John F. Kennedy seven months later.

The Dallas police found a spent bullet in the next room and concluded that the assassin had fired the shot into the first-floor window from an alley about fifty yards from the rear of the house. Officers took a series of photographs of Walker's home, but they had little else to go on.[5] There were witnesses to suspicious activity in the darkness that night. At the sound of the shot, one neighbor, fifteen-year-old Kirk Coleman, ran outside and pulled himself over a fence in the rear yard, looking toward a Mormon church parking lot close to Walker's home. He said he saw two men quickly drive away—one in a beige Ford and the other in a Chevrolet.[6]

Walker was not surprised that enemies had him in their crosshairs. While the Dallas Police Department investigated, Walker's supporters demanded the FBI get involved, given the general's notoriety as an anticommunist warrior. The first suspect was one William McEwan Duff, who had worked for Walker for about three months, mostly as a chauffeur. The thirty-two-year-old Duff was questioned by the Dallas police and passed a polygraph, saying he did not have a grudge against Walker and did not know who tried to kill him.[7] There was no evidence to charge Duff with the crime, though Walker later told the Warren Commission that Duff was a con man and someone who, if given the opportunity, would do just about anything for money. "I wouldn't believe 90 percent of what Duff said about anything."[8]

Born in Scotland, Duff was a drifter who knocked on Walker's door one evening in December 1962 looking for a place to live in exchange for work around the house. He had just left his wife after only a couple of months of marriage. Walker gave Duff an upstairs room, but after arguments with other members of Walker's staff, Duff left. It was only weeks before the shooting.[9]

Walker's longtime attorney Clyde Watts was sure Duff was guilty. With the help of two Oklahoma City private investigators, Watts began his own search for the man who had pulled the trigger.[10] The private investigators rented an apartment close to Duff's, befriended him, and according to a Dallas police report, "did quite a bit of drinking together." They came up with nothing, even after proposing to Duff that they conspire to kill his former boss.[11] "We couldn't get Duff to admit that he actually fired the shot, but he professed a readiness if someone would raise $5,000," Watts recalled.[12]

Aside from his suspicions about Duff, Walker viewed the attempt on his life as one more bit of evidence that Castro and his agents in the United States were out to murder anyone who stood in their way. Walker also put the blame on what he called "the anti-Americans—and there are plenty of them in this country." Magnifying the incident and thrusting himself into the center of a grand scheme to bring America to its knees, Walker said those who had targeted him were also determined to "destroy our local police and do away with our military forces."[13]

By the summer of 1963, President Kennedy was looking toward his reelection campaign. It didn't matter that the vice president was Texan Lyndon

Johnson; Dallas was a center of some of the most vicious attacks on Kennedy. Operating out of his home, Walker was leading a hard core of extremists with the aim of making any presidential visit to Dallas very uncomfortable.

A month before the planned campaign stop that cost him his life, Kennedy sent UN ambassador Adlai Stevenson to Dallas. What Stevenson found, when he arrived for a commemoration of United Nations Day on October 24, was a jeering mob, many of whom had attended a counterdemonstration the day before that was billed as the United States Day rally. Walker was the principal speaker at that event, with a tone that sounded like a threat: "Every street corner in Dallas is a virtual battleground against the United Nations." Walker also had an ominous prediction: the CIA was in the hands of the United Nations and was preparing to eliminate any opposition by patriotic Americans.[14]

Interestingly, Lee Harvey Oswald was among the 1,300 people in the audience, listening to the man he tried to shoot six months earlier.[15] Oswald even sent a letter to a member of the Communist Party confirming his attendance and observing that "political friction between Left and Right is very great here."[16] The *Washington Post* called it one of those "curious ironies" of the president's assassination.[17]

Walker's incendiary speech had sufficiently aroused what became an angry crowd as Stevenson began a full schedule of events the next morning. Stevenson first spoke at a UN Day luncheon at the Sheraton Dallas, held a press conference, and then went to an Eleanor Roosevelt Foundation reception. Even as he spoke at the Sheraton, a small plane overhead towed a banner that read "Get US Out of UN."

Trouble came at an evening speech to about five thousand at the city's Memorial Auditorium. Walker's supporters began heckling Stevenson, and some fistfights broke out in the audience. After the speech, Stevenson went to his car through a shoving crowd of almost one hundred protesters. In one case a woman struck Stevenson in the head with her picket sign. The UN ambassador and two-time presidential candidate also was spat upon.[18] Wiping his face he asked, "Are these human beings or are these animals?"[19]

It was an embarrassment, and the Dallas City Council did issue an official apology. Mayor Earle Cabell called on Dallas citizens to repudiate the current hate groups just as they had repudiated the Klan in the 1920s. Those who jeered

Stevenson, Cabell said, were not conservatives but radicals. "Let us look at these so-called patriots . . . see who they are . . . and where they are leading us."[20]

It was clear that Walker had stoked the violence that drove the UN ambassador out of Dallas. An organizer of Stevenson's visit called the assault "a concerted action by members of Edwin Walker's following and the John Birchers."[21] On the day of the protest, Walker had some of the picket signs stored in his home, and he contributed to the defense of a man who was charged with spitting at a police officer.[22] Walker tried to justify the attack by saying it reflected the feelings of many Americans that the United States was unfairly paying the largest share of the UN's budget. As for the battered Stevenson, Walker was dismissive. "Adlai got what's coming to him . . . Only a little man would turn a national protest into a personal affront."[23] Not surprisingly, activists of the Far Right were calling Stevenson the Communist Party's favored choice for secretary of state in the next Kennedy administration.[24]

Stevenson Warns JFK about Dallas

Not averse to strange behavior to generate publicity, Walker displayed the American flag upside down in front of his house for several days to protest the Dallas city officials' apologies to Stevenson. Walker said the flag was flown that way as a "distress signal, which is warranted when any other flag takes precedent over the flag of the United States." In this case, he was referring to the UN flag and his allegations that US policy is controlled by an "invisible government" in league with the UN.[25]

A week later, students from North Texas University who had joined the anti-Stevenson demonstration started planning a protest for a possible Kennedy visit. According to FBI files, four of the students apparently had visited Walker and were organizing a Friends of Walker club at the university. The FBI's Criminal Investigative Division noted that one of the students who met with Walker said that upon Kennedy's arrival in Dallas, "we will drag his dick in the dirt."[26]

On November 12, Kennedy told his advisers that because of the importance of Florida and Texas to winning in 1964, he would soon make campaign stops in those states. Stevenson advised Kennedy that visiting Dallas was risky and that the city was home to a dangerous extremism, much of it directed against the president. Stevenson told Kennedy confidant and historian Arthur Schlesinger that the president might reconsider a visit. "There was something very ugly and frightening about the atmosphere."[27]

At the same time Kennedy was preparing for his reelection, Barry Goldwater consolidated his position as the face of the Republican Right. Texas was a key state as it looked like the Republicans would break with moderates in the party and nominate Goldwater. His *Conscience of a Conservative*, published three years earlier, became the guidebook for conservatives unhappy with the centrist course of previous Republican stalwarts such as Nixon in 1960 and Eisenhower.

As it looked like Goldwater had a strong chance of capturing the nomination, he recognized the critical importance of wealthy donors with ties to the extreme Right. The Birchers enjoyed considerable support in Arizona, he said, and not just the "cactus drunks" but also some of the wealthiest Republicans in the state.[28] Although Goldwater would try to cast a wider net in a fractured Republican party during the 1964 campaign, some of his language in *Conscience of a Conservative* echoed Walker's "better dead than Red" refrain in lectures at the 24th Infantry Division. "The American people are being told that however valuable their freedom may be, it is even more important to live." That, Goldwater writes, "is a craven fear of death." Goldwater was careful not to make the same mistake as Walker in naming those in responsible government posts as traitors or unwitting dupes of the communist conspiracy. Instead, he used more tentative language, saying "traitors (and perhaps cowards) have at times occupied key positions in our government."[29]

On November 21, the president and First Lady Jacqueline Kennedy set out for a two-day, five-city visit to Texas. Before Dallas, Kennedy stopped for speeches in San Antonio, Houston, and Fort Worth. The next day, November 22, 1963, America was forever changed.

The morning went well as Kennedy greeted well-wishers outside his hotel. He spoke at a breakfast of the Fort Worth Chamber of Commerce, focusing on military preparedness and promising "the people of Texas will be in the lead."

As they arrived at Dallas's Love Field, the Kennedys were greeted by Governor John Connally and his wife, Nellie. In the limousine, the Connallys sat in the front and the Kennedys in the back. Vice President Johnson and wife, Lady Bird, were in another car in the motorcade. The procession left the airport and traveled along a ten-mile route that went through downtown Dallas on the way to the Trade Mart, where the president was scheduled to speak at a luncheon. The top to the limousine was open, a fatal mistake that cost the president his life.

Crowds lined the streets as the limousine turned off Main Street at Dealey Plaza around 12:30 p.m. As it was passing the Texas School Book Depository building, shots were fired from a window on the sixth floor. The president was shot in the head and neck. A bullet also struck Governor Connally. The car sped off to Parkland Memorial Hospital just a few minutes away, but the president died shortly afterward. On Air Force One, Lyndon Johnson took the oath of office.

Police arrested Lee Harvey Oswald, who worked at the book depository which allowed him access to the building. He was held for the assassination of the president and the fatal shooting of Patrolman J. D. Tippit. On Sunday morning, November 24, Oswald was scheduled to be transferred from police headquarters to the county jail. On live television, Americans saw Oswald shot and killed by a local nightclub owner named Jack Ruby. Oswald died two hours later at Parkland Hospital.

During the morning of November 22, Oswald's Russian-born wife, Marina, had followed President Kennedy's activities on television. She and a friend, Ruth Paine, cried when they heard that the president had been shot. Paine, who was studying Russian and was one of the few friends Marina had in Dallas, translated the news of the shooting as it came over the TV. When Marina heard that the shots were probably fired from the building where Lee worked, she began to suspect her husband was the assassin. Marina knew that Oswald had tried to kill Walker and that the rifle he had used was hidden under a blanket in Ruth Paine's garage. When the police arrived to question Marina, she led them to the garage to find his rifle. It was missing.[30]

Marina Nikolaevna Prusakova was nineteen years old when she met Oswald, who arrived in Russia in October 1959. His service in the Marines had just ended in September, and Oswald said he was a committed Marxist who wanted to renounce his American citizenship for citizenship in the Soviet Union. Authorities, suspicious of Oswald's motives but happy to have an American defector, kept him under surveillance but granted him a year-by-year visa. He was sent to Minsk, in present-day Belarus, to work in a radio factory, where he met Marina. They were married in April 1961. Likely disillusioned with the Soviet Union, Oswald applied to the US embassy to return to the United States with Marina and their daughter, born in February 1962. It took a while, but by June of that year the three were making Dallas their home.[31]

In April 1963, Oswald lost his job with a photography firm due to incompetence and poor relations with coworkers. It was just four days before his failed attempt to kill Walker. He had ordered the rifle through the mail several weeks earlier, under the assumed name of Alek Hidell. It was an Italian-made 6.5-millimeter Mannlicher–Carcano rifle available for $19.95 from Klein's Sporting Goods of Chicago. He told Marina that he intended to use it for hunting.[32] Oswald also ordered a Smith & Wesson .38 revolver from Los Angeles.

During this period, Oswald was attending typing classes three evenings a week. As he floated from job to job, he realized he needed an added skill. But, as with most things he did, Oswald attended the classes irregularly, and in the week before taking a shot at Walker, he quit entirely.[33]

Oswald was likely planning his assassination of Walker for almost two months. He was meticulous, outlining all the details in a notebook and studying bus schedules for his route to and from Walker's house, according to the Warren Commission report. Over the weekend of March 9 and 10, Oswald photographed the alley that ran behind Walker's home, and the rear of the house. He also took pictures of a nearby railroad track and right-of-way.[34] Marina Oswald said that in the days before the shooting Lee would take refuge in a closet with an improvised desk. "He told me not to bother him so he was quite secretive about it," she said. Marina was adamant that she did not know beforehand that her husband was contemplating an assassination.[35]

As he prepared for his attack on Walker, Oswald posed for a picture—the now infamous photo of the assassin holding the rifle that he used to fire through Walker's window and to murder President Kennedy. In his other hand was the Communist Party newspaper, *The Worker*, and the Socialist Workers Party newspaper, *The Militant*. Marina took the photo in their backyard sometime around March 27, about two weeks before he went out into the night to kill Walker. It was, in Marina's opinion, "a ridiculous picture. It was puzzling me why anybody would want to take a picture dressed like that with all the equipment."[36]

Oswald at first considered killing Walker on the weekend of April 6 and 7; however, he changed his mind, reasoning that the best time would be the night of Wednesday, April 10, when the Boy Scout meeting at the nearby church might create a diversion. On the night of the shooting, Marina remembered Oswald leaving their apartment shortly after dinner. She thought he was attending a class or was "on his own business."[37] Oswald was unusually late that night, and by 10:30 she went to his room looking for some clue to his whereabouts. "I was petrified and didn't know what to do," she recalled.[38]

Like Killing Hitler before He Took Power

That's when Marina found a disturbing note, which, according to the Warren Commission report, "appeared to be the work of a man expecting to be killed, or imprisoned, or to disappear." The letter, written almost entirely in less-than-perfect Russian, ended with instructions to Marina to go to the city jail "if I am alive and taken prisoner." He also told her he had paid the rent, water, and gas bills in advance. "I left you as much money as I could, $60 on the second of the month. You and the baby can live for another 2 months using $10 per week."[39]

After firing the shot, Oswald ran from Walker's house and ditched the rifle, hiding it in a field near a railroad track a little more than a half mile away. He then took the bus home. When Oswald finally returned, Marina confronted him. He was very pale, Marina recalled, and "he told me not to ask him any questions. He only told me he had shot at General Walker." Oswald said he was unsure if he actually hit his target that night, and when he learned the next day that Walker was not killed, Oswald told Marina he was "very sorry" the bullet had missed.[40] He assured Marina that he had taken separate bus routes to and from Walker's house. He had decided not to drive, saying that Americans always think they should have a car to get away from the scene of a crime.[41]

Marina, relieved to hear that Walker had not been hit, was angry and threatened to turn Lee in to the police if he tried killing someone else. "I told him, 'How dare you take somebody's life.'" Typically, Oswald saw himself as a man with a destiny, comparing his attempt on Walker's life to assassinating Hitler before he took power. In Oswald's words, Walker was America's "leading fascist."[42] The Warren Commission later concluded that Oswald had a "strong concern for his place in history," that he saw himself as a savior. While the commission questioned how much Oswald truly understood about communism or any political ideology, "it seems clear that his commitment to Marxism was an important factor influencing his conduct," and it probably influenced his decision to shoot at Edwin Walker.[43]

Within three days of his attempt on Walker's life, Oswald had retrieved the rifle, wrapping it in a raincoat. He also showed Marina the notebook of his detailed plans, complete with photographs of Walker's home and a map of the neighborhood. She told Warren Commission investigators that he promptly burned the evidence.[44] When the commission asked why she did not turn him in that night, she answered simply, "Because I am a wife." Nonetheless, the Oswald marriage was unraveling.[45]

Shortly thereafter, Marina's friends George and Jeanne de Mohrenschildt visited the Oswalds at their apartment for the first time. Jeanne saw the rifle in a closet as Marina showed her around, prompting George to jokingly ask Oswald if he had taken a shot at General Walker. The remark was followed by an uncomfortable silence. De Mohrenschildt recalled that Oswald's reaction was strange; he became speechless and tense, "sort of shriveled."[46] Oswald was not amused and assumed that Marina had told George about his attempt to kill Walker.[47] De Mohrenschildt, who was part of the small Dallas-area Russian community, later said that his comment was in jest and that some people had speculated Walker himself staged the shooting for publicity.[48] When de Mohrenschildt was questioned by Warren Commission investigators, he said Oswald did express his hatred for Walker. "You know," he said, "this was the period of General Walker's big showoff," referring to the attack against Stevenson.[49] While de Mohrenschildt was described as eccentric and an outspoken anticommunist, with ties to CIA covert operations in the Caribbean, the Warren Commission found no credible evidence that he had links to extremist organizations or was in any way connected with Oswald's assassination of the president.[50]

By April 24, the Oswalds had parted ways. Marina moved into Ruth Paine's home. Lee left for New Orleans for a brief time, getting out of town as the police investigated the Walker shooting.[51] When Lee Oswald returned to Dallas, living in rented rooms, he finally landed a job at the Texas School Book Depository. It was the last in a string of failures to earn a living. On November 22, 1963, carrying his rifle in a brown paper package, Oswald entered the sixth floor of the book depository building and waited for the presidential limousine. Following the assassination and Jack Ruby's brazen televised murder of Oswald, the investigation centered on the one person who had known the gunman on the most intimate basis—Marina, the twenty-two-year-old woman, now a widow, from Minsk.

On November 30—just eight days after the Kennedy assassination—the FBI requested the mangled bullet found in Walker's home for a ballistics examination. The bullet was so badly mutilated that the Dallas City-County Investigation Laboratory was unable to identify the weapon. The Dallas Police Department forwarded the bullet to federal investigators on December 2.[52]

Events tying Oswald to the Walker shooting were moving quickly. The White House was concerned that the *Chicago Sun-Times* was coming out with the story. Presidential press secretary Pierre Salinger asked for guidance from the Justice Department and was told to simply confirm that there was evidence that Oswald had made an attempt on Walker's life.[53]

On the same day the FBI received the bullet, Ruth Paine turned over to federal agents some of Oswald's belongings from her garage. Among them was a book in which Marina had hidden the letter Oswald wrote to her before he left for Walker's house. Agents also took possession of Oswald's photographs of Walker's house. Although Oswald had destroyed the notebook he used to lay out the details of his plot, several photographs remained. Two were taken from the rear of the house. It was clear that the gun had been fired from a position near the point where one of the photographs was taken. The third photograph showed the entrance to Walker's driveway from a back alley. Still another showed the railroad tracks less than a half mile from his home.[54]

Also critical in clearly identifying Oswald as the assailant was construction work on an apartment building that appeared in the background of one photograph. FBI agents inspected the construction company's log to confirm that the pictures were taken not long before the April 10 shooting.[55] A photography expert with the FBI also was able to determine that Oswald's camera was an Imperial Reflex.

Starting on December 3, Marina was interviewed extensively, telling federal agents for the first time about Oswald's plans to kill Walker. In a subsequent interview, in 1964, Marina said Oswald was a loner and that it would be out of character for him to have an accomplice in the Walker shooting.[56]

Oswald's Prologue to the Kennedy Assassination

The FBI also revisited Walker's neighbor Kirk Coleman, asking if either of the men he saw the night of the shooting resembled Lee Harvey Oswald. Coleman answered no, indicating that the two men he saw in the church parking lot were likely leaving from a Boy Scout meeting that was held that night.[57] The government concluded that Oswald was the man who shot through the window, narrowly missing Walker's head.[58] FBI ballistics expert Robert A. Frazier said that because of the bullet's condition, he could not say definitively whether it was fired from the same rifle Oswald used to assassinate the president. However, there were strong clues that suggested that it was used in both shootings. Frazier said it was a 6.5-millimeter bullet and that relatively few types of rifles could produce the characteristics found on the bullet. It was *probably* the same rifle, but the FBI and Dallas Police Department could not go any further.[59]

The Warren Commission saw the Walker shooting as a prologue to the Kennedy assassination. It certainly demonstrated Oswald's "propensity to act dramatically and, in this instance, violently in furtherance of his beliefs."[60] One theory about Oswald's attempt on Walker's life was floated by the CIA's chief of Clandestine Services for Mexico. In closed-door hearings in 1976, he told a Senate committee on intelligence activities that Oswald may have "used this heroic deed to build himself up" in the eyes of the Cuban government. Oswald was likely seeking notoriety from Castro himself. It was consistent, he said, with what he knew about "the psychology of psychopathic personalities."[61]

Even a half century later, the Kennedy assassination is the subject of books, movies, and conspiracy theories; not surprisingly, some involve Walker, who was vocal in his hatred of the president. Was Walker part of a Far Right plot to kill the president and was Oswald his trigger man? Did Oswald fire the shot at Walker as a cover? Within days of the Kennedy assassination, the FBI received letters from those who believed Walker was behind the murder. One letter came from a waiter at a downtown club who claimed to have overheard Walker discuss the plan to kill the president.[62] Walker also received death threats from people who suspected he was Oswald's accomplice. One warned him that he wouldn't "go quick like the President . . . don't forget, Walker you got 6 more months to go, so tidy up your affairs."[63] Walker was invited to speak at a "Friends of General Walker" event on Long Island until the Garden City Hotel canceled after receiving more than a dozen threatening phone calls. Hotel management said Kennedy's assassination only eight days earlier had made Walker's appearance "inappropriate."[64]

The Warren Commission put to rest any theories that Walker was either an acquaintance of Lee Harvey Oswald or was involved in the death of the president. Although Walker's phone number and address were found among Oswald's papers, it was most likely that Oswald had that information at the time he was preparing to murder Walker. The commission also dismissed a rumor that Jack Ruby had visited Walker at his home. It was a "totally unfounded" allegation made by Walker's disgruntled former employee, William Duff, who also accused Walker of diverting John Birch Society funds to his own personal account.[65]

The Warren Commission did look into one of Walker's associates, Robert Surrey. Surrey, who was Walker's partner in the American Eagle Publishing Company, had produced about five thousand handbills that were seen across the city during the Stevenson visit and several days before Kennedy came to Dallas.[66] Featuring the words "Wanted for Treason" and pictures of President Kennedy made to look like a MOST WANTED poster, the handbill's language mirrored Walker's rhetoric about an anti-American control apparatus. Kennedy was "charged with betraying the Constitution" and turning the sovereignty of the United States over to the Soviet-controlled United Nations. Walker kept many of these fliers in the backseat of his station wagon."[67]

The Warren Commission noted that Surrey, a thirty-eight-year-old printing salesman, was mostly involved in producing Walker's political and promotional literature, much of which was stored at Walker's home-based headquarters. As a close friend, Surrey was one of the first people Walker called after the April 10 shooting, and it was Surrey who told the police at the time that he saw two men peeking through Walker's windows in the alley behind his home two nights before the shooting. They left in an automobile, Surrey said, with the license plate missing. Surrey tried to follow the car but lost it in traffic.[68] In a letter to J. Edgar Hoover, J. Lee Rankin, general counsel for the Warren Commission, said he wanted more information about Surrey's story of the men staking out Walker's home. Could one of them be Oswald, and was the other an accomplice in both the Walker shooting and the Kennedy assassination? Surrey told the FBI that neither of the men he saw fit the description of Lee Harvey Oswald—they were a little older and a little heavier than Oswald.[69]

A Plan to Take Back Cuba

Walker, of course, had his own list of convoluted conspiracies that frustrated Warren Commission investigators. Just ten days after Kennedy's assassination, Walker held a press conference in Dallas to say that Fidel Castro had personally selected Oswald as the assassin. "God has given us a warning that no man alive can ignore."[70] In a swing through Shreveport, Louisiana, for one of Billy James Hargis's conferences in February 1964, Walker claimed that a communist cell was active in Dallas. The Fair Play for Cuba Committee, Jack Ruby, and the committed Marxists Lee Harvey and Marina Oswald were all active members. And, Walker said, "government investigators know about it."[71]

A chief obsession for Walker was Cuba. Speaking in Savannah, Georgia, during his Midnight Ride tour, Walker seemed ready to lead his own Bay of Pigs operation. "I challenge the commander-in-chief of the United States of America to take the 82nd Airborne Division . . . joined by Cubans to liquidate the scourge that has descended upon the island of Cuba."[72]

Though he was not launching his own invasion, Walker did have a tangential relationship with anti-Castro rebels. One of those was Carlos Bringuier, a Cuban exile who became Billy James Hargis's resident expert on Cuba. Walker attended a fundraiser in Dallas for Bringuier's anti-Castro Student Revolutionary Directorate, and both were featured speakers at Christian Crusade meetings in 1964, spinning the tale that Oswald was an agent of the Cuban government.[73]

In yet another odd twist in the Kennedy assassination, Oswald had been involved in a scuffle with Bringuier on a New Orleans street corner. On August 9, 1963, Oswald was passing out Fair Play for Cuba Committee leaflets when Bringuier approached him and a fight ensued. Later that month, Oswald and Bringuier debated briefly on a New Orleans radio call-in show.[74]

Walker also made the acquaintance of Loran Hall and Gerry Patrick Hemming, soldiers of fortune with ties to Cubans working to overthrow Castro. Walker met with Hemming about preparations to train exiles in South Florida for a proposed invasion of the island.[75] David Kaiser, in *The Road to Dallas*, says Hall and Hemming came to Dallas in 1963 looking for funds for a training camp. They met Congressman John Rousselot and one of Walker's close associates, attorney Robert Morris. Although these men put the pair in touch with those who could provide money, Hall and Hemming failed to raise enough and their ambitious plans fell through.[76] As in many of his dealings with extremists and soldiers of fortune, Walker told Hemming he did not want to participate in training anti-Castro rebels but would assist his efforts behind the scenes.[77]

Walker was spending much of his time after the Kennedy assassination chasing debunked conspiracies, and he was particularly interested in the case of Warren Reynolds, the owner of a used car lot. Reynolds said that soon after Kennedy was shot he saw a gunman fleeing the scene where officer J. D. Tippit was killed. Then, on January 23, 1964, Reynolds was wounded by a .22 rifle shot as he was closing for business. After Reynolds and Walker met, Walker requested that the FBI investigate. Walker believed the Reynolds shooting was part of the larger scheme to silence anyone who knew too much about the communist master plan against him and President Kennedy. Walker told the Warren Commission that of all the used car lot owners in Dallas, the "attempted assassination [of Reynolds], who had seen Oswald [on the street], makes this quite unusual."[78] In its final report, the Warren Commission found no evidence that the attack on Reynolds was connected with the events of November 22, 1963.[79]

Walker also repeated the claim from the supermarket tabloid *National Enquirer* that Ruby and Oswald were acquaintances and that together they had wanted an anticommunist like General Walker dead.[80] Walker told the Warren Commission that Oswald and Ruby knew each other well enough for Oswald to have picked up Ruby's car from a repair shop. When pressed, Walker could not provide any verification, saying, "I have been told that it happened." In what was a frustrating series of questions, Walker would not reveal the source of his information. "Another repairman, a friend of mine," was all he said. Finally, attorney Wesley Liebeler asked firmly, "My question is, do you know their names?" Walker's reply was bizarre: "Yes I do, but I'm not telling."[81]

Walker's answers to the Warren Commission were indicative of his distrust of the government. He went so far as to allege that there was a deal among the Warren Commission members to play down the role of communists behind the murder of the president. And one reason, he said, was that President Johnson did not want to upset relations with the Soviet Union. "We certainly would not expose anything that would embarrass our international relations . . . between Washington, DC, and Moscow," he said.[82]

Well after the release of the Warren Commission findings, Walker remained outspoken about what he imagined was a government cover-up. Walker called the Warren Commission "a sham and an insult to the American people . . . It is one big lie, cover to cover." He said that while the commission was correct in pinpointing Oswald, he was not the loner characterized by the report. "Oswald knew more national and international figures personally, particularly Leftist ones, than any other man his age."[83] As late as 1975, Walker asked Senator Frank Church to investigate whether the CIA was behind the attempt on his life.[84]

In his final interview, just weeks before his death in 1993, Walker weaved a fantasy that the Kennedys had known it was Oswald who tried to kill him that April evening. He told the *Dallas Observer* that the police had arrested Oswald shortly after he fired the shot at Walker but that Attorney General Robert Kennedy had him released. The Kennedys, he said, had it in for him.[85]

In the minds of many Americans, Walker and the radical Right in Dallas had fueled hatred of the Kennedys, leading to the attack on Stevenson and the death of the president. After President Kennedy's assassination, there were those who were convinced that Dallas deserved a reputation as a "city of hate," says Edward Miller in *Nut Country.* Even conservative Bruce Alger, who served in Congress from 1954 to 1964, came to realize that his city was becoming associated with the outliers, the John Birch Society and Edwin Walker.[86]

However, Walker insisted that blaming the right-wingers in Dallas was exactly what Castro wanted. "It is about time the [Warren] Commission cleared the city of Dallas."[87] In a recorded statement from his home, Walker said, "Dallas has been set up" by Castro, *Pravda,* and the Communist Party newspaper, *The Worker.* Their object was to spread "malicious and deceptive attacks on the conservative Right" and to hold the entire city responsible for Kennedy's murder.[88]

Although there were those who suspected Walker and others on the Far Right had conspired to kill the president, the Warren Commission came to no such conclusion. Commission attorney Liebeler, who interviewed Walker extensively, asked pointedly if he knew of any connection between those who "follow you as a political leader and the assassination of President Kennedy?" Walker answered no, but the line of Liebeler's questioning led to one group that Walker certainly knew well: the Minutemen, a loosely organized militia that was preparing for war against the government.[89] Although the Warren Commission could not tie the Minutemen to an anti-Kennedy conspiracy, the group was on J. Edgar Hoover's radar in the early 1960s. Walker's association with the Minutemen and other extremist groups in the years following the Kennedy assassination were also under FBI scrutiny.

10

The "Mad Hatter" of the Right

Edwin Walker never denied the charge that he was an extremist. "I see extremists as being inspired by something that will bring us out of the world situation today."[1] Rejecting the Republican Party of Richard Nixon after his 1960 defeat, Walker complained that Nixon's call for a moderate line was like walking down the middle of the street—"and see what happened to him. We have all we need of middle of the road leadership." As he prepared his run for Texas governor in 1962, Walker let it be known that his campaign would outflank even the Texas Right. "This country was not established by moderates," he said. "If it's super patriots and extremists we need, I suggest we get them."[2]

The extremists who made up the ecosystem of the militant Right in the early 1960s spanned a wide variety of ideologies and tactics. In 1962, Fletcher Knebel, author of *Seven Days in May,* said these radical factions had sprung up "like dandelions" in the two years since the election of President Kennedy.[3] A common thread of all these groups was the perception that the government was controlled by unseen forces that threatened the very foundation of Western civilization. It was a fantasy that differentiated the ultra Right from mainstream conservatism, and many residing on these outskirts of rational political discourse looked to Edwin Walker to lead them from the abyss.[4]

Along this spectrum of beliefs and prejudices, it is evident that Walker's sentiments were at the furthest reaches of the radical Right. Among the most prominent of these groups in the early to mid-1960s were the Minutemen, a forerunner of the militias that began to emerge in the 1990s. Led by Robert Bolivar DePugh of Norborne, Missouri, the Minutemen were armed, trained, and ready to rebuff what they viewed as an imminent invasion of the United States. As unbelievable as it sounded, a California Minuteman "commander" told columnist Drew Pearson in 1962 that thousands of Chinese troops, disguised in UN uniforms, were already on the Mexican border, preparing to take San Diego.[5] There were even whispers that control of the US armed forces would soon be turned over to a Russian colonel, a belief that anticipated today's black helicopter and QAnon conspiracies.[6]

Once they conquer us, the commander said, they will create insane asylums for anyone who resists. It was a distorted view of mental health as a political weapon that had been central to the Far Right's narrative about Walker's brief incarceration at a federal psychiatric facility after his arrest in Oxford. "Did you know," the Minuteman leader told Pearson, "that you can be arrested for speaking against the UN on the street corner and you'll be tried by the World Court?"[7] Walker and the Minutemen shared these delusions about a plot by hidden actors of the invisible government to subjugate America.

The number of Minutemen during the early 1960s is hard to pin down. DePugh made the unsubstantiated claim of 25,000 well-armed members across the country. DePugh said every member was required to fire at least five hundred rounds a year in target practice.[8] Because of their focus on armed resistance to their perceived enemies, these "grassroots guerillas," in Pearson's estimation, were opposed to any form of gun control legislation.[9]

Like some of today's decentralized and secretive militia groups, members preferred to stay anonymous and typically joined autonomous cells. As DePugh explained, "I tell them I don't want to know your names. When the takeover comes, these names can be a matter of life and death." Recruiting members from the John Birch Society was not successful. DePugh himself had been a member, but Birchers were not interested in arming themselves or in survivalist tactics, even while they agreed with the ideology of the militant Minutemen.[10] Regardless of their numbers, they clearly were a violent domestic terrorist group. Days after Barry Goldwater's defeat in 1964, DePugh urged Americans to reject the political process and join his underground army, which was ready to do battle as the country's "last line of defense."[11] The Minutemen, DePugh said, will take "any action no matter how brutal."[12]

In May 1962, several Minutemen training in Florida's isolated, swampy everglades were arrested for intending to dynamite synagogues in the Miami area and carry out assassinations of Florida political leaders. The hit list included a member of the Miami school board, who was under attack because he favored teaching students about the functions of the United Nations. These Florida Minutemen were also responsible for bombing the home of *Miami Herald* editor Don Shoemaker three months earlier.[13] In 1968, the FBI arrested seven Minutemen in Washington State for planning to rob four banks and dynamite a power plant as a diversion.[14]

One of the more frightening aspects of the Minutemen, aside from their guerrilla training in the woods and plans to murder public officials, was their desire to root out the "communists and subversives" next door. As DePugh explained, the Minutemen were "better positioned" than the FBI "to investigate our friends and neighbors. If there is a potential enemy among us, we want to be the first to uncover him."[15]

With groups like the Minutemen in mind, President Kennedy, in a speech to Democratic donors in mid-November 1961, warned of the rise of "discordant voices of extremism" and "armed bands of civilian guerillas" who would take on the role of local vigilantes. These are the radicals, Kennedy said, who believe that the real danger is from within. "They look suspiciously at their neighbors and their leaders. They call for a man on horseback because they do not trust the people." Kennedy then made a pointed reference to Edwin Walker, who had resigned from the army only two weeks earlier. The Far Right may object "quite rightly to politics intruding on the military—but they are very anxious for the military to engage in their kind of politics."[16]

Walker's supporters were making their own news that same day in Los Angeles, in what was billed as a National Indignation Convention at the Hollywood High School auditorium. The FBI and Secret Service were particularly concerned that Walker's appearance at the rally only ten blocks from the Palladium, where Kennedy was to speak, would pose a security threat to the president.[17] As Kennedy sounded the alarm over those who called for a dictator, a group dubbed *Friends of General Walker* was among the two thousand who converged around the Palladium on Sunset Boulevard waving placards. Although they were peaceful, *Washington Post* columnist Pearson described the scene as having "an angry snarl and an ominous overtone."[18] A week after Kennedy's address, his Republican predecessor, Dwight Eisenhower, said that extremists like those convening under Walker's banner were not honest patriots but were "advocating some form of dictatorship."[19]

Organized in September 1961 by thirty-two-year-old Dallas businessman Frank McGehee, the National Indignation Convention became Walker's platform to address a wider audience of the extreme Right. McGehee had contacted Walker only a day after the general's resignation from the army was announced.[20] McGehee, a member of the John Birch Society, said Walker was Kennedy's "political prisoner" after Walker's arrest at the University of Mississippi.[21] Attorney General Robert Kennedy expressed his opinion that McGehee's National Indignation Convention, with Walker as its celebrity speaker, "represents a tremendous danger to this country." The FBI also took note of Walker's interest in McGehee's organization.[22] Chief among McGehee's grievances was the sale of 135 surplus fighter planes to Yugoslavia and the training of four Yugoslav pilots at Perrin Air Force Base in Texas. This was the issue that gave McGehee legitimacy among the conservative establishment, as well as among the outliers.

In October 1961, one of McGehee's first actions was a forty-five-minute protest at the front gates of the air force base. Although he had only eight others with him, the picket line garnered his National Indignation Convention the publicity and endorsements he was seeking from members of Congress. The *Dallas Morning News* reported that with word of McGehee's protest, "countless enraged citizens" flooded the switchboard.[23] Just days later, the Kennedy administration announced that it would take "a microscopic look at any future economic and military cooperation with Tito's Yugoslavia.[24] By December, the National Indignation Convention was considered among the country's fastest-growing ultraconservative organizations as it also pushed for a hard line against Cuba and a boycott of products made in communist states.[25]

The moderate conservatives of *National Review* were not hesitant about sharing the stage with Walker at a National Indignation Convention rally at the Dallas Memorial Auditorium, one week after its vocal demonstration in Los Angeles. The magazine's publisher, William Rusher, came to Walker's defense, saying that Kennedy's "polished oratory" about right-wing extremists should be directed "to the cause of preventing further onslaughts by communism." By telephone hookup, the convention also heard from Eddie Rickenbacker, who predicted that only another Teddy Roosevelt could stand in the way of a "socialistic dictator."[26]

In January 1962, Walker was again the featured speaker at a National Indignation Convention rally, which was broadcast across the country through a long-distance telephone connection with one hundred radio stations. He warned of national suicide if the United States disarmed in the face of what he called a "world army." But he said he was optimistic because there were plenty of Americans "awakened to communist infiltration."[27] McGehee and his convention were so enamored with Walker that they led an effort to persuade him to run for president in 1964. This was before his poor showing in the Democratic primary for the Texas governor's race had left Walker's political career stillborn.[28]

It was Walker's arrest for sedition following the riot on the campus of Ole Miss, and his help a year later for those who heckled and assaulted Adlai Stevenson, that made the ex-general a focal point of the FBI's surveillance of the militant Right. Was Walker giving financial or other assistance to terrorists such as the Minutemen, the Ku Klux Klan, or others who advocated armed insurrection against the United States government? Was Walker a behind-the-scenes actor—the "mad hatter," in the words of an anonymous letter to the FBI office in Dallas?[29]

Although the FBI was not able to definitively connect Walker with Minutemen activities, there were clues that he was lending his counsel, and possibly his money, to cells in Texas. The FBI noted that Walker was in contact with Minutemen leaders in several states, and in the days leading up to the riot at the University of Mississippi, well-armed Minutemen, answering Walker's call for volunteers, had been intercepted by the Dallas Police Department.[30] An informant who had infiltrated the group two years later told the FBI that "Gen. Walker [is] a very important person in the Minutemen" and that "several members of the group are personally acquainted with General Walker and he apparently has a capacity of being an adviser." The FBI also noted that a member of the Minutemen and "a personal and close friend of Edwin Walker" had been implicated in the firebombing of the offices of the *Midlothian Mirror* in Texas in 1962.[31]

Keep Your Guns Cleaned and Oiled

Walker may have been more than an adviser to the Texas Minutemen. In October 1964, an FBI informant notified the Dallas office that Minutemen from Fort Worth had paid a visit to Walker's property near his hometown of Center Point and "stated that a great many firearms were stored" there. The FBI in Dallas found a number of inconsistencies in the informant's story, especially the location of the property and whether Walker himself resided there or had leased it to a tenant. However, the Dallas agents were interested in "recent rumors" that Walker was working with Minutemen and Klan factions planning antigovernment attacks following the election of Lyndon Johnson.[32]

Always careful to mask any calls for insurrection since his arrest at Ole Miss, Walker nonetheless had a warning following Johnson's election to the presidency, telling an audience in Florida that although he was not advocating arming for an uprising, "you'd better keep the guns you have cleaned and oiled; you might need them."[33] The FBI and Secret Service were aware that Walker's not-so-subtle language could put the president at risk and that Klan factions in Alabama and Mississippi were looking to Walker to lead a revolution.[34] Although the FBI was unable to uncover an organized terrorist plot, federal agents were busy investigating Walker's ties to the Ku Klux Klan.[35]

Walker was advertised as one of the "old give 'em hell speakers" at a Citizens' Council "We—the White People" rally on the Louisiana State Capitol steps in Baton Rouge on July 4, 1965.[36] It was well attended by a resurgent KKK, particularly Robert Shelton's United Klans of America, protesting Louisiana governor John McKeithen's weak position on segregation.[37] That same week, Attorney General Nicholas Katzenbach announced that he would work with his Alabama counterpart and the House Un-American Activities Committee to investigate Klan activity throughout the South.[38]

Later that year, Shelton and Walker met in Shreveport, a center of extremist groups. Shelton, an air conditioner salesman who carried the exalted title of Imperial Wizard, offered Walker an equally exalted position of Grand Dragon for the state of Texas. Walker apparently demurred, most likely preferring to keep a safe distance from Justice Department scrutiny and to repair his image.[39]

Yet Walker was not averse to working secretly with a number of groups, some acting as fronts for the Klan, with names such as American Royal Rangers, the Dixie Council, and the Western American Security Police. The American Royal Rangers was a reorganized Original Knights of the Ku Klux Klan, trading white robes for paramilitary khaki uniforms and Confederate flag medallions. While the American Royal Rangers had Walker's active support, the FBI noted, he "will remain in the background and will not be openly connected with it."[40]

Likewise, although Walker was careful to avoid lending his name publicly to groups of the neofascist Right, he was praised by some of the most notorious anti-Semites of the early 1960s, such as Conde McGinley, who said America had fought on the wrong side in World War II and that "the Jews screamed for us to go to war against Germany." McGinley dubbed Kennedy's New Frontier the "Jew Frontier," and as for Walker, he had been intentionally targeted by *Overseas Weekly*, which was "owned and directed by Jews."[41]

The National States' Rights Party, which featured the Nazi thunderbolt on the cover of its newsletter, offered a tape of Walker's speeches to "patriotic groups all over the country." Taking a prayerful approach, the anti-Semitic group asked "may God give us more men like General Walker."[42] Throughout the mid-1960s, there were radicals willing to go with Walker down any winding rabbit hole. One loyalist, who signed his letter "A Revolutionist," said he was ready to die in service to the former army commander. "I don't want to go now, but if it will serve a purpose, I am ready. I will gladly follow your program without question, GENERAL, there are millions of others that will follow you too."[43] A prominent leader of the National States' Rights Party in Florida, Oren Potito, had heeded Walker's calls for volunteers at the University of Mississippi. Potito, who was well armed, was among those arrested by federal marshals the day of the riot.[44]

Even some of the men Walker coached at Augsburg later joined the ranks of extremist groups. Major Arch Roberts, who was Walker's top aide at the 24th Infantry Division, became a prolific mailer of John Birch Society attacks on the Kennedy administration.[45] In 1962, he was relieved of military duty for a rogue speech before the Daughters of the American Revolution in which he accused Los Angeles mayor Sam Yorty of having a "communist background."[46] In the 1970s, Roberts headed the benign-sounding Committee to Restore the

Constitution. Louisiana congressman John Rarick, who called Walker "a symbol of courage to all Americans," entered into the *Congressional Record* a long tract, written by Roberts, that was replete with anti-Semitic tropes. Roberts repeated many of the Pro-Blue talking points, predicting that America's independence would soon be extinguished by "an invisible monetary power." And the mastermind of this invisible power? "Foreigners, international money lenders" and, of course, the Jewish Rothschilds.[47]

Whether he was secretly winning friends in the Klan or openly lending his name to the Citizens' Council, Walker remained an unrepentant racist throughout his life. In the years after the riot at Ole Miss, he continued his war against the civil rights movement. On the tenth anniversary of the Supreme Court's ruling in *Brown v. Board of Education,* Walker was invited by the Citizens' Council to speak at a rally in Little Rock to denounce what he called "Black Monday." Walker was scheduled to speak on the steps of Central High School, the very steps he had protected as the Little Rock Nine made their historic journey through the schoolhouse door in 1957. The Little Rock school board told Walker he was not welcome and he was denied access to the campus. Instead, he addressed a meeting of the Citizens' Council, which billed his talk "An American Soldier's Battle with the World Police State."[48]

As the Texas delegate to the Citizens' Council's national leadership conference in October 1963, Walker was the featured luncheon speaker, serving up a menu of conspiratorial and racist rhetoric. "The Kennedys have liqui dated the government and you will be voting with the *nigras* from now on," he said.[49] And referring to Eisenhower and Kennedy, Walker said, "One ordered troops into Little Rock and one into Mississippi. Both run at the beck and call of Khrushchev."[50] To Walker, Martin Luther King was "an agent of the UN with instructions coming from the communist and Black countries to get control of the Revolution."[51] While Walker used the word *nigras* in public, he was not above using the more egregious slur even when speaking with the press.[52]

Walker under FBI Surveillance

On August 28, 1963, as Dr. King delivered his "I Have a Dream" speech, denizens of the ultra Right were dreaming of a time before desegregation. The March on Washington, which brought more than 200,000 to the nation's capital for jobs and freedom, was successful in pressuring the Kennedy administration to initiate a strong federal civil rights bill in Congress. In the weeks before August 28th, the FBI was keeping a close eye on racist factions intent on a violent confrontation. A lengthy report on hate groups and individuals who posed a threat included various iterations of the Ku Klux Klan, George Lincoln Rockwell's Nazis, the National States' Rights Party, Billy James Hargis's Christian Crusade, and Edwin Walker, who was hinting that he might make an appearance at the Washington Mall, calling the March "the Negro attack on Washington."[53] Rockwell asked the police department for a permit to stage a counterdemonstration, which was denied. Courting Walker to join his swastika-wearing Nazis, Rockwell said the man who led the insurrection at Ole Miss could mobilize ten thousand whites.[54]

At a Christian Crusade conference in Oklahoma City in early August, Walker was among the headliners, but he was cagey when asked if he would go to the March on Washington, saying, "I will go where the spirit moves me." The FBI was listening, and Walker probably knew that. As one FBI source observed, "Walker considers himself the leader of all groups against integration . . . but indicated he learned a lesson at Oxford and will do nothing to incite a riot."[55]

Despite his careful words about the March, Walker was unafraid to accuse FBI Director J. Edgar Hoover of not revealing communist conspirators behind Martin Luther King, "probably at the direction of the Kennedys."[56] As the March on Washington drew closer, FBI agents were keeping track of Walker's whereabouts. Just a day before, the FBI surveilled Walker's Dallas home to see if he was still there and noticed five automobiles parked in the back.[57]

Although Walker did not make the drive to Washington, he was again proving himself a provocateur at civil rights rallies. In Austin, Walker was among a dozen segregationists from the local Citizens' Council who were standing on the sidelines as about six hundred walked to the Texas State Capitol building in a call for civil rights legislation. Walker told reporters he was there as an observer. Looking at the marchers, who were led by the Texas Southern Christian Leadership Conference, he commented sarcastically, "If that's all the supporters Kennedy has here, he's sure flopped."[58]

Walker also joined the racist Right in defending Byron De La Beckwith, the murderer of Medgar Evers. Evers, who served as the NAACP's Mississippi field secretary and was one of the people James Meredith had called as he attempted to register as a student at Ole Miss, was assassinated outside his home in Jackson on June 12, 1963. Evers had just returned from a civil rights rally when he was shot in the back as he walked from his driveway. De La Beckwith was arrested after his fingerprints were found on a rifle sight at the scene. The district attorney described De La Beckwith's ambush of Evers as "the most cold-blooded killing."[59] A Klansman with a violent past of domestic abuse, De La Beckwith had heeded Walker's call to join the attack at the University of Mississippi. He had been stopped on his way to Oxford from Greenwood with a car loaded with weapons.[60]

A parade of white supremacists, including former governor Ross Barnett, paid a visit to De La Beckwith as he awaited the jury's verdict. Walker was there too, in September 1963, meeting with Evers's killer as he sat in jail. Walker, who was to speak at a Citizens' Council rally in Jackson, told reporters that De La Beckwith was "in good spirits and very courageous."[61] When he was asked whether he thought De La Beckwith was guilty, Walker responded with what sounded like a justification for the assassination. "Evers was working against the good of the country." Civil rights activists were outraged that a Klansman and likely murderer was being treated like royalty in the Hinds County jail, with a defense fund in the thousands of dollars.[62]

On February 7, 1964, the day the jury was to come back with its decision, Walker was in the courtroom, again shaking De La Beckwith's hand and greeting the defendant's estranged wife. Soon thereafter, an all-white jury, after deliberating eleven hours, announced it could not reach a verdict, ending the case in a mistrial.[63] University of Mississippi historian James Silver called Walker's and Barnett's visits "as public as daylight"—a clear sign that uncompromising segregationists were not above condoning murder.[64]

Violent men were part of the legacy of the militant Right of the 1960s, but they could be unwelcome guests as Walker and Hargis, striving for respectability, toured the country in the spring of 1963. The two were occasionally embarrassed by someone in the audience with neo-Nazi propaganda or a swastika armband.[65] However, others just as radical, but who might wear a plain business suit, often had a place on the stage. Among the featured speakers at a Christian Crusade convention in Tulsa, for instance, was Willis Carto, a leader of the anti-Semitic Liberty Lobby, who called Hitler's defeat a historical tragedy.[66] One contributor to Hargis's *Christian Crusader* weekly was General Charles A. Willoughby, who had served as General Douglas MacArthur's intelligence chief in occupied Japan. Willoughby peddled tales of an international Red conspiracy masterminded by Jews.[67]

An Attraction for the "Bitter and Vindictive"

The John Birch Society's Robert Welch tried to keep the most extreme element at arm's length, but that did not fully clear the Birchers in the eyes of some. Welch might have been overstating his case when he claimed that Birch chapters accepted "only men and women of good character" and rejected racists of any stripe. Welch would point to a "small but growing" number of African American Birchers, "working so courageously, to show how the Negroes are being used today by the communists."[68] Welch also was adamant that his members did not stockpile weapons. "Our people are not riff-raff. They're good people [and] not wild characters."[69]

For some in Congress, the danger was clearly the wild characters on the Right. Ohio senator Stephen Young condemned what he termed "the fascist John Birch Society." America was fertile soil for right-wing radicalism, said Young, because it had held an attraction for "the bitter and the vindictive."[70] On the floor of the House, California congressman Ronald Brooks Cameron sounded a warning eerily familiar six decades later: "We are all aware that democracy is under attack by the radical Right." In a dire prediction, Cameron said, "It is tomorrow that concerns me . . . Sooner than any of us would like to believe," he said, the United States could experience "a torrent of suspicion, hate, fear, and distrust unlike anything this country has seen." Cameron was worried that while Welch was "attempting to improve the ignoble image" of the John Birch Society by keeping a safe distance from homegrown fascists like Gerald L. K. Smith, these militants see an opportunity. Smith, whose affiliation with hate groups began in the 1930s, urged his followers to ignore for now Welch's "naïveté about the Jewish issue." He encouraged them to attend John Birch Society meetings in an effort to push the Birchers even further to the extremes.[71]

As Welch struggled to gain acceptance among mainstream conservatives, the editorial board of the *Houston Post* concluded that the Birchers were "potentially dangerous because democracy is rejected in favor of authoritarianism." The editors sensed that many Americans were victim to delusions that occur when "a substantial number of people become badly frightened, frustrated and disturbed."[72] Edwin Walker was adept at exploiting that fear, especially in the South, as the walls of segregation came tumbling down. In July 1966, he was the keynote speaker for the Americans for the Preservation of the White Race at Whitworth College in Brookhaven, Mississippi. Organizers of the event trafficked in not only white supremacy but also in anti-Semitic conspiracies, referring to the "communist-Jewish control" of the Democratic Party.[73] Walker, echoing the virulent anti-Semitism of Carto's Liberty Lobby, also referred to "Jew-controlled" senators and to Israel "doing everything in their power to force the United States to declare war on the Arabs."[74]

Walker might have tried to project an image of respectability, especially in his dealings with members of Congress, but as his statements betrayed ideas that were beyond the pale, he lost even those few friends on Capitol Hill. Although he was a veteran of World War II, Walker told an audience in Tampa during his Midnight Ride tour that "Hitler didn't declare war on us; we declared war on him."[75] The Battle of Stalingrad, Walker said, was a "trumped-up story" to persuade Americans that Russia suffered from the war, to "cause Americans to feel sorry for them."[76] Referring to Rudolph Hess, the imprisoned former Hitler deputy, Walker said cryptically, "Hess has a message . . . He was a very astute man"[77] One of Walker's most consistent defenders, Dan Smoot, bemoaned the "hate Germans propaganda" in press coverage of the Adolf Eichmann trial in Israel.[78] Sounding like Charles Lindbergh's America First Committee, Smoot believed the United States should have stayed out of the fight against Hitler. In Smoot's view, America had been dragged into the war by the invisible government and by Franklin Roosevelt's "incurable ambition to get in that war and become President of the world." Though Smoot was not outwardly anti-Semitic, his position that World War II "put the Soviet Union astride the globe like a menacing colossus" seemed to minimize the consequences of a Nazi victory in Europe and the Holocaust.[79]

Walker's investment in the *American Mercury* also is revealing about his association with those who denied the Holocaust or longed for the Third Reich. A once highly respected magazine, founded by H. L. Mencken, by the 1950s it had fallen into the hands of neofascists. The Anti-Defamation League called it "the single most important anti-Semitic publication in the United States."[80] In the days leading up to the riot at Ole Miss, Walker was listed as one of the magazine's purchasers. The *American Mercury* was now owned by the Legion for the Survival of Freedom, based in McAllen, Texas. Aside from being an investor in the publication, which sold for $200,000, Walker was named military editor and analyst.[81]

Through the 1960s, the *American Mercury* would align with a number of groups and individuals on the lunatic fringe, including Carto's Liberty Lobby. Because the magazine was clearly in the orbit of the most radical elements, its fortunes fell rapidly. The conservative intellectuals leading *National Review* rejected contributions from anyone affiliated with the *American Mercury*, calling it "reprehensible and irresponsible."[82]

Walker's involvement with Robert and Mary Surrey is yet another clue to his complex relationship with the militant Right. Robert Surrey was Walker's closest confidante and American Eagle partner. Mary worked in Walker's home as his personal secretary. Robert Surrey accompanied Walker to the University of Mississippi during the chaotic days of September 30 and October 1, 1962, and both Surreys were members of Rockwell's American Nazi Party.[83] During the span of his career, from 1958 to 1967, Rockwell was the most widely publicized hate group leader in America, according to biographer Frederick Simonelli. Based in Arlington, Virginia, Rockwell's Nazis were frequent speakers on the Washington Mall.[84] Surrey printed a number of Walker's pamphlets as well as the KENNEDY WANTED FOR TREASON poster. He also was Rockwell's printer, putting him under FBI scrutiny.[85]

However, Walker's partnership with the Surreys ended in early 1965, when Mary left Walker's employ after he refused to join the Nazis, which likely was a disappointment to Rockwell.[86] Three years earlier, Rockwell had been ejected from the Senate committee room where Walker was testifying, declaring, "I came here to defend Walker, the only patriot brave enough to stand up and refuse to condemn me."[87] Walker neither publicly condemned nor condoned Rockwell. Of course, that did not stop Rockwell from making vain attempts to recruit Walker, complimenting him on "his inspiring courage and actions," even if he might be put off by "my ogreish reputation."[88]

Generally, Walker felt more at home with the far less ogreish Citizens' Councils, which preferred golf shirts and country clubs to white hoods and cross burnings but upheld the same racist ideas. Walker sympathized with some of the more radical elements, but he also sought the approval of the establishment Right. It was behavior that reflected Walker's eccentric personality and fear of losing status as a commanding officer in two wars. There was another factor at play. According to one FBI source, it would have been out of character for the secretive Walker to join a factional group "as he is very much a loner."[89] Walker may also have feared that joining any organization carried the risk that he might be outed as gay.

11

The Outing of General Walker

With the discrediting of the John Birch Society, and as a new generation of politically savvy conservatives emerged in the late 1960s, Edwin Walker's popularity on the American Right began to vanish. Any hope for elected office had been dashed in 1962, when he came in dead last in the Texas Democratic party primary.

As Walker faded into obscurity, he continued to carry a deep secret, until it was uncovered by an arrest at a Dallas park: Walker was a closeted homosexual at a time when being gay would derail a military career and result in ridicule in right-wing circles.

Walker's reputation as a confirmed bachelor often led to suspicion about his cloistered personal life, but he made every effort to portray the image of the tough Texan who had braved some of the worst fighting of two wars. To Walker, the elite and effete men of the Kennedy administration lacked the manliness to confront Fidel Castro or Nikita Khrushchev.

Sexuality and politics intersected in the 1950s, and well into the 1960s, with the perception of the homosexual as a threat to national security. In June 1950, the Senate authorized a formal inquiry into the employment of "homosexuals and other moral perverts" in government. State Department investigators were diligent about firing anyone suspected of being gay—just being unmarried or not quite fitting into prescribed gender norms was enough to be persecuted. Between 1949 and 1950, the State Department fired 203 people who were deemed "security risks," and of that number, ninety-one were labeled possible perverts.[1] Two years later, the American Psychiatric Association diagnosed homosexuality as "pathological behavior." Gay men and women were barred from federal employment, purged from the armed forces, and harassed by police in cities across the country. At the root of Cold War homophobia were unfounded fears that gays with access to classified material were vulnerable to blackmail by Soviet agents or that their "sexual overindulgence" made them susceptible to the immoral ideology of communism.[2]

To the ultra Right, homosexuality was a sinister deviance working with a sinister ideology to undermine the sacred American values of marriage and family. Like communist professors on campus, homosexuals were recruiting wholesome young men and women. South Dakota senator Karl Mundt said communism could never appeal to soldiers like Walker, but only to "sex deviates." Firing them from government jobs kept America safe. "Down through the ages that is the way spies have been made and recruited."[3]

Barry Goldwater, who projected the image of the straight-talking Westerner, connected anticommunism with manliness. He defended Walker's use of strong words to his troops about being prepared to sacrifice their lives if it came down to war with the Soviet Union. Diplomats and negotiators, Goldwater said, were not the kind of men who could defeat US enemies in Moscow, who had already declared, "We will bury you." As for the Kennedy men in the State and Defense Departments, Goldwater again reverted to the language of a virile—and purposefully heterosexual—hypermasculinity. Instead of taking on the communist threat, these effeminate East Coast appeasers only "hide behind their squaws' skirts."[4]

This culture of hypermasculinity was inherent in the organizations of the radical and racist Right. Robert Welch lectured on what he labeled the sexually aberrant behavior of homosexuality and interracial dating. American Nazi leader George Lincoln Rockwell, who also may have had hidden homosexual relationships, often bragged about his own manliness in a way that revealed a sense of insecurity, saying, "It takes a MAN to be a Nazi." According to one acquaintance, Rockwell "had a fixation on homosexuality and tried to tar all his opponents with that brush . . . He said that he had problems with that in his own organization . . . He was so rabid on the point that I often wondered if he were not himself so inclined."[5] Walker also made a very conscious effort to project an aura of soldierly masculinity, saying, "The world I live in is to do or die—making men of soldiers and soldiers of men."[6]

Although he likely would never identify as a homosexual, he did engage in sexual encounters with other men. On the evening of June 23, 1976, Walker was arrested in a Dallas park restroom for making a sexual advance to an undercover vice officer who was responding to complaints of homosexual liaisons in the park. The undercover officer said Walker "fondled his genitals."[7]

Walker went on trial for the misdemeanor charge of public lewdness, pleaded no contest, was fined, and was placed on probation for a year. Responding to the arrest, Walker would only say that with the Supreme Court ruling on his case against the Associated Press, he was a public figure and "can be libeled at will."[8] Walker's arrest was not the only high-profile case made by vice officers that year. G. Harold Carswell, Nixon's Supreme Court nominee who had been rejected by the Senate, was found guilty of making sexual advances to a male vice officer in a Tallahassee men's room.[9] On March 16, 1977, Walker was again arrested in a Dallas park restroom for approaching an undercover officer with an offer to engage in sexual activity.[10]

Walker's long-held secret was out, but to some it came as no surprise. There had been rumors before, whispered in polite language. Newspaper accounts of Walker's command of troops at Little Rock and during the crisis at the University of Mississippi would on occasion pointedly refer to Walker's bachelor status.[11]

Did the FBI suspect Walker was a homosexual? As the FBI collected articles about Walker, one passage was underlined in obvious fashion: "He [Walker] is not married." Walker's appearance at the campus of Ole Miss provided other clues at a time when any liaison between an older man and a younger one raised suspicions in the notoriously homophobic FBI. According to an FBI report, Walker was in the company "of a man about 20 years old who refused to give his name." The man, who had befriended Walker during his campaign for governor, accompanied him to his hotel the day before the riot at the Ole Mis campus.[12] One FBI agent's description of "a youthful male assistant" was a coded implication of a possible homosexual relationship.[13]

The repeated mention of Walker's bachelorhood was enough for one of his supporters in Congress, Samuel Devine of Ohio. "Somebody says he is not a married man and has no children. J. Edgar Hoover is a bachelor, and he is one of the greatest Americans of our time," Devine said. Those thinly veiled remarks about Walker's sexuality, Devine said, were a case of "guilt by innuendo."[14] Hoover's own closeted homosexuality might have been the reason these particular comments from the *Congressional Record* made it to Hoover's desk.[15] At times, Walker would get defensive when asked about his marital status. In response to an invitation to participate in a military ceremony, Walker seemed testy: "There is no Mrs. Walker. There never has been."[16]

Among the peculiar annals of the ultra Right was an anonymous tract called the "Deguello Report," a mimeographed manifesto written in 1976. Likely written by an insider in one of the many extremist groups, possibly the National States' Rights Party, the report alleges that Walker was "a sincere American Nationalist . . . but known to his enemies as a secret homosexual." The accuracy of this exposé is far from verified, but the author writes that there had been homosexual relationships between Walker and the young men who came through his compound in Dallas.[17] In another instance, a prominent British journalist who visited Walker in his home made a pointed reference to a young man who "waited upon Walker not as a servant but as a friend, bringing us coffee and biscuits." As she conducted the interview in the comfort of Walker's spacious residence, she observed that "the young man watched Walker like a hypnotized rabbit."[18]

Among all of Walker's close associates, it is Billy James Hargis who figures in another case of furtive homosexual affairs. Like others in the religious Right who equated homosexuality with communism, Hargis made sexuality a central topic of his sermons. In 1968, his Christian Crusade published a bestseller, *Is the School House the Proper Place to Teach Raw Sex?,* which sold 250,000 copies.[19] In 1970, Hargis followed up with *The Sex Revolution in the United States,* as he shifted from a singular focus on communist infiltration to sexual politics.

Hargis's homosexuality was revealed only a few months before Walker's first arrest. Five of Hargis's students, four of them men, came forward publicly to say they had had sexual relations with the Tulsa preacher over a period of three years, at his American Christian College in Tulsa, at his farm in the Ozarks, or during his tours with a college choir called the All-American Kids. Hargis denied the accusations but admitted cryptically, through a lawyer, "I have made more than my share of mistakes. I'm not proud of them."[20]

Queerness and Hypermasculinity

Hargis, like Walker, tried to portray himself as rustic and masculine, a job made difficult by his pudgy face and less-than-manly features, which contrasted sharply with Walker's rugged good looks. On the cover of his 1965 biography, *Crusading Preacher from the West,* by Cuban exile Fernando Penabaz, Hargis tried to create a more masculine image. He is pictured standing beside a white horse, a potent symbol of the American frontier. It was a part of the country unspoiled by East Coast liberals and homosexuals living in the sinful canyons of New York high-rise buildings. The American West was a real man's landscape, imbued with conservative virtues. Indeed, the two leading conservative politicians of the 1960s, Barry Goldwater and Ronald Reagan, were often pictured like Hollywood icons on horseback. Hence, an outward portrayal of manliness was a convenient cover for Walker and Hargis. As Carol Mason points out in *Oklahomo: Lessons in Unqueering America,* if you were manly, you weren't queer.[21]

Walker and Hargis had traveled across the country for six weeks in 1963 on their Midnight Ride speaking tour, but there were no allegations or rumors that the two were involved in a love affair. At the time, both had kept their sexual preferences under wraps.

The scandal did take its toll on Hargis, as the leadership of the Christian Crusade was turned over to its vice president David Noebel. Noebel not only found subversive messages in the music of the Beatles but also wrote *The Homosexual Revolution* in 1977. In a fashion typical of the evangelical Right, Noebel raised the specter of "youth seduced by expert male homosexuals who skillfully initiate their victims into a world of absolute vileness and degradation."[22] Without the charismatic Hargis, the Crusade was finished.

As for Walker, even before his arrest in the park restrooms, he had already become a peripheral character of the American Right. He tried to make a living through $500 speaking fees and continued to warn of communist professors on American campuses and the fast-approaching race war being orchestrated by the United Nations, the NAACP, and the press.[23]

In the same spirit as his jeremiads about a defeatist policy in Korea, Walker charged the Johnson administration with "waging [the Vietnam] war without intending to win." Vietnam was worse than Korea, he said, "a chaotic situation where men are fed into a meat grinder without any discernible objective. We should win or get out." He even returned to his most frightening proposal: using nuclear weapons, particularly the oddly named Davy Crockett, a small nuclear warhead that could be fired from artillery. The Davy Crockett was first deployed in Europe when Walker was commanding troops at Augsburg. Although it proved to be a poorly conceived weapon and was removed from US forces in 1967, Walker praised what he called the "atomic bazooka." Despite the fact that army leaders had concluded it would present an unacceptable hazard to allied troops, Walker pronounced it "ideal for conditions in Vietnam."[24]

Walker's position on Vietnam meant that many of his appearances were met by antiwar protesters, but by the mid-1960s Walker was increasingly viewed by the FBI as an eccentric curiosity and less as a dangerous insurrectionist. When he spoke at a high school auditorium in Long Beach, California, the FBI was there as well, but agents were more interested in antiwar activists than in Walker.[25] In his private and public writings, Walker was a man quickly losing touch with reality, writing, for example, "Will the people of Dallas be surprised when they find out that long hair, beards, and bare flesh are a front [and] disguise of revolution?"[26]

Under the illusion that he had a private channel to J. Edgar Hoover, Walker sent a strangely worded letter critical of President Nixon and what he termed "the ratpack campus professors and clergy" who were responsible for the antiwar protests on college campuses. The president, Walker said, should be concerned about the communist enemy at home. "Why go to a jungle or desert to fight an enemy? We have a pretty good fight on the campuses," he said. In one eerie remark, Walker warns of "another [Lee Harvey] Oswald in the form of a soldier who has hijacked an airplane loaded with bombs which could be used to overthrow the US Senate capitol." The letter was so incoherent that FBI officials advised that it not be answered, noting that Walker shows "signs of grandiosity, [and] confusion."[27]

Another letter, addressed to "Catholic Senator Mike Mansfield," again exhibited increasingly strange behavior. He referred to "booby tube generals" and "presidents, dead, assassinated, ditched and rattling on." Walker attacked the clergy, saying that the "police states have their state pulpiteers," a reference to Billy Graham, who "cozied to Lyndon Johnson when he was president." With Nixon, Graham had "a permanent Washington suite in the White House."[28]

During the Nixon administration, Walker took particular aim at Secretary of State Henry Kissinger with the peculiar remark that there were two intelligence agencies, the KGB and the CIA, and "when I speak of Henry Kissinger, I speak of both." Kissinger's confirmation by the Senate in 1973 prompted Walker to charge, "I am speaking of treason in the Senate." In this fantasy, Kissinger was purging the CIA with the help of the Kremlin—"clearing the deck for KGB operations in the US."[29]

Arkansas journalist Harry Ashmore writes that in the late 1960s and early 1970s, Walker was "a sort of wandering segregationist minstrel."[30] With Goldwater's overwhelming defeat in 1964, mainstream conservatives and Republicans worked to shed the image of extremism by expelling Birchers from leadership positions in local party organizations. The Goldwater campaign had earlier attempted to distance itself from the outliers of the Right, denying Walker a seat on the Texas delegation to the 1964 Republican convention.[31] In Arlington, Virginia, a "Beat-the-Birchers Committee" declared that the organization's methods and views were not compatible with GOP principles.[32]

Even before the Goldwater defeat, Walker was pushing for a third-party movement, saying Democrats and Republicans were indistinguishable. "It wouldn't surprise me if Rockefeller money didn't support Kennedy, and if Kennedy saw he was going to lose, wouldn't support Rockefeller."[33] In May 1965, a coalition of Rightist groups from across the country gathered in Chicago to devise a third-party strategy. The goal of the Congress of Conservatives was to create "anticommunist parties" at the state and national levels. The platform was a recipe for World War III, including proposals such as invading Cuba, seeking to overthrow Mao Zedong's government, and breaking all relations with the Soviet Union and communist regimes in Eastern Europe. The coalition was organized by Birch Society leader Medford Evans, who had sat at Walker's side during Senate hearings three years earlier.[34]

Walker, a featured speaker, said there were no patriotic political parties at that time. Instead, "we have only a [one-party] dictatorship."[35] According to the *Chicago Daily News,* Walker gave "the most spectacular, if near-grotesque performance of the meeting." Like so many appearances before, Walker was described as repeating himself, pausing at awkward moments, tossing out "a string of run-on sentences, then graciously thank[ing] the communist-controlled reporters for coming." The sense that Walker was mentally unbalanced was not lost on the press. One reporter brought along a colleague to take down "Walker's irregular torrent of words on a shorthand machine."[36]

George Wallace: "A Man of God"

Among the other headliners was Lester Maddox, who would be elected governor of Georgia in 1966. Maddox rode to the governorship on his reputation as an Atlanta restaurateur who barred African Americans with a gun. Maddox threw plenty of red meat to his audience, using words that might find resonance today in the quarters of the Far Right. "You know why I pulled a gun?" Maddox asked. "Because the Constitution gives me the right to keep and bear arms."[37]

But it was Alabama governor George Wallace who met the expectations of the ultra Right as a presidential candidate who would best articulate the fear of integration, riots in major cities, and antiwar protests. With the refrain that there "isn't a dime's worth of difference" between the two parties, Wallace ran in 1968 as the candidate of his own American Independent Party. Wallace surrounded himself with some of the more radical elements of the racist Right, including Asa Carter. An organizer of the Alabama Citizens' Council, Carter was also closely connected with Ku Klux Klan factions in the state.[38]

Walker made a swing through several southern states for Wallace's campaign, and at a Labor Day rally in Chesapeake, Virginia, he called Lyndon Johnson "the rear end of a jackass." As for the GOP candidate, Richard Nixon, he was a "warmed-over Quaker." Turning to Democrat Hubert Humphrey, Walker labeled him "a warmed-over socialist." Both Democrats and Republicans, he said, had sold out to the communists. The segregationist governor of Alabama, on the other hand, was in Walker's words "a man of God."[39]

Among Wallace's positions that particularly pleased Walker—aside from opposition to integration—was his support for the apartheid regime in South Africa and for withdrawing from the United Nations. To this enthusiastic Virginia audience, Walker repeated Wallace's threat that if elected President "the first anarchist that lies in front of my car—it's going to be the last car he ever lays down in front of." As for the war in Vietnam, Walker said, "Retreat and defeat in Vietnam is a victory for the revolutionists in the United States."[40]

Winning nearly 10 million votes, about 13 percent of the total, Wallace carried five southern states and won forty-six electoral votes. Wallace was appreciative of Walker's support in 1968 and enlisted him in what would be a second national campaign, in 1972.[41] Walker was a welcome adviser to the Wallace campaign and provided his recommendations to the American Independent Party chairman, suggesting that the platform "does not have to appeal to every pet project. We have those people. It has to be acceptable to the disenchanted."[42] Wallace's 1972 campaign was cut short on May 15 by an assassination attempt in Maryland that left him partially paralyzed. Walker led a nightly prayer vigil in a Dallas park but was arrested for refusing to leave at midnight. The park was under a curfew following drug raids.[43]

Because Walker had forgone his pension in resigning from the army, his financial problems started to mount in the early 1970s. He expressed his frustration in 1977, saying that his three years of weekly telephone messages, which cost him $35 a month, did not yield a single donation. Typical of his recorded "message of the week," he warned of attempts by the government to "register, control, and confiscate firearms . . . What right," he asked, "has the federal government to assume the responsibility for you and your family?"[44] One of his admirers suggested a General Walker Foundation to raise money to assist Walker financially and to provide the funds for his speaking tours. "You are living like a gypsy," he wrote Walker, "with your neck stuck out four hundred miles."[45] Walker did receive the occasional correspondence from someone who still saw him as a heroic soldier battling the unseen enemy. "The hour is late," wrote one die-hard follower. "I feel the country is fast being led down the road to socialism."[46]

Walker's Descent into Obscurity

A little more than a decade after Walker was packing convention halls in Texas and California, he was a bitter and largely forgotten recluse. The *Dallas Times-*

Herald called his house, with its cryptic billboards facing the street, "notorious for its front yard messages." Walker said he paid $500 in legal fees to keep his signs up, like the one that read "Sodom Gomorrah Or Wallace." Typically defiant, he said, "Four times we went through [court hearings] and I'm still the winner."[47] One passerby wrote to Walker to say that he made it a point to drive by Walker's house to view the latest addition to the lawn, and to express his interest in "the man behind the signs."[48]

Texas Monthly writer Gary Cartwright said that, like downtown Dallas, the general was calmer these days compared with the tumultuous year of the Kennedy assassination and Walker's narrow escape from Lee Harvey Oswald's rifle. Ken Latimer, an actor with the Dallas Theater Center in the mid-1970s, agreed. "General Walker and his people used to picket us fairly regularly, but they've been quiet for some time now."[49]

In 1978, Walker moved from the large, fourteen-room, two-story home at 4011 Turtle Creek Boulevard that he had rented since December 1961. He placed a sign in the yard that read "Memorial to Oswald Ruby Warren Conspiracy." It was reported that he took one souvenir from the house: the window through which Oswald took his shot. Walker told the *Dallas Morning News* he wanted to move to a more modest home. He said that in the process of moving to a smaller residence, he would be shipping some of his belongings "to people I care about" in Houston and Colorado. In one odd turn of phrase, he told the newspaper, "I do better keeping you all straight if I have less here."[50]

In 1983, Walker's financial situation improved markedly when the army restored his pension, bringing him $45,120 a year. In granting the pension, the army called him "a truly dedicated American soldier who firmly believed that insufficient action was being taken within the military establishment to combat the threat of Communism."[51] Saying that his quarrel was not with the army but with the Kennedy administration, Walker boasted, "I got everything back."[52] The following year, he made a donation to the National Rifle Association that prompted the director of the NRA to tell Walker it was the largest single donation from an individual in almost two years.[53]

Walker did have good things to say about Ronald Reagan, writing to one congressman in 1985 that "the president has been right on every initiative he has taken, every single one." However, Walker's deteriorating mental state could be surmised from a strangely worded reference to his decision to "decline nomination, in retaining my own direct methods of assistance."[54]

Edwin A. Walker died at the age of eighty-three, "in obscurity," said Robert Wilonsky of the *Dallas Observer,* who was the last to interview him. Because he thought he was never given a fair shake by the media, Walker gave few interviews. Visitors were not allowed in, although his address and phone number were still listed in the city directory. Wilonsky said that as Walker approached his last days, he agreed to one final opportunity to present his case to the press, but by phone.[55]

Walker died on Halloween, October 31, 1993, from lung disease, "no doubt from a chain-smoking habit," and his only survivor was a nephew, George Walker. By that point, Walker had been silent for so long that many thought he had already died. "He spent the last years of his life like an aging boxer, too tough, and too proud, and too punch-drunk to hear the bell."[56]

Walker told Wilonsky that by the 1990s, with the end of communism in Russia and the dissolution of the Soviet Union, conditions were different from the 1960s. "Our fight is not necessary now in the way it was then." However, Walker remained an unapologetic white supremacist. In a confusing stream of logic, he said that integration "infers force and the other [desegregation] doesn't and that's all I have to say on the subject."[57]

Wilonsky described the voice as quivering, brittle, phlegmy, the voice "of a man who had seen his share of bloodshed and fighting in and out of uniform." Sometimes, Wilonsky said, Walker "mumbled gibberish," particularly when he spoke of his historical legacy. In his mind he was still a warrior, but "the more he would elaborate, the more murky the answer would become." Most of the last interview of his life was a "mishmash of right-wing code words, out-of-date rhetoric, rallying cries long forgotten." Assessing his life's work, Walker told the *Dallas Observer,* "Back then, I had a bit more influence . . . 'Course you young people don't remember that."[58]

Learning of Walker's death, his one-time partner on the Midnight Ride, Billy James Hargis, said, "I lost one of my best friends." Hargis, who died in 2004, said of Midnight Ride, "Nothing in my 50-year career of standing up for Christ and fighting satanic communism equaled the success of that undertaking."[59]

Wilonsky saw Walker as a "grim reminder of an ugly, mean-spirited time," but there's no denying Walker's place in history. For one brief moment, Major General Edwin Anderson Walker *was* Dallas, and he took the city's eccentricities to a national audience.[60]

Epilogue

Sixty years after the *Houston Post* declared the John Birch Society "a strange product of a strange time," we are again in a strange time. The insurrectionists who stormed the Capitol on January 6, 2021, as well as followers of QAnon and various conspiracy theorists on the Right, have held on to much of Edwin Walker's belief that there is an unseen plot to rob Americans of their liberty.

After the collapse of the Soviet Union, the Birchers found new life in the antiglobalist politics of the early 2000s. Like Walker, today's John Birch Society views the glass headquarters of the United Nations as a Trojan horse intent on subjugating freedom-loving Americans. William Jasper, senior editor of the Birch Society's magazine, *The New American,* says "powerful elites, American elites" are at the root of a scheme to end this nation's sovereignty. They may appear well-meaning and idealistic, Jasper writes, but "behind the humanitarian rhetoric, a much more sinister agenda is at work."[1]

While Walker's "control apparatus" was taking orders from Russian puppet masters, the modern John Birch Society's deep state actors are a bit more ambiguous, but all-pervasive. It is "a highly organized cabal" that has gained control of "the levers of power in the federal government, both political parties, universities, media, major corporations," Jasper writes in his 2001 book, *The United Nations Exposed.*[2]

The paranoid Right, in the 1960s and today, imagines enemies intending to disarm Americans through gun control legislation while preparing to enslave the nation under a worldwide dictatorship. That conspiracy theory took on a life of its own in 1963, when extremists, including General Pedro del Valle, said an army exercise in Georgia, dubbed Water Moccasin III, was really a rehearsal for that inevitable UN attack against the United States. Not only the

United Nations but even NATO was involved in the plot. Central to the fear-mongering was an appeal to the most egregious forms of racism. Letters to Capitol Hill offices warned of "African Negro troops who are cannables [*sic*] stationed in Georgia . . . We know of the UN plans to place Mongolian and Congolese troops over our dear United States."[3]

A half century later, in April 2015, that very same fantasy was the stuff of right-wing bloggers at "the outer edges of political paranoia." An eight-week US military training exercise across several states called Jade Helm 15 raised fear in some parts of rural Texas that it was a covert attempt by the Obama administration to seize Texans' guns, declare martial law, and even imprison some in abandoned Walmarts for "total population control."[4]

With this belief fueled on the Internet by the now-disgraced Alex Jones's Infowars, some buried their firearms as they waited for an apocalyptic battle against unmarked UN choppers and foreign troops. Governor Greg Abbott, who relied on Far Right political support, deployed the Texas State Guard to monitor the military exercise, while also saying there was nothing to worry about. One former Texas legislator said Abbott's response demonstrated how far Republican politics in Texas has been radicalized.[5]

Also in 2015, in a move that would have pleased Edwin Walker, the Texas state legislature proposed a bill that would forbid any government entity from participating in United Nations Agenda 21, a voluntary agreement among member countries to address environmental issues. Agenda 21, the modern Birchers say, is central to the "UN's plan to establish control over all human activity."[6] The mainstream conservatives of the Heritage Foundation also paint a picture of a dystopian landscape if "radical environmentalists" adopt the policies embedded in Agenda 21. They will compel people, the Heritage Foundation writes, "to give up their cars in favor of subways, trolleys, buses and bicycles."[7] Warnings about Agenda 21 were even written into the Republican party's 2016 platform, which called it "erosive of American sovereignty."[8]

Extremism garners its strength during periods of accelerated change, which may be demographic, political, economic, or in many cases a combination of the three. In the midst of these changes, protests arise from those who believe they have lost status and are determined to regain what they feel is rightfully theirs. In the early 1960s, the emerging civil rights movement, youth culture, and the tensions of the Cold War gave the ultra Right a platform to register the frustrations of those who claimed the United States was not their country anymore.

In 1961, *Washington Post* editorial writer Alan Barth said the radical Right was not a wave of the future but "a voice of frustration and despair."[9] What they called for was a national purification and a return to the past. Militancy on the Right has reemerged in the second decade of the twenty-first century for many of the same reasons that it arose in the early 1960s—a transforming America. In 1963, California congressman Ronald Brooks Cameron cautioned members of the House of Representatives that "under normal circumstances the appeals of demagogues have attraction only to the lunatic fringe, but during a crisis . . . extremist panaceas become a real threat to democracy."[10]

One particularly toxic twenty-first-century invention of the paranoid Right is QAnon, a natural successor to Edwin Walker's worldview. QAnon puts the United Nations at the center of the one-world master plan with a few twists that not even Walker could have dreamed. Supermarket bar codes, the COVID-19 vaccine, and Social Security numbers are all part of the effort to control our thoughts—shades of Walker's alarm about brainwashing. QAnon message boards hummed with speculation that the coronavirus was a creation of the elites in the deep state and media determined to destroy the Trump presidency. *Atlantic Monthly* editor Adrienne LaFrance, in a revealing investigation of QAnon, found it to be "emblematic of modern America's susceptibility to conspiracy theories."[11]

In Edwin Walker's imagination, Robert Kennedy was secretly leading the rebellious youth of the 1960s, preparing them for revolution, and the attempted assassination of George Wallace in 1972 was the work of Richard Nixon and the Republican Party.[12] The major difference between disinformation hatched in the minds of Edwin Walker or Robert Welch and that of QAnon today is the ease and speed with which falsehoods can travel and metastasize through social media.

Today's anti-vaxxers on ultra Right channels have their predecessor in the John Birch Society's Kent and Phoebe Courtney, who went so far as to warn parents about vaccinating children against polio. To the Courtneys, the UN's World Health Organization was using the Salk vaccine to create a generation of Americans too weak to enlist in the military. That would allow the communists to "walk in and take over."[13] Even today, the World Health Organization remains a lightning rod for those who suspect it is aligned against American interests. Life in the conspiracy wonderland comes down to a struggle between absolute good and evil. A defining characteristic is suspicion that something has been withheld, that what we see isn't all there is to be revealed.[14]

A Battle against Satan Himself

In the darkest recesses of the extreme Right, the devil takes center stage as a political actor in the service of the deep state. In 1972, Hargis said America faced a "conspiracy so monstrous it staggers the human mind," and that behind it all is "Satan himself."[15] Walker told segregationists in Mississippi that they were "armed with the Bible and Christian faith" against the godless communists.[16] Today, the devil is still pulling the strings, as one Alabama pastor told his congregation that witchcraft was being used to undermine President Trump. John A. Kilpatrick of the Church of His Presence spoke of a coming battle of biblical proportions. Sounding a bit like Hargis, Kilpatrick predicted that "the deep state is about to manifest, and it's going to be a showdown like you can't believe."[17]

This study of Major General Edwin A. Walker began with the words "Unhappy is the land in need of heroes." The Cold War fears of the 1960s led those on the outer limits of political discourse to seek a hero with the power to reveal the hidden truths and to lead America back to an idealized past. With Walker in mind, John F. Kennedy was concerned about those who "call for a man on horseback."[18]

For some, Walker was that leader who would rescue America's traditions and way of life. Throughout history, the "man on horseback" has been an image of one who restores order—a Napoleon riding to save the French republic. Unlike the John Birch Society's Robert Welch, who made his fortune selling sweets, or the overweight preacher Billy James Hargis, it seemed Walker was that man in uniform who could lead the charge.

Yet those who watched Walker closely were confident that he was simply too off the rails to mount any serious threat to democracy in this country.

Washington Post columnist Chalmers Roberts wrote that the Senate hearings in April 1962 revealed that Walker did not have the mental dexterity to be a dictator in waiting.[19] Nationally syndicated columnist Doris Fleeson, who also sat in that Senate hearing room, came to the same conclusion. "He will not even do as a man on horseback."[20]

Walker and others on the edges of American politics, Left and Right, reject democratic institutions. Authority derived directly from the people results in what the Birchers labeled "mobocracy." As the editors of *Time* magazine wrote in 1961, the rhetoric of the John Birch Society was "barely a goose step away" from using intimidating tactics against perceived enemies.[21] After hearing Walker's address at a Christian Crusade convention in Oklahoma City, one local newspaper reporter wondered whether the Birchers were averse to "using force and violence if necessary" to remake America in their image.[22] When Walker was asked if he would consider extralegal means to achieve his ends, his reply was that the young interviewer was being brainwashed by liberals and communists.[23] Despite Walker's puzzling remark, his followers well understood the message.

On January 6, 2021, a new populist Right also saw democracy as a fraud, and, closer than just a goose step away, they marched to the US Capitol. It was an attack that Edwin Walker, America's first modern insurrectionist, likely would have approved. Several years after his resignation from the army, he referred to Congress as "a bunch of clowns . . . They may be your elected officials in Washington but they are not mine."[24] In December 2021, three retired generals warned of a threat from *inside* the military as they looked toward the 2024 presidential election. "We are chilled to our bones at the thought of a coup succeeding next time."[25]

Six decades before the Trump movement, journalist Alan Barth struck a chord of optimism by predicting that the extreme Right "will no doubt seek to capture control of the Republican party but they are unlikely to succeed." Genuine conservatives, he said, devoted to the nation's values and institutions, will be reluctant to make common cause with extremists. True Republicans "will not care to forsake the traditions of their party for a forlorn kind of fascism."[26]

Barth, sadly, may have been mistaken. The question today is whether the Republican Party will be beholden to the most militant elements of American conservatism for electoral success. In the aftermath of the Capitol insurrection, some ask whether the Republican party will indeed move to the radical fringe, something that even General Edwin A. Walker could not have imagined.

NOTES

Introduction

1. Edwin Walker, *Twenty Questions*, Edwin A. Walker Papers, box 97-021, folder 4.

2. Schlesinger, *Robert Kennedy and His Times*, 450.

3. *Christian Century*, September 20, 1961.

4. Abcarian and Stanage, "Alienation and the Radical Right," 783.

5. Knebel, "Who's on the Far Right?," *Look*, March 13, 1962.

6. Medford Evans, in Huntington, *Far-Right Vanguard*, 125.

7. Lowndes, *From the New Deal to the Far Right*, 49.

8. Huntington, *Far-Right Vanguard*, 219.

9. Robert Bolivar DePugh, in George and Wilcox, *Nazis, Communists, Klansmen, and Others on the Fringe*, 274.

10. Knebel, "Who's on the Far Right?"

11. Barth, "Report on the Rampageous Right," *New York Times*, November 26, 1961.

12. Hemmer, *Messengers of the Right*, 120.

13. Perlstein, "I Thought I Understood the American Right. Trump Proved Me Wrong," *New York Times*, April 16, 2017.

14. *Congressional Record*, May 20, 1963, 8958.

15. Ibid.

16. Hemmer, *Messengers of the Right*, 110–111; Miller, *A Conspiratorial Life*, 334–335.

17. Miller, *A Conspiratorial Life*, 220.

18. Smoot, *Invisible Government*, 141.

19. *Congressional Record*, May 20, 1963, 8958.

20. *Dan Smoot Report*, July 17, 1961.

21. Miller, *A Conspiratorial Life*, 5.

22. Ibid., 371.

23. Quoted in Abcarian and Stanage, "Alienation and the Radical Right," 779.

24. Goldwater, *Conscience of a Conservative*, 71.

25. Abcarian and Stanage, "Alienation and the Radical Right," 780.

26. Quoted in Abcarian and Stanage, "Alienation and the Radical Right," 786.

27. Edwin A. Walker, *The American Eagle: Weapons for Freedom,* 16, Edwin A. Walker Papers, box 97-021, folder 4.

1. From Anzio to Little Rock

1. *Arkansas Gazette,* May 12, 1959.
2. Ashmore, *Hearts and Minds,* 285.
3. Scheips, *Role of Federal Military Forces,* 44, 50.
4. Ashmore, *Hearts and Minds,* 285.
5. Norrell, *The House I Live In,* 172.
6. Ibid., 162.
7. Doyle, *An American Insurrection,* 10–12.
8. Ibid., 12.
9. Ambrose, *Eisenhower: The President,* 444.
10. Doyle, *An American Insurrection,* 58.
11. Silver, "Mississippi: The Closed Society," 4.
12. Brownell, *Advising Ike,* 206.
13. *Time,* September 16, 1957.
14. Blossom, *It Has Happened Here,* 62.
15. *Time,* September 16, 1957.
16. Proclamation State of Arkansas, September 2, 1957, Dwight D. Eisenhower Library, Records as President, Official Files, box 615, official file 142-A-5-A.
17. Blossom, *It Has Happened Here,* 78–79.
18. Ibid., 80–81.
19. Jacoway, *Turn Away Thy Son,* 138.
20. Brownell, *Advising Ike,* 207.
21. Telegram from Governor Orval Faubus to Dwight Eisenhower, September 4, 1957, Dwight D. Eisenhower Library, Records as President, box 615, official file 142-A-5-A.
22. Telegram from Dwight Eisenhower to Governor Orval Faubus, September 5, 1957, Dwight D. Eisenhower, Records as President, box 615, official file 142-A-5-A.
23. Brownell, *Advising Ike,* 209.
24. *Time,* September 23, 1957.
25. Ashmore, *Hearts and Minds,* 263–264.
26. Statement by the President, September 21, 1957, Dwight D. Eisenhower Library, Gerald D. Morgan Records, box 6, civil rights file 2.
27. Scheips, *Role of Federal Military Forces,* 41, 43.
28. Reed, *Faubus,* 229.
29. Scheips, *Role of Federal Military Forces,* 41.
30. Ibid., 44.
31. *New York Times,* September 24, 1957.
32. Telegram from Mayor W. W. Mann to President Dwight Eisenhower, September 23, 1957, Dwight D. Eisenhower Library, Records as President, box 615, official file 142-A-5-A.

33. Ashmore, *Hearts and Minds*, 264.

34. *Time*, October 7, 1957.

35. *New York Times*, September 24, 1957.

36. "Obstruction of Justice in the State of Arkansas," A Proclamation by the President of the United States, US Naval Base Newport, Rhode Island, September 23, 1957, Dwight D. Eisenhower Library, Kevin McCann Collection of Press and Radio Conferences and Press Releases, box 20.

37. *New York Times*, September 24, 1957. George Washington was the first president to use federal troops to put down a domestic insurrection, during the 1794 Whiskey Rebellion. Washington's order to 13,000 soldiers to crush the tax rebellion on the western frontier was the precedent both for Eisenhower's use of troops at Little Rock and for Kennedy's at the University of Mississippi, in 1962.

38. Eisenhower, *Waging Peace*, 171.

39. Scheips, *Role of Federal Military Forces*, 44–45.

40. Jacoway, *Turn Away Thy Son*, 176; Scheips, *Role of Federal Military Forces*, 45.

41. Telegram from W. W. Mann to Dwight Eisenhower, September 24, 1957, Dwight D. Eisenhower Library, Records as President, box 615, official file 142-A-5-A (2).

42. Ashmore, *Hearts and Minds*, 267.

43. Jacoway, *Turn Away Thy Son*, 9–10, 139.

44. *New York Times*, September 25, 1957; Jacoway, *Turn Away Thy Son*, 178–179.

45. Address by the President of the United States, Tuesday, September 24, 1957, Dwight D. Eisenhower Library, Kevin McCann Collection of Press and Radio Conferences and Press Releases, box 20. The 101st was under the command of General Maxwell Taylor at the Battle of the Bulge. After being deactivated, it was reorganized in 1955 to become the army's first modern division trained to use nuclear or conventional weapons and organized for mobile warfare. Its forte was "small brush-fire wars." *New York Times*, September 25, 1957.

46. Text of Governor Orval Faubus's televised address, in *Arkansas Gazette*, September 27, 1957.

47. Address by the President of the United States, Tuesday, September 24, 1957.

48. *Washington Star*, September 25, 1957.

49. General Maxwell Taylor, in Jacoway, *Turn Away Thy Son*, 178.

50. Walker, Statement to Senate Armed Services Committee, November 2, 1961, Edwin A. Walker Papers, box 96-30, folder 2.

51. *New York Times*, September 26, 1957.

52. Troop Information Program, Operations Order No. 1, Edwin A. Walker Papers, box 96-30, folder 31.

53. *New York Times*, September 26, 1957.

54. Doyle, *An American Insurrection*, 13.

55. *New York Times*, September 26, 1957.

56. Ibid.; Scheips, *Role of Federal Military Forces*, 52.

57. Text of address by General Edwin A. Walker to students of Central High School, Edwin A. Walker Papers, box 96-30, folder 31.

58. *Los Angeles Times*, May 9, 1958.

59. Text of address by General Edwin A. Walker to students of Central High School.

60. *New York Times,* September 26, 1957.

61. Blossom, *It Has Happened Here,* 114.

62. *New York Times,* September 26, 1957.

63. Jacoway, *Turn Away Thy Son,* 185–186.

64. Godfrey, "Bayonets, Brainwashing, and Bathrooms," 62–64; *New York Times,* October 8, 1957.

65. *Arkansas Gazette,* September 27, 1957.

66. *Time,* October 7, 1957.

67. Letter from Governor Orval Faubus to General Edwin Walker, October 7, 1957; and Response from Army Secretary Wilber Brucker to Governor Orval Faubus, October 7, 1957, Edwin A. Walker Papers, box 96-30, folder 1; *New York Times,* October 8, 1957.

68. Letter from Army Secretary Wilber Brucker to Governor Orval Faubus, October 26, 1957, Edwin A. Walker Papers, box 96-30, folder 1.

69. *Time,* October 21, 1957.

70. Cope, "Dedicated People," 17.

71. *Arkansas Democrat,* May 21, 1959.

72. Cope, "Dedicated People," 30.

73. Telegram from Congressman Kenneth Roberts to the White House, October 2, 1957; and Telegram from Senator Richard B. Russell to Dwight Eisenhower, September 26, 1957, Dwight D. Eisenhower Library, Papers as President, Administration Series, box 23, Little Rock, Arkansas, file 2.

74. Letter from Dwight Eisenhower to Senator Richard B. Russell, September 27, 1957, Dwight D. Eisenhower Library, Papers as President, Administration Series, box 23, Little Rock, Arkansas, file 2.

75. United States Senate, Hearings Before the Committee on Armed Services on Senate Resolution 191, September 6, 1961, 40.

76. *New York Times,* October 4, 1957.

77. *Dallas Morning News,* September 27, 1957; October 2, 1957.

78. *Memphis Commercial Appeal,* September 26, 1957.

79. *Arkansas Gazette,* July 24, 1958.

80. *Arkansas Democrat,* July 22, 1958.

81. Jacoway, *Turn Away Thy Son,* 186.

82. *Washington Post,* October 2, 1957.

83. Jacoway, *Turn Away Thy Son,* 192.

84. Ibid.

85. Scheips, *Role of Federal Military Forces,* 59.

86. Stockley, *Daisy Bates,* 155.

87. Scheips, *Role of Federal Military Forces,* 59.

88. *New York Times,* October 17, 1957.

89. Scheips, *Role of Federal Military Forces,* 60, 62–63.

90. Blossom, *It Has Happened Here,* 154–155.

91. Scheips, *Role of Federal Military Forces,* 64.

92. *Arkansas Democrat,* May 28, 1958.

93. Scheips, *Role of Federal Military Forces,* 65–66.

94. *Arkansas Gazette,* May 30, 1958.

95. *Arkansas Gazette,* May 21, 1958.

96. *Arkansas Gazette,* May 13, 1959.

97. Godfrey, "Bayonets, Brainwashing, and Bathrooms," 57.

98. Hearings Before the Senate Special Preparedness Subcommittee: Military Cold War Education and Speech Review Policies, April 4, 1962, 1411–1412.

99. *New York Times,* November 4, 1961.

100. Hearings Before the Senate Special Preparedness Subcommittee, April 4, 1962, 1410.

101. *Newsweek,* December 4, 1961.

102. "First Special Service Force," 1.

103. *Arkansas Democrat,* August 11, 1958.

104. "First Special Service Force," 1.

105. *New York Times,* September 25, 1957.

106. "First Special Service Force," 1.

107. Blumenson, *United States Army in World War II,* 266–267.

108. "First Special Service Force," 1. In 1968, *The Devil's Brigade* came to the big screen, starring William Holden. The movie was based on the 1966 book of the same name. The film dramatizes the brigade's Italian campaign.

109. Breuer, *Operation Dragoon,* 13; Fisher, *United States Army in World War II,* 5–6.

110. Breuer, *Operation Dragoon,* 37, 43.

111. Ibid., 44.

112. Ibid., 84.

113. Ibid., 84–85.

114. Ibid., 85–86.

115. *New York Herald Tribune,* August 17, 1944.

116. Breuer, *Operation Dragoon,* 88.

117. Ibid., 246–247.

118. Walker, Statement to Senate Armed Services Committee, November 2, 1961.

119. *Congressional Record,* appendix, September 5, 1961, A6982. Walker would later complain that the First Special Service Force was being transformed into "nation-builders . . . to make [them] more suitable to UN control." *The Military Purge: An Analysis by Edwin A. Walker,* Edwin A. Walker Papers, box 97-021, folder 4.

120. *New York Times,* September 25, 1957.

121. *Congressional Record,* August 30, 1961, 17573.

122. *Congressional Record,* appendix, September 5, 1961, A6982.

123. *Newsweek,* December 4, 1961.

124. Hearings Before the Senate Special Preparedness Subcommittee, April 4, 1962, 1409.

125. Ibid.

126. Manchester, *American Caesar,* 634–636.

127. Hearings Before the Senate Special Preparedness Subcommittee, April 4, 1962, 1489, 1491.

128. Walker, Statement to Senate Armed Services Committee, November 2, 1961. In recounting his years in combat, Walker could be moved to poetry, telling an audience in Dallas, "The gallant youth of Texas learned hard and learned it well, the give and take of gunfire, the heat and cold of hell, but never learned the reason why—they died for a parallel." Walker, speech delivered in Dallas, December 12, 1961, Edwin A. Walker Papers, box 97-021, folder 4.

129. Walker, *In Reflection,* Edwin A. Walker Papers, undated, box 97-021, folder 4.

130. Walker, draft, May 7, 1961, Edwin A. Walker Papers, box 93-402, folder 2.

131. Walker, Statement to Senate Armed Services Committee, November 2, 1961.

132. Hearings Before the Senate Special Preparedness Subcommittee, April 4, 1962, 1473; Walker, speech delivered in Dallas, December 12, 1961.

2. Pro-Blue and the Red Conspiracy

1. Hearings Before the Senate Special Preparedness Subcommittee, April 4, 1962, 1394.

2. Ibid., 1474; *Arkansas Democrat,* April 23, 1961.

3. Ibid., 1468–1469.

4. *Citizen News,* January 12, 1962, Edwin A. Walker Papers, box 96-30, folder 2.

5. Hearings Before the Senate Special Preparedness Subcommittee, April 4, 1962, 1431.

6. *Time,* March 10, 1961.

7. Forster and Epstein, *Danger on the Right,* 18.

8. *Houston Press,* March 30, 1961.

9. "The Life of John Birch," in *American Opinion,* March 1960.

10. Robert Welch, in Forster and Epstein, *Danger on the Right,* 41.

11. *Houston Post,* April 1, 1961.

12. Letter from FBI Director J. Edgar Hoover to [Recipient's name removed in redaction], April 19, 1962, Federal Bureau of Investigation Files, 165-494-24.

13. *Overseas Weekly,* April 14–16, 1961, Edwin A. Walker Papers, box 96-30, folder 15.

14. Ibid. Schlamm was also known for his prescient review of *Mein Kampf* in the book review section of the *New York Times,* on October 17, 1943. "So here it is in the definitive new translation selling for $3.50, which is quite a lot of money for a bad book, but far less than what it is going to cost the Germans."

15. *Washington Post,* November 29, 1961; draft Weekly Message, August 25, 1975, Edwin A. Walker Papers, box 2005-084, folder 1.

16. Walker, Statement to Senate Armed Services Committee, November 2, 1961.

17. Hearings Before the Senate Special Preparedness Subcommittee, April 4, 1962, 1417.

18. "Commanding General Urges Use of Most Powerful Weapon," *Taro Leaf,* October 8, 1960, Edwin A. Walker Papers, box 96-30, folder 15.

19. Hearings Before the Senate Special Preparedness Subcommittee, April 4, 1962, 1454.

20. *Congressional Record,* May 20, 1963, 8948, 8956.

21. *Congressional Record,* May 20, 1963, 8956.

22. Forster and Epstein, *Danger on the Right,* 177, 184–185; *Congressional Record,* May 20, 1963, 8956.

23. *Congressional Record,* May 20, 1963, 8946–8947, 8957.

24. *Congressional Record,* May 20, 1963, 8947, 8954–8955.

25. United States Senate, Hearings Before the Committee on Armed Services, September 6, 1961, 12. While the *Overseas Weekly* quoted Walker as saying that Harry Truman, Dean Acheson, and Eleanor Roosevelt were "definitely pink," there is disagreement about whether those were his exact words. The official army investigation concluded that Walker referred to these prominent Americans in less colorful language— as Leftist-influenced or -affiliated. *Congressional Record,* July 31, 1961, 14174. Former president Truman found the accusations ludicrous, referring to the Birchers as "nothing but the Ku Klux Klan without the nightshirts." *Associated Press,* December 7, 1961.

26. *Houston Chronicle,* April 18, 1961.

27. *University of New Mexico Daily Lobo,* May 17, 1962.

28. *Houston Chronicle,* April 18, 1961.

29. *Congressional Record,* May 20, 1963, 8956.

30. *Houston Post,* April 4, 1965. Aside from the PTA, the John Birch Society saw an opening in school boards, turning elections into heated ideological debates.

31. "Walker Speaks . . . on Textbooks," Edwin A. Walker Papers, box 97-021, folder 4.

32. *Washington Post,* November 24, 1961; Arch Roberts, *Victory Denied,* in *Congressional Record,* November 8, 1967, 31863.

33. *American Opinion,* January 1959.

34. Hearings Before the Senate Special Preparedness Subcommittee, April 4, 1962, 1391, 1405.

35. United Press International, April 17, 1962.

36. Hearings Before the Senate Special Preparedness Subcommittee, April 4, 1962, 1461.

37. Edwin A. Walker, "The American Eagle Is Not a Dead Duck," speech delivered in Chicago, February 9, 1962, Edwin A. Walker Papers, box 97-021, folder 4.

38. Hearings Before the Senate Special Preparedness Subcommittee, April 5, 1962, 1522.

39. *Walker, American Eagle.*

40. *Congressional Record,* April 14, 1961, 5576–5577.

41. *Washington Post,* November 29, 1961.

42. J. Edgar Hoover, in *Washington Daily News,* November 27, 1965.

43. *New York Times,* April 22, 1961.

44. President John F. Kennedy press conference, transcript, *New York Times,* April 22, 1961.

45. Walker, *American Eagle.*

46. Kennedy press conference, April 22, 1961.

47. *New York Times,* April 18, 1961; Hearings Before the Senate Special Preparedness Subcommittee, April 4, 1962, 1414.

48. *Houston Press,* June 12, 1961; *New York Times,* April 14, 1961.

49. *Washington Post,* November 28, 1961.

50. "Walker Speaks . . . on Textbooks."

51. *Congressional Record,* May 24, 1961, 8850.

52. Hearings Before the Senate Special Preparedness Subcommittee, April 4, 1962, 1392–1394; Walker, *The Walker Story,* August 7, 1965, Edwin A. Walker Papers, box 96-30, folder 10.

53. US Army Admonishment of Major General Edwin A. Walker, June 12, 1961, Edwin A. Walker Papers, box 97-021, folder 3; United States Senate, Hearings Before the Committee on Armed Services, September 6, 1961, 14.

54. US Army Admonishment, June 12, 1961.

55. Inspector General Report, in United States Senate, Hearings Before the Committee on Armed Services, September 6, 1961, 12.

56. *Washington Post,* November 29, 1961.

57. *Washington Post,* November 28, 1961; November 29, 1961.

58. *Taro Leaf,* in *New York Times,* April 14, 1961.

59. Inspector General Report, in United States Senate, Hearings Before the Committee on Armed Services, September 6, 1961, 12.

60. *Congressional Record,* July 31, 1961, 14174.

61. Jim Lucas, Scripps-Howard Newspapers, November 18, 1961; Senator Strom Thurmond, Citizens Council Radio, transcript, undated.

62. Inspector General Report, in United States Senate, Hearings Before the Committee on Armed Services, September 6, 1961, 13–14.

63. Hearings Before the Senate Special Preparedness Subcommittee, April 4, 1962, 1419, 1399.

64. *Washington Post,* December 7, 1961.

65. Inspector General Report, in United States Senate, Hearings Before the Committee on Armed Services, September 6, 1961, 14; *New York Times,* January 14, 1962.

66. Inspector General Report, in United States Senate, Hearings Before the Committee on Armed Services, September 6, 1961, 14.

67. Hearings Before the Senate Special Preparedness Subcommittee, April 4, 1962, 1398–1399.

68. *New York Herald Tribune,* April 19, 1961.

69. *New York Mirror,* September 12, 1961, in *Congressional Record,* September 14, 1961, A7252.

70. *New York Daily News,* April 19, 1961.

71. *Congressional Record,* April 14, 1961, 5577; May 24, 1961, 8254; Personal Papers, undated, Edwin A. Walker Papers, box 93-402, folder 2.

72. Hearings Before the Senate Special Preparedness Subcommittee, April 4, 1962, 1395, 1621.

73. Ibid., 1395–1396.

74. United Press International, September 22, 1961; *Congressional Record,* May 24, 1961, 8254.

75. Hearings Before the Senate Special Preparedness Subcommittee, April 4, 1962, 1395, 1401.

76. *New York Times,* September 23, 1961; September 27, 1961.

77. *New York Times,* September 30, 1961; Walker, *American Eagle,* 4.

78. Hearings Before the Senate Special Preparedness Subcommittee, April 5, 1962, 1506.

79. United States Senate, Hearings Before the Committee on Armed Services, September 7, 1961, 232.

80. Hearings Before the Senate Special Preparedness Subcommittee, April 4, 1962, 1402.

81. *Washington Post,* April 6, 1962. Dan Smoot, who came to Walker's defense, took the low road, writing that *Overseas Weekly* publisher Marion von Rospach "herself enjoys the nude and semi-nude girlie pictures." *Dan Smoot Report,* August 28, 1961, Edwin A. Walker Papers, box 93-402, folder 2.

82. United States Senate, Hearings Before the Committee on Armed Services, September 6, 1961, 43.

83. *Congressional Record,* September 5, 1961, 6983; *Congressional Record,* May 24, 1961, 8254.

84. Hearings Before the Senate Special Preparedness Subcommittee, April 4, 1962, 1395.

85. *New York Times,* April 17, 1961.

86. *Washington Post,* January 7, 1962.

87. *Washington Star,* November 8, 1961. Walker claimed he received as many as two thousand letters of support from "patriotic and fighting Americans—only two in opposition." Letter from Edwin Walker to Frederick Ayer, July 10, 1961, Edwin A. Walker Papers, box 93-402, folder 2.

88. Letter from William D. Kelley to "Friends of Walker," November 20, 1961, Edwin A. Walker Papers, box 93-402, folder 2. A California American Legion post came to Walker's defense, saying Pro-Blue "aroused the ire of communists and their sympathizers." Resolution of San Gabriel American Legion Post, September 14, 1961, Edwin A. Walker Papers, box 93-402, folder 2.

89. Hearings Before the Senate Special Preparedness Subcommittee, April 4, 1962, 1397.

90. *Charleston News and Courier,* August 9, 1961.

91. *Arkansas Democrat,* April 23, 1961.

92. *Congressional Record,* August 30, 1961, 17549.

93. *New York Herald Tribune,* September 22, 1961.

94. Resolution of the Texas Senate, in *Congressional Record,* August 1, 1961, 14197.

95. United States Senate, Hearings Before the Committee on Armed Services, September 6, 1961, 43, 47.

96. United Press International, November 17, 1961.

97. *New York Times,* September 7, 1961; United States Senate, Hearings Before the Committee on Armed Services, September 6, 1961, 37.

98. Hearings Before the Senate Special Preparedness Subcommittee, April 4, 1962, 1412, 1471.

99. *New York Times,* November 4, 1961.

100. Hearings Before the Senate Special Preparedness Subcommittee, April 4, 1962, 1406.

101. Walker, "The American Eagle Is Not a Dead Duck."

102. George H. Decker interview, transcript, September 18, 1968, John F. Kennedy Library Oral History Program.

103. Walker, Statement to Senate Armed Services Committee, November 2, 1961.

104. Simonelli, *American Fuehrer,* 40–41.

105. Walker, *The Military Purge: An Analysis,* Edwin A. Walker Papers, box 97-021, folder 4.

106. Walker, *The Victory Purge: An Analysis,* Edwin A. Walker Papers, box 97-021, folder 4.

107. *New York Times,* November 26, 1961.

108. *Congressional Record,* September 21, 1961, 19288–19289.

109. Walker, text of speech dated December 12, 1961, Edwin A. Walker Papers, box 97-021, folder 4.

110. Clyde J. Watts, "The True Story of the Walker Case," 8–9, Edwin A. Walker Papers, box 97-021, folder 1.

111. *Air Force Magazine,* July 1, 2006; Manchester, *American Caesar,* 136–137.

112. Manchester, *American Caesar,* 630.

113. Hearings Before the Senate Special Preparedness Subcommittee, April 4, 1962, 1406–1407.

114. Douglas MacArthur, in Manchester, *American Caesar,* 631.

115. Associated Press, December 7, 1961; *New York Times,* November 6, 1961.

116. *New York Times,* October 25, 1961; *Washington Post,* November 28, 1961.

117. United Press International, September 21, 1961.

118. Interview with Senator John Stennis, Citizens Council Radio, transcript, undated.

119. Hearings Before the Senate Special Preparedness Subcommittee, April 4, 1962, 1449.

120. Ibid., 1420.

121. Ibid., 1431.

122. Ibid., 1480–1481.

123. Ibid., 1454.

124. Ibid., 1405, 1449.

125. Ibid., 1513–1514.

126. *National Review,* April 10, 1962.

127. Hearings Before the Senate Special Preparedness Subcommittee, April 4, 1962, 1405.

128. Ibid., 1498.

129. Ibid., 1512.

130. *Washington Star,* April 5, 1962.

131. Walker, *Victory Purge.*

132. Hearings Before the Senate Special Preparedness Subcommittee, April 5, 1962, 1513, 1523; *Washington Star,* April 5, 1962.

133. Hearings Before the Senate Special Preparedness Subcommittee, April 5, 1962, 1522–1523.

134. *Oklahoma Courier,* August 9, 1963, in *Congressional Record,* August 15, 1963, 15131; United Press International, April 17, 1962.

135. Hearings Before the Senate Special Preparedness Subcommittee, April 4, 1962, 1457.

136. United Press International, April 4, 1962; *Washington Post,* April 5, 1962.

137. United Press International, April 4, 1962.

138. Hearings Before the Senate Special Preparedness Subcommittee, April 4, 1962, 1492.

139. *Washington Post,* April 6, 1962.

140. Evans and Novak, in *Congressional Record,* August 11, 1964, A4247.

141. *Washington Star,* April 5, 1962.

142. *Washington Star,* April 6, 1962; *Washington Post,* April 7, 1962.

143. *Washington Post,* April 7, 1962.

144. *Washington Star,* April 5, 1962.

145. United Press International, April 4, 1962.

146. *Detroit News,* February 12, 1962.

3. Military Men on the Fringe

1. Hearings Before the Senate Special Preparedness Subcommittee, January 25, 1962, 144.

2. Ibid., 147.

3. *Washington Post,* January 23, 1962.

4. United States Senate, Hearings Before the Committee on Armed Services, September 6, 1961, 6.

5. Ibid., 30.

6. Jim Lucas, Scripps-Howard Newspapers, November 18, 1961.

7. *New York Times,* January 14, 1962.

8. United States Senate, Hearings Before the Committee on Armed Services, September 6, 1961, 122–123, 125.

9. United States Senate, Hearings Before the Committee on Armed Services, September 7, 1961, 175.

10. *New York Herald Tribune,* September 22, 1961.

11. Jim Lucas, Scripps-Howard Newspapers, November 18, 1961.

12. *Augusta Chronicle-Herald,* August 6, 1961.

13. Hearings Before the Senate Special Preparedness Subcommittee, January 24, 1962, 30–31, 38.

14. *Washington Post,* September 26, 1961.

15. *New York Times,* October 9, 1961.

16. "Defense Department Directive: Principles of Public Information Policy," May 31, 1961, in United States Senate, Hearings Before the Committee on Armed Services, September 7, 1961, 237.

17. United States Senate, Hearings Before the Committee on Armed Services, September 6, 1961, 20–21, 27.

18. *Congressional Record,* August 2, 1961, 14433.

19. *New York Times,* June 18, 1961.

20. Bogle, *Pentagon's Battle for the American Mind,* 156–159.

21. Hearings Before the Senate Special Preparedness Subcommittee, April 12, 1962, 1803.

22. *New York Times,* November 22, 1961.

23. Bogle, *Pentagon's Battle for the American Mind,* 160.

24. Walker, Statement to Senate Armed Services Committee, November 2, 1961.

25. Sherwin, *The Extremists,* 128; *New York Times,* September 2, 1950.

26. Walker, text of speech dated December 12, 1961.

27. Drew Pearson, WTOP radio, Washington, DC, transcript, January 20, 1962.

28. Reuther, "Radical Right in America Today," 14.

29. United States Senate, Hearings Before the Committee on Armed Services, September 7, 1961, 153.

30. *Congressional Record,* August 2, 1961, 14434–14435.

31. *New York Times,* June 18, 1961.

32. Jim Lucas, Scripps-Howard Newspapers, November 18, 1961.

33. *Congressional Record,* August 30, 1961, 17547.

34. United States Senate, Hearings Before the Committee on Armed Services, September 6, 1961, 131.

35. Ibid., 5, 33.

36. Hearings Before the Senate Special Preparedness Subcommittee, April 4, 1962, 1392; Walker, text of speech dated December 12, 1961.

37. United States Senate, Hearings Before the Committee on Armed Services, September 6, 1961, 3–4.

38. *Congressional Record,* July 31, 1961, 14174.

39. Quoted in Peel, "The Wackacobi: Extremists of Our Times," 575.

40. Meyer, *Fulbright of Arkansas,* 227–229; *Congressional Record,* August 2, 1961, 14433–14434.

41. *Congressional Record,* August 2, 1961, 14433–14434.

42. Meyer, *Fulbright of Arkansas,* 227–229.

43. Hearings Before the Senate Special Preparedness Subcommittee, April 4, 1962, 1411.

44. Draft letter, undated, Edwin A. Walker Papers, box 96-30, folder 10; Walker, *What Is Counterinsurgency?,* May 2, 1962, Edwin A. Walker Papers, box 97-021, folder 4.

45. Walker, *What Is Counterinsurgency?*

46. *Congressional Record,* August 2, 1961, 14433–14434.

47. Ibid.

48. *New York Times,* November 26, 1961.

49. *Washington Post,* November 24, 1961.

50. Letter from Hilaire Du Berrier to Senator William Fulbright, October 14, 1961, Edwin A. Walker Papers, box 93-402, folder 2.

51. *Congressional Record,* June 12, 1961, 10109. Kowalski, like others who were concerned about the influence of the ultra Right in the military, received his share of hate mail. One telegram warned, "Keep your dirty old fingers off of Major General Edwin Walker. I would suggest you keep your opinion to yourself." Telegram to Pentagon, Washington, DC, May 10, 1961, Edwin A. Walker Papers, box 96-30, folder 2.

52. *Christian Century,* September 20, 1961.

53. Interview with Laura Bergquist Knebel, transcript, John F. Kennedy Library Oral History Program.

54. Schlesinger, *Robert Kennedy and His Times,* 450.

55. Ibid.

56. The fight for the mind and heart of the military man long precedes Eisenhower's National Security Directive. In 1928, the War Department issued its *Citizenship Training Manual,* which praised thrift, good judgment in choosing one's friends, and the early pioneer spirit—

characterized as no "hardship too severe to hold them back." The manual also lauded "individualism as opposed to that misguided philosophy of collectivism." The army leadership believed that new recruits from immigrant families might be carriers of communist ideology. "It cannot be expected that foreign-born parents, lacking knowledge or inspiration of American ideals, will . . . give such instruction to their own children." Quaintly, the army referred to the State Department as "the friendly relations department of our government"—a far cry from Walker's Pro-Blue, with its allegations of traitors in policy-making positions. *Citizenship Training Manual,* 4–5, 14, 19, 29, 31.

57. *Congressional Record,* August 2, 1961, 14434.

58. *New York Times,* September 21, 1961.

59. *Congressional Record,* July 31, 1961, 14174.

60. Interview with Representative Dale Alford, Citizens Council Radio, transcript, undated.

61. Soviet Ministry of Defense daily *Krasnaya Zvezda,* July 18, 1961, in *Congressional Record,* August 30, 1961, 17549.

62. *Greenville News,* August 2, 1961.

63. *New York Times,* January 14, 1962.

64. Ryan, *Earl Browder and the Communist Party,* 265, 272. The Communist Party newspaper, the *Daily Worker,* described Walker as an "American Fuehrer" waiting for the chance to take power. "The general was assembling a coalition of white supremacists, capitalists, and soldiers to bring fascism to America." The Communist Party and Walker's followers in the John Birch Society seemed to live in alternate worlds of conspiracy theories. While Walker charged that *Time* was under the spell of communist propaganda, the *Daily Worker* saw Henry Luce and his *Time–Life* "magazine empire" behind Walker's plans for a fascist coup. *Daily Worker,* November 12, 1961.

65. United States Senate, Hearings Before the Committee on Armed Services, September 6, 1961, 127.

66. *New York Daily News,* November 13, 1961.

67. Hearings Before the Senate Special Preparedness Subcommittee, April 4, 1962, 1391

68. United States Senate, Hearings Before the Committee on Armed Services, September 6, 1961, 4. It was not until 1973 that the term *Stockholm syndrome* was coined to describe how hostages and prisoners, under severe mental stress, may cooperate and even sympathize with their captors.

69. Interview with Edwin A. Walker, Citizens Council Radio, transcript, undated.

70. Hearings Before the Senate Special Preparedness Subcommittee, April 4, 1962, 1391, 1406.

71. *New York Times,* October 6, 1961.

72. Walker, *Victory Purge.*

73. Walker, *Twenty Questions.*

74. Reuther, "Radical Right in America Today," 11.

75. Ibid., 11–13.

76. Ibid.

77. Hearings Before the Senate Special Preparedness Subcommittee, April 4, 1962, 1435.

78. Webb, *Rabble Rousers,* 104.

79. *New York Times,* November 12, 1996.

80. Webb, *Rabble Rousers,* 114.

81. Ibid., 138–139; Bendersky, *Jewish Threat,* 412.

82. *Washington Post,* November 24, 1961.

83. *Oklahoma Courier,* August 9, 1963, in *Congressional Record,* August 15, 1963, 15130.

84. Forster and Epstein, *Danger on the Right,* 151–153.

85. *Independent American,* August 7, 1963.

86. Walker, Statement to Senate Armed Services Committee, November 2, 1961.

4. Thunder on the Right

1. *Washington Post,* November 6, 1961.

2. Walker, text of speech dated December 12, 1961.

3. Walker radio address, transcript, undated, Edwin A. Walker Papers, box 2005-084, folder 1.

4. *New York Times,* February 4, 1962. Walker did not appear to be interested in advancing the fortunes of any particular party. When asked, he recalled voting for Eisenhower in 1952 and 1956, and Richard Nixon in 1960. Surprisingly, he said, "I am sure I voted once for Roosevelt."

5. United Press International, February 3, 1962; *Time,* February 9, 1962.

6. *Time,* February 9, 1962.

7. *New York Daily News,* February 4, 1962.

8. *Time,* February 9, 1962.

9. *Chicago Tribune,* February 10, 1962. One admirer, writing to Walker from Bayonne, New Jersey, said, as for the 1964 presidential election, "the American people must wake up and follow, you, General . . . Our only hope is YOU." Letter from W. English to Edwin Walker, April 13, 1962, Edwin A. Walker Papers, box 2005-084, folder 1.

10. *Washington Post,* February 4, 1962.

11. Walker, "The American Eagle Is Not a Dead Duck." In the midst of the campaign, Walker directed his attention to the trade of Soviet spy Rudolf Abel for downed American U-2 pilot Francis Powers. To Walker, Kennedy was bowing to Moscow's claim that Powers was a spy, saying, "The entire Powers case was worked to Soviet advantage and aroused wonderment at what kind of collaboration exists between Moscow and Washington." *Washington Star,* February 11, 1962.

12. Platform of Edwin A. Walker, Candidate for Governor of Texas, Edwin A. Walker Papers, box 2005–084, folder 1.

13. Walker, "The American Eagle Is Not a Dead Duck."

14. United Press International, January 20, 1962; Platform of Edwin A. Walker. Lazaro Cárdenas served as Mexico's president from 1934 to 1940, carrying out wide-ranging social and economic reforms, including land redistribution and nationalization of foreign-owned industries. He served as minister of national defense from 1943 to 1945. Cárdenas remained the major figure of the Mexican Left and the chief opponent of US economic and political influence in Mexico through the 1960s. After the Cuban revolution in 1959, Cárdenas did support Castro allies in Mexico.

15. *Pecos Daily News,* March 14, 1962, Edwin A. Walker Papers, box 2005-084, folder 1.

16. *Washington Post,* February 4, 1962; United Press International, February 3, 1962.

17. *Washington Post,* April 4, 1962.

18. *Washington Star,* February 5, 1962.

19. *National Review,* May 6, 1961.

20. *National Review,* November 18, 1961; *Dallas Morning News,* November 23, 1961.

21. Quoted in Huntington, *Far-Right Vanguard,* 109.

22. Ibid., 118–119.

23. Miller, *A Conspiratorial Life,* 164.

24. Ibid., 258–259.

25. Huntington, *Far-Right Vanguard,* 219.

26. Miller, *A Conspiratorial Life,* 209–210. *National Review* editors, making a case for limiting the powers of the federal government, were natural allies of southern governors Ross Barnett and George Wallace, who used states' rights as their justification for opposing integration. While trying to refrain from the explicit racism of George Wallace, Buckley's rhetoric, in Miller's estimation, could be just as incendiary and racist. For Miller, it suggests that the concept of a "responsible Right" was itself a delusion. Miller, *A Conspiratorial Life,* 257.

27. *New York Daily News,* February 4, 1962.

28. *Newsweek,* December 4, 1961.

29. *New York Times,* February 14, 1962; *New York Post,* March 8, 1962. New York City detective Tony Ulasewicz provided the FBI with the American Nazis' plans that day. A decade later, Ulasewicz would be a key figure in the Watergate cover-up. John F. Kennedy Presidential Library, John F. Kennedy Assassination Records Archives 1 (1964), 4.

30. *New York Daily News,* February 4, 1962.

31. Bruce Alger, in Miller, *Nut Country,* 100.

32. *Pecos Daily News,* March 14, 1962.

33. Letter to Contributors, undated, Edwin A. Walker Papers, box 2005-084, folder 1.

34. *Washington Post,* February 4, 1962.

35. *New York Daily News,* February 4, 1962.

36. M. L. Hall, "As I See It This Week," *Lubbock Sun,* March 25, 1962, Edwin A. Walker Papers, box 2005-084, folder 1.

37. Koeppen, "Republican Radical Right," 81; Reuther, "Radical Right in America Today," 4.

38. *Washington Post,* February 4, 1962.

39. Letter to Supporters, Walker Campaign Headquarters, undated, Edwin A. Walker Papers, box 2005-084, folder 1.

40. *Houston Chronicle,* April 18, 1961.

41. Quoted in Miller, *Nut Country,* 7.

42. *Washington Post,* November 19, 1961.

43. *Dallas Morning News,* April 11, 1962.

44. Walker, "The American Eagle Is Not a Dead Duck."

45. Texas Voters for Enforcing the Constitution, pamphlet, Edwin A. Walker Papers, box 2005-084, folder 1.

46. Ibid.

47. *Dallas Times-Herald,* May 3, 1962; Letter from Edwin Walker to Governors' Conference, July 3, 1962, Edwin A. Walker Papers, box 2005-084, folder 1.

48. Webb, *Rabble Rousers,* 144.

49. Walker radio address, undated.

50. "Letter to Citizens of the Republic," April 26, 1962, Edwin A. Walker Papers, box 2005-084, folder 1.

51. Dallas County Headquarters for Walker, "An Appeal to Your Conscience," undated, Edwin A. Walker Papers, box 2005-084, folder 1.

52. Walker radio address, undated.

53. "Walker Speaks . . . on Textbooks."

54. Walker radio address, undated.

55. Letter to Contributors, undated.

56. Walker, *American Eagle.*

57. *Dallas Morning News,* April 11, 1962.

58. Ibid.

59. Quoted in Miller, *Nut Country,* 98.

60. Letter to Supporters, undated. Walker's campaign was not without its kitschy elements, including a campaign jingle, "We're Gonna Win in a Walk with Walker." His campaign also used the slogan "Ayes on Walker." "Walk with Walker," undated, Edwin A. Walker Papers, box 2005-084, folder 1.

61. Letter to Supporters, undated.

62. *Washington Post,* April 7, 1962.

63. Letter from Senator John Tower to J. C. Phillips, editor, *Borger News-Herald,* November 24, 1965, Edwin A. Walker Papers, box 2005-084, folder 1.

64. *Washington Post,* April 7, 1962.

65. *Time,* May 18, 1962.

66. *Dallas Morning News,* April 11, 1962.

67. Quoted in Miller, *Nut Country,* 100.

68. *Dallas Morning News,* November 7, 1962. Anticipating the Republican Party's southern strategy, Walker said, "I have great support in the Republican Party, which represents a drift from the Democratic Party." *Washington Star,* April 4, 1962. That drift would become a tide with Goldwater's campaign in 1964 and Nixon's win in 1968.

69. *New York Times,* October 10, 1962.

5. Insurrection at Ole Miss

1. *The Ole Miss Annual,* 1961–1962, 2.

2. Ibid., 50.

3. *Time,* October 5, 1962.

4. Doyle, *An American Insurrection,* 52; *Time,* October 5, 1962.

5. Doyle, *An American Insurrection,* 22.

6. Silver, "Mississippi: The Closed Society," 31.

7. Ibid., 18.

8. *Wall Street Journal,* September 28, 1962; *Saturday Evening Post,* November 10, 1962.

9. Silver, *Mississippi: The Closed Society,* 151.

10. Silver "Mississippi: The Closed Society," 19.

11. Ibid., 10.

12. Doyle, *An American Insurrection,* 52–53.

13. Ibid., 30.

14. Ibid.

15. Quoted in Doyle, *An American Insurrection,* 21.

16. Doyle, *An American Insurrection,* 34.

17. Silver, "Mississippi: The Closed Society," 20.

18. Doyle, *An American Insurrection,* 49.

19. Silver, *Mississippi: The Closed Society,* 138.

20. Governor Ross Barnett, Declaration to the People of Mississippi, September 13, 1962, John F. Kennedy Library Digital Archives, Burke Marshall Papers, Mississippi File, September–October 1962.

21. *Jackson Clarion-Ledger,* September 17, 1962.

22. *Washington Post,* September 21, 1962.

23. *Time,* October 5, 1962.

24. Silver, "Mississippi: The Closed Society," 22.

25. Doyle, *An American Insurrection,* 70.

26. Memorandum from Theodore Sorensen to the President, September 28, 1962, John F. Kennedy Library Digital Archives, President's Office Files, Civil Rights, Mississippi, September 27, 1962–September 30, 1962.

27. Doyle, *An American Insurrection,* 67.

28. *Time,* October 5, 1962.

29. Ibid.; Paul Johnson, in *Washington Post,* September 27, 1962.

30. Telegram from John Patterson to John F. Kennedy, September 27, 1962, John F. Kennedy Library Digital Archives, President's Office Files, Civil Rights, Mississippi, October 1–November 1, 1962.

31. Eagles, *Price of Defiance,* 326–327.

32. *Time,* October 5, 1962.

33. Doyle, *An American Insurrection,* 96–101.

34. White House press release, September 29, 1962, John F. Kennedy Library Digital Archives, President's Office Files, Civil Rights, Mississippi, September 27–September 30, 1962.

35. Scheips, *Role of Federal Military Forces,* 83, 88; *Washington Post,* September 29, 1962.

36. Scheips, *Role of Federal Military Forces,* 121.

37. Ibid., 92.

38. *New York Times,* October 1, 1962; Eagles, *Price of Defiance,* 352.

39. *New York Times,* October 1, 1962; *Saturday Evening Post,* November 10, 1962.

40. Text of Governor Ross Barnett's statement, in *New York Times,* October 1, 1962.

41. *New York Times,* October 2, 1962.

42. *New York Times,* October 1, 1962; Ed Guthman, NBC News broadcast transcript, October 1, 1962, John F. Kennedy Library Digital Archives, Burke Marshall papers, Mississippi File, September–October 1962. The Lyceum, which was at the center of the insurrection, was built in 1848 and is the sole survivor of the university's five original buildings. During the Civil War, the Lyceum was used as a hospital. The Confederate statue, built by the Daughters of the Confederacy in 1906, at the dawn of the Jim Crow era, was removed by the university in July 2020, during the national debate about Confederate monuments.

43. Quoted in *Saturday Evening Post,* November 10, 1962.

44. *Jackson Clarion-Ledger,* December 30, 1961.

45. Speech delivered December 29, 1961, Jackson, Mississippi, Edwin A. Walker Papers, box 97-021, folder 4.

46. Special Agent in Charge, New Orleans, to FBI Director, September 30, 1962, FBI Memorandum 157-401-356.

47. Walker, speech delivered December 29, 1961.

48. WNOE radio interview with Edwin Walker, transcript, September 28, 1962, Edwin A. Walker Papers, box 97-021, folder 1.

49. Ibid.

50. *New York Times,* September 29, 1962.

51. *New York Times,* September 28, 1962.

52. United Press International, September 28, 1962.

53. *New York Times,* September 28, 1962.

54. *New York Times,* September 30, 1962.

55. Doyle, *An American Insurrection,* 97.

56. Special Agent in Charge, Dallas, to FBI Director, December 10, 1962, FBI teletype 157-401-1681.

57. *Jackson Clarion-Ledger,* September 17, 1962.

58. "Possible Minutemen Activities," Department of the Army to FBI Director, October 17, 1962, Department of the Army Memorandum 157-401-1549; *New York Times,* October 2, 1962.

59. "Desegregation of University of Mississippi," Special Agent in Charge, Houston, to FBI Director, October 1, 1962, FBI Memorandum 157-401-550.

60. Edwin Walker press conference, September 30, 1962, Oxford, Mississippi, FBI Transcript 157-401-1948; Eagles, *Price of Defiance,* 346.

61. Scheips, *Role of Federal Military Forces,* 102.

62. Telephone conversation between Ross Barnett and John F. Kennedy, September 30, 1962, John F. Kennedy Library Digital Archives, President's Office Files, Civil Rights, Mississippi, September 27, 1962–September 30, 1962.

63. John F. Kennedy televised address to the nation, September 30, 1962, John F. Kennedy Library Digital Archives, Speech Files, Civil Rights, Mississippi, September 27–September 30, 1962.

64. *Dallas Times-Herald,* June 12, 1964; Doyle, *An American Insurrection,* 155.

65. WLBT radio report, Oxford, Mississippi, transcript, September 30, 1962, Mississippi Department of Archives and History.

66. *New York Times,* October 1, 1962.

67. *Look,* December 31, 1962.

68. *Fort Worth Press,* June 10, 1964.

69. *Washington Post,* October 6, 1962; *Saturday Evening Post,* November 10, 1962.

70. *St. Louis Post-Dispatch,* October 1, 1962.

71. *Fort Worth Star-Telegram,* June 9, 1964; June 10, 1964.

72. *Look,* December 31, 1962.

73. *Fort Worth Star-Telegram,* June 17, 1964.

74. *Washington Post,* October 2, 1962; *Time,* June 26, 1964.

75. *Richmond News Leader,* October 1, 1962.

76. Memorandum to Attorney General Robert Kennedy from Burke Marshall, Assistant Attorney General, Civil Rights Division, September 13, 1962, John F. Kennedy Library Digital Archives, Burke Marshall Papers, Mississippi File, September–October 1962.

77. *Fort Worth Star-Telegram,* June 17, 1964.

78. Ibid.

79. "Desegregation of the University of Mississippi," Special Agent in Charge, St. Louis, to US Attorney, Oxford, Mississippi, November 8, 1962, FBI Memorandum 157-401-1400.

80. "Edwin A. Walker and Desegregation of University of Mississippi," December 4, 1962, FBI Memorandum 157-401-1690; *Washington Post,* October 6, 1962.

81. "Desegregation of the University of Mississippi," to US Attorney, Oxford, Mississippi, October 9, 1962, FBI Memorandum 157-401-866; "Desegregation of the University of Mississippi," to US Attorney, Oxford, Mississippi, October 16, 1962, FBI Memorandum 157-401-1041.

82. "Desegregation of the University of Mississippi," Special Agent in Charge, Memphis, November 27, 1962, FBI Memorandum 157-401-1537; *Washington Post,* October 6, 1962.

83. *Washington Post,* October 6, 1962.

84. John F. Kennedy, in Doyle, *An American Insurrection,* 191.

85. Scheips, *Role of Federal Military Forces,* 104; *Look,* December 31, 1962.

86. *New York Times,* October 1, 1962.

87. *New York Times,* October 2, 1962.

88. Telephone call between John F. Kennedy and Ross Barnett, transcript, September 30, 1962, John F. Kennedy Library Digital Archives, President's Office Files, Civil Rights, Mississippi, September 27–September 30, 1962.

89. *New York Times,* October 1, 1962.

90. Silver, "Mississippi: The Closed Society," 30.

91. *New York Times,* October 2, 1962.

92. *Saturday Evening Post,* November 10, 1962.

93. *Washington Post,* October 2, 1962; *Time,* October 12, 1962. Recalcitrant segregationists such as Mississippi congressman John Bell Williams falsely accused soldiers of "needlessly beat-

ing citizens with rifle butts." An army investigation found "that at no time was any brutality observed." In addition, there were unsubstantiated rumors of marshals invading the women's dormitories. As in the case of the Little Rock crisis, the false claim that armed agents of the federal government were fulfilling their prurient interests was another flash point in these confrontations at the intersection of race, class, and gender. Scheips, *Role of Federal Military Forces,* 119; *Washington Post,* October 2, 1962.

94. *New York Times,* October 5, 1962.

95. Scheips, *Role of Federal Military Forces,* 117. Deputy Sheriff Talmadge Witt would recall two years later that the students did "a good job" of fighting the marshals. He said he counted sixteen burned cars on campus the morning of October 1. *Fort Worth Press,* June 10, 1964.

96. Special Agent in Charge, Memphis, to FBI Director, Marked "Urgent," October 1, 1962, FBI Teletype 157-401-441.

97. Special Agent in Charge, Memphis, October 9, 1962, FBI Report 157-401-147; *Dallas Times-Herald,* June 10, 1964.

98. WLBT radio report, Oxford, Mississippi, transcript, October 1, 1962, Mississippi Department of Archives and History.

99. United Press International, October 1, 1962; "Desegregation of University of Mississippi," November 21, 1962, FBI memorandum 157-401-1541.

100. *Washington Post,* October 2, 1962.

101. Charles Shockley, in Doyle, *An American Insurrection,* 267.

102. "Edwin Walker and Desegregation of University of Mississippi," from A. H. Belmont to Clyde Tolson, October 3, 1962, FBI Memo 157-401-381.

103. Robert A. Surrey, "The Law of the Land," 1, Edwin A. Walker Papers, box 97-021, folder 4; *New York Times,* October 2, 1962.

104. *United States v. Edwin Walker,* United States District Court, Northern District of Mississippi, Violation of US Code, Title 18, Edwin A. Walker Papers, box 2005-084, folder 2; *New York Times,* October 2, 1962. Walker was charged under Title 18, United States Code, sections 111, 372, 2383, and 2384. Section 111 refers to assaulting, opposing, or interfering with federal officers while engaged in official duties. Section 372 refers to conspiring to prevent a federal officer from discharging official duties. Section 2383 refers to rebellion or insurrection against the United States. Section 2384 refers to seditious conspiracy to overthrow, put down, or to destroy by force the government of the United States.

105. Walsh, "A Postscript to the Meredith Case," 463. While Jacob Coxey's army was peaceful, some at the time feared a repeat of the radical violence of the Haymarket bombing that had occurred eight years before. The depression that started in 1893 lasted through most of the decade, with the unemployment rate reaching 20 percent. Organized by Coxey, from Ohio, the marchers wanted the US government to hire the unemployed on public works projects, an anticipation of the New Deal programs of the 1930s. When they reached Washington, Coxey was arrested on a minor charge and the protest fizzled.

106. *New York Times,* October 2, 1962; *Washington Post,* October 3, 1962.

107. United Press International, October 1, 1962.

108. White House press conference, transcript, October 1, 1962, John F. Kennedy Digital Archives, President's Office Files, Civil Rights, Mississippi October 1–November 1, 1962. The day Walker was arrested in Mississippi, a freelance photographer was assaulted and had his camera confiscated as he tried to take photos of the general's Dallas home. The photographer, who said he was shooting the pictures from the sidewalk, was knocked to the ground by two men who emerged from Walker's home. *Wall Street Journal,* October 2, 1962. A photo of Walker under arrest and led away at bayonet point won a first prize for United Press International photographer Pete Fisher. *Washington Post,* November 21, 1962.

109. *New York Times,* October 2, 1962.

110. *St. Louis Post-Dispatch,* October 1, 1962. Walker's arrest inspired a song for the civil rights movement's Freedom Songs: "Edwin Walker hit the campus with his guns and his troops, / And all the hating students joined in the group / And there was shouting' and screamin' / And bullets were a-flyin' / And on that old college ground two men lay a-dyin'." Edwin A. Walker Papers, box 97-021, folder 1.

111. *Philadelphia Inquirer,* October 2, 1962.

112. *Jackson Clarion-Ledger,* October 2, 1962; *Waller County Record,* quoted in *Washington Post,* October 10, 1962.

113. *Richmond News Leader,* May 3, 1963. Kilpatrick would make his television debut in the 1970s in the "Point/Counterpoint" segment of *60 Minutes.* It was a short debate with liberal journalist Shana Alexander on political issues. *Saturday Night Live* parodied the pair, with Dan Aykroyd playing the part of Kilpatrick.

114. *Richmond News Leader,* July 9, 1963.

115. *Charlotte Observer,* October 2, 1962; *Louisville Courier-Journal,* March 15, 1963.

116. Watts, "True Story of the Walker Case," 7.

117. Letter from the Englewood Anti-Communist League to Edwin Walker, October 22, 1962, Edwin A. Walker Papers, box 96-30, folder 2.

118. Letter from Representative John Dowdy to President John F. Kennedy, October 8, 1962, John F. Kennedy Digital Archives, White House Central Files, October 26–November 10, 1962.

119. Letter from Burke Marshall to Representative John Dowdy, November 1, 1962, John F. Kennedy Digital Archives, White House Central Files, October 26–November 10, 1962.

120. Surrey, "Law of the Land."

121. Letter from Clyde Watts to Porter Johnson, October 30, 1962, Edwin A. Walker Papers, box 96-30, folder 33.

122. Resolution signed by Clyde J. Watts, undated, Edwin A. Walker Papers, box 97-021, folder 4; Walsh, "A Postscript to the Meredith Case," 464.

123. Letter from Burke Marshall to Representative John Dowdy, November 1, 1962.

124. Surrey, "Law of the Land."

125. *New York Times,* October 2, 1962.

126. USIA telegram, October 17, 1962, John F. Kennedy Digital Archives, President's Office Files, Civil Rights, Mississippi, October 1–November 1, 1962. The riot at Ole Miss made headlines in Europe, with the French daily *Le Monde* comparing Walker to the French military men who

plotted to overthrow the government over policy in Algeria. The Leftist Paris newspaper *Combat* praised Kennedy for "routing the racist and fascist clique howling around Barnett and Walker." The Cuban press was more than pleased that the virulently anti-Castro Walker was committed, calling him "the head of a bunch of hoodlums." The East German *Neues Deutschland* called Walker and Barnett "the successors of the slaveholders . . . Ultras? Yes, they are ultras because the fascist groups of the whole country, the radical Rightist elements, are allied with the southern racists." With the predictable talking points of the Communist bloc, *Neues Deutschland* called the events at Oxford a "sampling of what would happen if the ultras gained unlimited control and plunged America into the night of fascism." USIA telegrams, John F. Kennedy Digital Archives, President's Office Files, Civil Rights, Mississippi, October 1–November 1, 1962.

6. "Standing on the Brink of the Pit of Hell"

1. *New York Times,* October 3, 1962. Walker was held under Title 18, United States Code, section 4244, which allows an examination of a defendant's mental competence after arrest and before trial.

2. Watts, "True Story of the Walker Case," 3.

3. *New York Times,* October 3, 1962.

4. Ibid.; *Washington Post,* October 3, 1962.

5. Watts, "True Story of the Walker Case," 4.

6. *New York Times,* October 5, 1962.

7. *Congressional Record,* October 3, 1962, 21862.

8. *Washington Post,* October 4, 1962; *New York Times,* October 4, 1962. From 1956 to 1958, Robert Morris was chief counsel for Senator Pat McCarran's Internal Security subcommittee. At the time, Morris was operating in the "world of respectable intellectual conservatism," according to Edward Miller's study of right-wing politics in Texas. But by the time he came to Dallas in 1961 as president of the University of Dallas, Morris had embraced the John Birch Society conspiracy theory that the United States would soon lose its sovereignty to the UN's backers in the Kremlin. Miller, *Nut Country,* 104. The Walker case further radicalized Morris. He worked with individuals and groups who needed introductions to conservative donors in Dallas, including oil millionaire H. L. Hunt.

9. *Washington Star,* October 3, 1962.

10. *Wall Street Journal,* October 12, 1962.

11. Ernest Angell, in *New York Times,* October 5, 1962.

12. "The Truth About General Walker," October 5, 1962, FBI File 157-401-678.

13. Transcript from Hearing, November 20–21, 1962, US District Court for the Northern District of Mississippi, Edwin A. Walker Papers, box 2005-084, folder 2.

14. Letter from Assistant Attorney General Herbert J. Miller to Dr. and Mrs. Charles Kring, October 12, 1962, Edwin A. Walker Papers, box 96-30, folder 33.

15. Affidavit of Dr. Charles E. Smith, October 2, 1962, Edwin A. Walker Papers, box 2005-084, folder 2.

16. H. M. Ray to William F. Walsh, May 11, 1964, in Walsh, "A Postscript to the Meredith Case," 468.

17. Motion filed by US Attorney H. M. Ray, October 2, 1962, in US District Court for the Northern District of Mississippi, reprinted in Walsh, "A Postscript to the Meredith Case," 472.

18. Quoted in *St. Louis Post-Dispatch,* October 7, 1962.

19. Ibid.

20. "American Medical Association Opinion of the Judicial Council Concerning the Complaints Received Against Charles E. Smith, MD," May 27, 1963, Edwin A. Walker Papers, box 96-30, folder 3; *New York Times,* July 5, 1963.

21. *Dallas Times-Herald,* April 29, 1963.

22. "American Medical Association Opinion."

23. Walsh, "A Postscript to the Meredith Case," 465.

24. Appearance to Post Bond, US District Court, Northern District of Missouri, October 6, 1962, Edwin A. Walker Papers, box 2005-084, folder 2; *New York Times,* October 7, 1962.

25. Watts, "True Story of the Walker Case," 4.

26. *St. Louis Post-Dispatch,* October 7, 1962.

27. *New York Times,* October 8, 1962.

28. Ibid.

29. Edwin Walker interview with KRLD, Dallas, at Love Field, transcript, October 7, 1962, Edwin A. Walker Papers, box 97-021, folder 1.

30. *New York Times,* October 9, 1962.

31. *New York Times,* October 13, 1962.

32. Letter from Dr. Robert Stubblefield to Judge Claude Clayton, US District Judge, Northern District of Mississippi, October 20, 1962, Edwin A. Walker Papers, box 96-30, folder 9.

33. Edwin A. Walker Psychiatric Report, Submitted to the US District Court for the Northern District of Mississippi, November 20, 1962, Edwin A. Walker Papers, box 96-30, folder 9. Two years later, Dr. Stubblefield would conduct a psychiatric evaluation of Jack Ruby, the man who assassinated Lee Harvey Oswald.

34. "Desegregation of University of Mississippi: Edwin A. Walker," December 18, 1962, FBI Memo 157-401-1816. Walker's mother appears protective of her son in letters as the army disciplined him for the Pro-Blue program. In a letter to Walker signed, "Always devotedly, Mother," she writes, "I hope to receive a letter from you so I shall know that you are OK. No stomach ulcers." She urges Walker, in another letter, not to get into "a nervous tizzy [and] get the required amount of sleep." Letters from Charlotte Walker to Edwin A. Walker, April 19, 1961, and September 9, 1961, Edwin A. Walker Papers, box 93-402, folder 2.

35. *Washington Post,* November 22, 1962.

36. *New York Times,* November 21, 1962.

37. Transcript from Hearing, November 20–21, 1962.

38. Ibid.

39. Watts, "True Story of the Walker Case," 8.

40. Transcript from Hearing, November 20–21, 1962.

41. *New York Times,* November 21, 1962. In another odd twist in the Walker case, after returning to Texas the day after his court appearance, Walker helped rescue a home from a fire. He directed firefighters and was credited with saving the two-story home of a farmer about fourteen miles from Gainesville, Texas. Walker assisted in the firefighting and in carrying out furniture and personal belongings. *New York Times,* November 23, 1962.

42. *New York Times,* January 22, 1963; Clyde Watts, "Resolution: In an Effort to Regain the Constitutional Rights of Every American Citizen," undated, Edwin A. Walker Papers, box 2005-084, folder 2.

43. Statement of Robert Morris on the Dismissal of Charges Against General Edwin A. Walker, undated, Edwin A. Walker Papers, box 2005-084, folder 2.

44. "Resolution." Clyde Watts sent his resolution to Congress and the Department of Justice, requesting that the existing law be changed to eliminate the possibility of committing an American citizen, "without notice, without counsel and without a hearing to a prison hospital for the criminally insane."

45. *Mississippi Free Press,* January 26, 1963.

46. Walker, *American Eagle.*

47. *New York Times,* October 4, 1962.

48. Ibid.

49. Transcript from Hearing, November 20–21, 1962.

50. *New York Times,* October 4, 1962.

51. Ashmore, *Hearts and Minds,* 285.

52. *Washington Star,* April 5, 1962.

53. *Washington Post,* April 5, 1962.

54. *Detroit News,* February 11, 1962.

55. Call from Edwin Walker to Joe Fribley, moderator, "Party Line," KWKH, Shreveport, Louisiana, September 26, 1962, Edwin A. Walker Papers, box 97-021, folder 1.

56. Ibid.

57. Walker, in *Dan Smoot Report,* May 8, 1961.

58. To FBI Director J. Edgar Hoover from Special Agent in Charge, Oklahoma City: "Christian Crusade," August 5–6, 1963, FBI Report 157-970-74; *Oklahoma Courier,* August 9, 1963, in *Congressional Record,* August 15, 1963, 15130.

59. *Daily Oklahoman,* August 4, 1963.

60. Transcript from Hearing, November 20–21, 1962. Walker had a sense of his political power that was far beyond the bounds of reality. In 1961, after his resignation from the army, Walker told supporters, "I am the program, I am influencing every day of my life and if I wasn't I wouldn't be a commander." *Newsweek,* December 4, 1961.

61. Transcript from Hearing, November 20–21, 1962.

62. "Desegregation, University of Mississippi, Edwin Walker, Obstruction of Justice, November 2, 1962," FBI Report 157-401-1494; Transcript from Hearing, November 20–21, 1962.

63. *Washington Star,* April 5, 1962.

64. Ibid.

65. *Washington Star,* April 6, 1962.

66. *Washington Daily News,* April 6, 1962; *Washington Post,* April 11, 1962.

67. *New York World Telegram,* April 14, 1962.

68. *Washington Post,* April 11, 1962.

69. Report of Special Agent in Charge, Dallas, to FBI Director, November 21, 1963, FBI Teletype 157-218-474.

70. *Washington Star,* December 13, 1961.

71. Special Agent in Charge, San Antonio, to FBI Director, October 5, 1962, FBI Report 116-165-494.

72. *New York Times,* October 8, 1962.

73. "Statement of Robert Morris."

74. *Dallas Morning News,* October 9, 1962.

75. "American Medical Association Opinion." Newspaper columnist Walter Winchell went a step further, saying that a conviction for sedition could carry the death penalty. "Walker's friends don't know how really lucky he is. The government is giving him a break trying to have him declared gluggy." Szasz, *Psychiatric Justice,* 185.

76. Richard P. Bergen, executive secretary of the AMA committee on Medicolegal Problems, in Walsh, "A Postscript to the Meredith Case," 467.

77. Clyde Watts to William F. Walsh, May 12, 1964, in Walsh, "A Postscript to the Meredith Case," 469–470.

78. Watts, "True Story of the Walker Case," 4.

79. *Amarillo Daily News,* March 28, 1963.

80. *Miami News,* February 28, 1963.

81. *Nashville Tennessean,* March 14, 1963.

82. Webb, *Rabble Rousers,* 112.

83. Buckley, *Flying High,* 69–70.

84. "Current Communist Goals," Linden, Indiana, chapter of the John Birch Society, undated, Edwin A. Walker Papers, box 96-30, folder 10.

85. Noebel, *Communism, Hypnotism and the Beatles,* 3.

86. *Oklahoma Courier,* August 9, 1963, in *Congressional Record,* August 15, 1963, 15131.

87. Hartley, "Whose Mental Health?," 270.

88. Statement of Robert Morris, President and Counsel for Defenders of American Liberties, undated, Edwin A. Walker Papers, box 97-021, folder 1.

89. Naske, "Bob Bartlett and the Alaska Mental Health Act," 33–34, 37–38.

90. "Siberia USA," advertisement, in Hearings Before the Senate Subcommittee on Territories and Insular Affairs, February 21, 1956, 142.

91. Ibid., 141–142.

92. *American Mercury,* March 1960, in Hartley, "Whose Mental Health?," 275.

93. Hearings Before the Senate Subcommittee on Territories and Insular Affairs, February 21, 1956, 137–138, 264.

94. Hearings Before the Senate Subcommittee on Territories and Insular Affairs, March 5, 1956, 264.

95. "Resolution."

96. *Dan Smoot Report,* October 15, 1962.

97. Walker, *Twenty Questions.*

98. Szasz, "Psychiatry's Threat to Civil Liberties." Testifying before Senate hearings on the Alaska mental health bill was an anti-Semitic agitator named John Kasper, who befriended Ezra Pound at St. Elizabeth's Hospital. Kasper wanted Crommelin and other reactionary military leaders, including Pedro del Valle, to help secure Pound's release. Kasper, a New Jersey bookseller, called psychiatry a "Jewish science." Naske, "Bob Bartlett and the Alaska Mental Health Act," 38; Hearings Before the Senate Subcommittee on Territories and Insular Affairs, February 21, 1956, 168–169.

99. Szasz, "Psychiatry's Threat to Civil Liberties."

100. Szasz, "The Shame of Medicine."

101. Banks, "Immediate Appeal of Pretrial Commitment Orders," 807–808.

102. Szasz, *Psychiatric Justice,* 224–225.

103. *The New Yorker,* August 23, 2017.

7. Into the Vortex

1. Walker, speech delivered in Dallas, December 12, 1961.

2. Kimble, "Mutually Assured Disparagement: Enmification and Enlightenment in Early 1950s *Mad,*" 131.

3. *New York Times,* October 1, 1963; October 2, 1963.

4. *Independent American,* October 29, 1962.

5. Rusher, *Rise of the Right,* 125–126.

6. *Dallas Morning News,* June 3, 1964.

7. *Time,* June 26, 1964.

8. *Fort Worth Star-Telegram,* June 9, 1964.

9. *Fort Worth Star-Telegram,* June 15, 1964.

10. *Louisville Courier-Journal,* March 15, 1963.

11. United Press in *Jackson Clarion-Ledger,* October 2, 1963.

12. *Fort Worth Star-Telegram,* June 9, 1964.

13. Ibid.

14. *Fort Worth Star-Telegram,* June 16, 1964.

15. *Fort Worth Star-Telegram,* June 9, 1964.

16. Ibid.

17. *Fort Worth Star-Telegram,* June 17, 1964.

18. *Fort Worth Star-Telegram,* June 18, 1964.

19. *Fort Worth Star-Telegram,* June 19, 1964.

20. *Time,* June 26, 1964.

21. *Fort Worth Star-Telegram,* June 19, 1964.

22. *Dallas Morning News,* June 20, 1964.

23. *Fort Worth Star-Telegram,* June 20, 1964. Walker's suits against publications that used the

AP dispatches suffered a setback later that summer when the case against *Newsweek* was dismissed. *New York Times,* August 20, 1964.

24. *Daily Oklahoman,* October 8, 1962.

25. *Fort Worth Press,* June 14, 1964. In 1961, Watts wrote "Strategy for Survival," in which he said, "We are at war . . . Soviet Russia's intentions are aided by the communist conspiracy in the United States with awesome capabilities." In this tract, he called student protests in San Francisco against the House Committee on Un-American Activities "communist-organized, engineered, and financed." Watts, "Strategy for Survival," Edwin A. Walker Papers, box 96-30, folder 10.

26. *Fort Worth Press,* June 21, 1964.

27. *Fort Worth Star-Telegram,* July 23, 1964.

28. *Dallas Times-Herald,* July 30, 1964.

29. *Fort Worth Star-Telegram,* September 1, 1964.

30. *Dallas Morning News,* October 1, 1964.

31. "Defamation a Deux," 246–247.

32. *Washington Post,* June 3, 1967.

33. US Supreme Court, *Curtis Publishing Co. v. Butts* together with *Associated Press v. Walker,* Edwin A. Walker Papers, box 96-30, folder 33.

34. Ibid.

35. Text of Brief Submitted to the US Supreme Court, October Term 1965, Edwin A. Walker Papers, box 96-30, folder 33

36. US Supreme Court, *Curtis Publishing Co. v Butts* together with *Associated Press v. Walker.*

37. Ibid.

38. Ibid.

39. *Washington Post,* June 13, 1967.

40. *New York Times,* June 18, 1967. The Supreme Court of Louisiana, in dismissing Walker's suit against the *New Orleans Times-Picayune,* ruled that the newspaper could not be held liable for publishing the AP reports: "This theory of vicarious liability cannot stand." Supreme Court of Louisiana, *Walker v. Associated Press,* Edwin A. Walker Papers, box 96-30, folder 33.

41. Edmondson, "In Sullivan's Shadow," 130–131.

42. Walker statement on Associated Press suit, undated, Edwin A. Walker Papers, box 96-30, folder 33. Walker also faced a years-long battle with the IRS. In 1965, the IRS claimed that Walker owed $3,863 on his 1961 income taxes and had failed to report $540 in rents he collected on a piece of property and another $400 of income from a hunting license. Walker not only denied that he owed the government money but also insisted he had a refund coming. Walker told the *Dallas Morning News* that the IRS "spent more money trying to retrieve what they allege they deserve than what the total amount is worth." *Dallas Morning News,* October 21, 1965.

43. *Dan Smoot Report,* July 10, 1967.

44. *Congressional Record,* June 21, 1967, 16702. Walker's mother, Charlotte, was one of those taking issue with the Supreme Court's decision. In a letter to the hometown paper, the *Kerrville Daily Times,* she quoted from Rarick's remarks in the *Congressional Record.* "As you request letters to you, I shall appreciate the publication of mine," she wrote. The letter was clipped and sent to

Walker, "With love from C.T.W." Charlotte Walker, letter to the editor, *Kerrville Daily Times,* June 29, 1967, Edwin A. Walker Papers, box 96-30, folder 33.

45. *Los Angeles Times,* December 17, 1962.

46. Walker, "Why Be a Person of the Press?," undated draft, Edwin A. Walker Papers, box 96-30, folder 10.

8. Midnight Riders of the Ultra Right

1. *Montgomery Advertiser,* March 10, 1963.

2. Midnight Ride poster, Edwin A. Walker Papers, box 96-30, folder 8.

3. *Tampa Times,* March 5, 1963.

4. *Independent American,* February 19, 1963.

5. "Walker Speaks . . . on Textbooks," 5.

6. *Christian Century,* in Forster and Epstein, *Danger on the Right,* 85.

7. Forster and Epstein, *Danger on the Right,* 72–73.

8. *Oklahoma Courier,* August 9, 1963, in Congressional Record, August 15, 1963, 15131-15132.

9. Ibid., 15130; Forster and Epstein, *Danger on the Right,* 68–69.

10. Forster and Epstein, *Danger on the Right,* 68–69.

11. Ibid., 75.

12. *Santa Ana Register,* October 12, 1962.

13. *New York Times,* January 30, 1962.

14. Hearings Before the Senate Special Preparedness Subcommittee, April 5, 1962, 1525.

15. "Operation Midnight Ride Daily Report," March 5, 1963, Edwin A. Walker Papers, box 96-30, folder 8.

16. Quoted in Levitas, *Terrorist Next Door,* 78.

17. *Tampa Times,* March 5, 1963.

18. *Miami News,* February 28, 1963.

19. "You Can Join in our Fight for Survival," Florida Coalition of Patriotic Societies, undated, Edwin A. Walker Papers, box 96-30, folder 8.

20. "Operation Midnight Ride Daily Report," March 2, 1963, box 96-30, folder 8.

21. *Palm Beach Post,* March 2, 1963.

22. Ibid.

23. "Operation Midnight Ride Daily Report," March 2, 1963.

24. "Operation Midnight Ride Daily Report," March 5, 1963.

25. *Montgomery Advertiser,* March 10, 1963.

26. *Birmingham News,* March 9, 1963.

27. "Operation Midnight Ride Daily Report," March 20, 1963, Edwin A. Walker Papers, box 96-30, folder 8. Describing Denver as a "hotbed of communist activity," Walker and Hargis were met by more than 1,200 supporters packed into a local high school auditorium as well as about two hundred picketers outside representing groups as diverse as the National Association for the Advancement of Colored People, the Congress of Racial Equality, the Student Peace Union from

the University of Denver, and the Socialist Workers Party. Those outside, Hargis told his audience, "are marching, intentionally or unintentionally, to the call of Khrushchev." *Rocky Mountain News,* March 27, 1963.

28. "Operation Midnight Ride Daily Report," March 6, 1963, Edwin A. Walker Papers, box 96-30, folder 8.

29. *Deseret News,* May 15, 1963.

30. *Greenville News,* March 13, 1963.

31. *Greenville News,* March 13, 1963. Throughout its century-long history, Bob Jones University has had a controversial record on race. Founded in 1926, the university moved to Greenville, South Carolina, in 1947 after being on shaky financial ground. The school was at the doctrinal extreme of Christian fundamentalism, with a strong anti-Catholic bias, and up until the 1970s did not admit Black students. Bob Jones University lost its tax-exempt status because of its prohibition on interracial dating, a policy that ended only in 2000. In 2008, the university apologized for its history of race bigotry.

32. *Tampa Times,* March 5, 1963.

33. Associated Press, November 21, 1961.

34. "Operation Midnight Ride Daily Report," March 6, 1963.

35. Ruotsila, "Russia's Most Effective Fifth Column," 1024.

36. *Montgomery Advertiser,* March 10, 1963.

37. *Cincinnati Enquirer,* March 19, 1963.

38. *Greenville News,* March 13, 1963.

39. *Montgomery Advertiser,* March 10, 1963.

40. "Operation Midnight Ride Daily Report," March 6, 1963.

41. *Cincinnati Enquirer,* March 18, 1963; March 19, 1963.

42. "Operation Midnight Ride Daily Report," March 18, 1963, Edwin A. Walker Papers, box 96-30, folder 8.

43. *Los Angeles Herald Examiner,* April 4, 1963.

44. Ibid.

45. Forster and Epstein, *Danger on the Right,* 83.

46. "Operation Midnight Ride Daily Report," March 5, 1963.

47. *Oklahoma Courier,* August 9, 1963, in Congressional Record, August 15, 1963, 15131.

48. *New York Times,* August 6, 1963.

49. *Los Angeles Times,* January 11, 1962; *Los Angeles Herald Examiner,* January 12, 1962.

50. *Redondo Daily Breeze,* January 14, 1962.

51. *New York Times,* April 14, 1963.

52. *Houston Post,* March 29, 1961.

53. Bele, "Legacy of the Involvement of the Democratic Republic of the Congo," 1.

54. Hearings Before the Senate Special Preparedness Subcommittee, April 5, 1962, 1523.

55. Walker, speech delivered in Dallas, December 12, 1961.

56. "Beliefs and Principles of the John Birch Society," John Birch Society flier, June 12, 1962, Edwin A. Walker Papers, box 96-30, folder 10.

57. *Los Angeles Herald Examiner,* April 4, 1963.

58. *Louisville Courier-Journal,* March 15, 1963.

59. Draft of speech, March 31, 1961, Edwin A. Walker Papers, box 93-402, folder 2.

60. Hearings Before the Senate Special Preparedness Subcommittee, April 5, 1962, 1523–1524.

61. Walker, *Twenty Questions.*

62. Hearings Before the Senate Special Preparedness Subcommittee, April 5, 1962, 1525.

63. *Los Angeles Herald Examiner,* January 12, 1962.

64. Hearings Before the Senate Special Preparedness Subcommittee, April 5, 1962, 1525, 1531.

65. Weekly messages, August 10, 1975, Edwin A. Walker Papers, box 2005-084, folder 1.

66. *New York Times,* December 13, 1961.

67. *New York Times,* October 27, 1963.

68. Forster and Epstein, *Danger on the Right,* 75.

69. Walker, *American Eagle.*

70. Vinz, "Politics of Protestant Fundamentalism," 247.

71. Ibid., 240, 252.

72. Ibid., 239.

73. Letter from John P. Patrick to Edwin Walker, July 8, 1966, Edwin A. Walker Papers, box 2005-084, folder 1.

74. Hargis, *The Truth About UNESCO,* 1.

75. Hargis, *United Nations,* 1, 5.

76. Ruotsila, "Russia's Most Effective Fifth Column," 1034.

77. Walker, in Doyle, *An American Insurrection,* 97.

78. Associated Press, November 2, 1963.

79. *New York Times,* December 10, 1961.

80. Congressional Record, May 20, 1963, 8950.

81. *Louisville Courier-Journal,* March 15, 1963.

9. Edwin Walker: America's "Leading Fascist"

1. Testimony of Major General Edwin A. Walker and General Clyde Watts, July 23, 1964, *Hearings Before the President's Commission on the Assassination of President John F. Kennedy,* 11:405.

2. Ibid.

3. *Washington Post,* April 12, 1963.

4. *New York Times,* December 7, 1963.

5. *Hearings Before the President's Commission,* 23:758; *Washington Post,* December 7, 1963.

6. *Hearings Before the President's Commission,* 23:761.

7. Dallas Police Department, "Subject: William McEwan Duff Polygraph Examination," December 31, 1963, Edwin A. Walker Papers, box 96-30, folder 37.

8. Testimony of Major General Edwin A. Walker and General Clyde Watts, July 23, 1964, 11:415.

9. Ibid., 11:413.

10. Ibid., 11:414.

11. Dallas Police Department, "Supplemental Offense Report," June 6, 1963, Edwin A. Walker Papers, box 96-30, folder 37.

12. Testimony of Major General Edwin A. Walker and General Clyde Watts, July 23, 1964, 11:414–415.

13. "April 11, 1963—General Edwin Walker Interviewed After Shooting Incident," Helmer-Reenberg, video.

14. *Dallas Morning News,* October 24, 1963.

15. Testimony of Major General Edwin A. Walker and General Clyde Watts, July 23, 1964, 11:400.

16. *Report of the President's Commission on the Assassination of President John F. Kennedy,* 416.

17. *Washington Post,* December 9, 1963.

18. *Dallas Morning News,* October 25, 1963; *New York Times,* October 25, 1963.

19. McKeever, *Adlai Stevenson,* 539.

20. *Dallas Times-Herald,* October 27, 1963.

21. *New York Times,* October 25, 1963.

22. *Dallas Times-Herald,* October 27, 1963.

23. *The Remarker,* November 15, 1963, Edwin A. Walker Papers, box 96-30, folder 37; Associated Press, November 2, 1963.

24. *Christian Crusade Weekly,* December 8, 1960.

25. Associated Press, November 2, 1963.

26. "Lee Harvey Oswald," June 18, 1964, FBI Report 105-8255-460.

27. McKeever, *Adlai Stevenson,* 538–539.

28. Buckley, *Flying High,* 68–70.

29. Goldwater, *Conscience of a Conservative,* 90–91.

30. *Report of the President's Commission,* 14–15.

31. Ibid., 12–13.

32. *Hearings Before the President's Commission,* 1:13.

33. *Hearings Before the President's Commission,* 23:394.

34. *Hearings Before the President's Commission,* 1:14–17.

35. US House of Representatives, *Hearings Before the Select Committee on Assassinations,* 12:383.

36. Ibid., 12:382.

37. *Report of the President's Commission,* 814, 724.

38. US House of Representatives, *Hearings Before the Select Committee on Assassinations,* 12:383.

39. *Report of the President's Commission,* 183–184; *Hearings Before the President's Commission,* 23:393, 395.

40. *Report of the President's Commission,* 184–187.

41. Memo from Forrest Sorrels, Special Agent, United States Secret Service, to Jesse Curry, Chief of Police, Dallas, December 26, 1963, Edwin A. Walker Papers, box 96-30, folder 37.

42. US House of Representatives, *Hearings Before the Select Committee on Assassinations*, 12:383.

43. *Report of the President's Commission*, 376, 404–406.

44. *Hearings Before the President's Commission*, 11:292–293.

45. *Washington Post*, February 8, 1964.

46. US House of Representatives, *Hearings Before the Select Committee on Assassinations*, 12:52.

47. *Report of the President's Commission*, 724.

48. Ibid., 283; De Mohrenschildt, *I Am a Patsy*, 130.

49. *Hearings Before the President's Commission*, 9:250.

50. *Report of the President's Commission*, 283–284.

51. Ibid., 725.

52. Ibid., 186.

53. "Assassination of the President," December 6, 1963, FBI Memorandum, 116-1654-556.

54. *Report of the President's Commission*, 183, 185–186.

55. *Hearings Before the President's Commission*, 22:585.

56. Ibid., 23:772.

57. Ibid., 23:762–763.

58. Ibid., 23:185–187; *New York Times*, December 7, 1963.

59. *Hearings Before the President's Commission*, 3:502–503; *Report of the President's Commission*, 562.

60. *Report of the President's Commission*, 404.

61. Hearings Held Before the Senate Select Committee to Study Governmental Operations with Respect to Intelligence Activities, John F. Kennedy Presidential Library, John F. Kennedy Assassination Records Archives 1 (May 7, 1976), 33.

62. Letter addressed to FBI Director J. Edgar Hoover, undated, FBI Memorandum 62-1090-36.

63. "Major General Edwin A. Walker," December 16, 1963, FBI Report 159-218-51.

64. *New York Times*, December 1, 1963.

65. *Report of the President's Commission*, 368, 663.

66. *Hearings Before the President's Commission*, 5:428.

67. "Wanted for Treason," handbill, Edwin A. Walker Papers, box 96-30, folder 37; *Hearings Before the President's Commission*, 5:529.

68. *Hearings Before the President's Commission*, 5:446–449.

69. Letter from J. Lee Rankin, General Counsel, the President's Commission, to FBI Director J. Edgar Hoover, May 20, 1964, FBI Memorandum 116-1165-75.

70. *Dallas Morning News*, December 3, 1963.

71. *Dallas Times-Herald*, February 13, 1964.

72. Associated Press, March 6, 1963.

73. "Information Concerning the Assassination of John Fitzgerald Kennedy," June 18, 1964, FBI Memorandum 157-218-115.

74. *Report of the President's Commission*, 407.

75. Kaiser, *Road to Dallas,* 2; Letter from Tom Lutz to Edwin Walker, July 26, 1977, Edwin A. Walker Papers, box 96-30, folder 37.

76. Kaiser, *Road to Dallas,* 162–163, 250.

77. John F. Kennedy Presidential Library, John F. Kennedy Assassination Records Archives 1 (May 1, 1967), 5.

78. *Hearings Before the President's Commission,* 11:418–419.

79. *Report of the President's Commission,* 663.

80. *National Enquirer,* May 17,1964.

81. *Hearings Before the President's Commission,* 11:421. Equally strange, and for no apparent reason, Walker displayed the flag at full-staff despite the half-staff mourning period for President Kennedy. *Washington Post,* December 12, 1963.

82. Interview with Edwin Walker, Citizens Council Radio, audiotape, 1964.

83. *Zephyrhills* (Florida) *News,* September 30, 1965.

84. Letter from Edwin Walker to Senator Frank Church, June 23, 1975, Edwin A. Walker Papers, box 96-30, folder 37.

85. *Dallas Observer,* November 18–24, 1993.

86. Miller, *Nut Country,* 113–114.

87. "Testimony of Major General Edwin A. Walker and General Clyde Watts," 428.

88. "December 2, 1963—General Edwin Walker After the Assassination of President John F. Kennedy," HelmerReenberg, video. The US Communist Party daily, *The Worker,* called Dallas "the company headquarters for the wild men of the ultra-Right." *The Worker,* November 26, 1963.

89. Testimony of Major General Edwin A. Walker and General Clyde Watts, July 23, 1964, 11:424.

10. The "Mad Hatter" of the Right

1. *New York Times,* December 4, 1961.
2. *Los Angeles Times,* January 11, 1962.
3. Knebel, "Who's on the Far Right?"
4. Cullen and Wilkison, *The Texas Right,* 104.
5. *Washington Post,* March 6, 1962.
6. *New York Times,* July 21, 1963.
7. *Washington Post,* March 6, 1962.
8. *New York Times,* November 12, 1964.
9. *Washington Post,* December 3, 1962.
10. Sherwin, *The Extremists,* 161.
11. *New York Times,* November 12, 1964.
12. Robert DePugh, in Sherwin, *The Extremists,* 166.
13. *Washington Post,* May 12, 1962.
14. US Department of Justice Release, January 26, 1968.
15. Sherwin, *The Extremists,* 165.

16. "Address of the President at the Dinner Honoring Him by the Democratic Party of California," November 18, 1961, John F. Kennedy Library Digital Archives, President's Office Files, Papers of John F. Kennedy.

17. "Information Concerning General Edwin A. Walker," November 9, 1961, FBI Memorandum 62-1074-1.

18. *Washington Post,* November 24, 1961; New York Times, November 19, 1961.

19. *New York Times,* November 24, 1961.

20. *Dallas Morning News,* November 4, 1961.

21. *Dallas Morning News,* October 14, 1962; *Time,* December 8, 1961.

22. "Information Concerning Frank B. McGehee," November 13, 1961, FBI Memorandum 105-1246-35; Robert Kennedy, in *Dallas Times-Herald,* November 15, 1961.

23. *Dallas Morning News,* October 14, 1961.

24. Ibid., October 15, 1961. President Eisenhower had initiated the sale of fighter planes to Yugoslavia in 1957 to support Josip Tito's policy of independence from Moscow.

25. *Newsweek,* December 4, 1961.

26. *Dallas Morning News,* November 23, 1961.

27. National Indignation Convention press release, January 17, 1962, Edwin A. Walker Papers, box 96-30, folder 37; *Birmingham News,* January 21, 1962.

28. United Press International, November 13, 1961.

29. Letter to Bureau, Dallas, October 2, 1962, FBI Memorandum 63-4296-12.

30. "Information Concerning Minutemen," February 14, 1964, FBI Memorandum 105-1264-84.

31. "Minutemen," November 27, 1964, FBI Report 105-1280-153.

32. "Edwin A. Walker," January 22, 1965, FBI Memorandum 157-218-167.

33. *Zephyrhills* (Florida) *News,* September 30, 1965.

34. To Chief United States Secret Service: "Major General Edwin A. Walker," May 3, 1965, FBI Memorandum 116-1654-105.

35. To FBI Director J. Edgar Hoover from Special Agent in Charge, Jackson, Mississippi: "Alleged Klan Participation in Insurrection Plot," March 4, 1965, FBI Report 157-2138-107.

36. "We the White People Rally," flier, Edwin A. Walker Papers, box 96-30, folder 10.

37. To FBI Director J. Edgar Hoover from Special Agent in Charge, New Orleans: "Rally of Segregation Groups, Baton Rouge," July 8, 1965, FBI Memorandum 157-33-3129.

38. *New York Times,* July 7, 1965.

39. To FBI Director J. Edgar Hoover from Special Agent in Charge, Birmingham: "United Klans of America," November 1, 1965, FBI Memorandum 157-370-40. In September 1965, another group, the National Knights of the KKK, sought to unite the disparate Klan groups across the country. They considered Walker a leader, but again there is no evidence that Walker was interested in affiliating with the Klan, at least not overtly.

40. To Special Agent in Charge, New Orleans: "American Royal Rangers," July 22, 1965, FBI Report 157-2905-29.

41. *Common Sense,* September 1, 1961, Edwin A. Walker Papers, box 96-30, folder 2.

42. Arkansas National States' Rights Party newsletter, February 1962; March 1962.

43. Letter from Dal Givens to Edwin Walker, August 28, 1965, Edwin A. Walker Papers, box 2005-084, folder 1.

44. John F. Kennedy Presidential Library, John F. Kennedy Assassinations Records Archives 1 (May 1, 1967), 3.

45. *Washington Post,* November 24, 1961.

46. United Press International, April 27, 1962.

47. *Congressional Record,* April 19, 1971, 10850–10852.

48. *Dallas Times-Herald,* May 18, 1964.

49. *New York Times,* October 27, 1963.

50. "Midnight Ride Tampa," March 7, 1963, FBI Report, 157-218-5.

51. Walker, "Art of Artifice," 2, Edwin A. Walker Papers, box 97-021, folder 4.

52. *Oklahoma Courier,* August 9, 1963, in *Congressional Record,* August 15, 1963, 15130.

53. "Christian Crusade," August 5–6, 1963, FBI Report 157-970-74.

54. *Washington Post,* July 11, 1963.

55. "Christian Crusade," August 5–6, 1963.

56. *Daily Oklahoman,* August 3, 1963.

57. Special Agent in Charge, Dallas: "March on Washington," August 27, 1963, FBI Memorandum 157-218-24.

58. *Dallas Morning News,* August 29, 1963.

59. *New York Times,* February 7, 1964.

60. Massengill, *Portrait of a Racist,* 116.

61. Ibid., 164, 201.

62. *Knoxville Crusader,* January 15, 1964.

63. *New York Times,* February 8, 1964.

64. Silver, *Mississippi: The Closed Society,* 239. De La Beckwith was not convicted of the murder until 1994, and he died in prison in 2001 at age eighty.

65. *Cincinnati Enquirer,* March 19, 1963.

66. Forster and Epstein, *Danger on the Right,* 79; *Washington Post,* January 6, 1967.

67. Bendersky, *Jewish Threat,* 397–398.

68. Welch, "What Is the John Birch Society?," advertisement, *Washington Post,* December 12, 1965.

69. *Houston Chronicle,* April 18, 1961.

70. *Saturday Evening Post,* January 13, 1962.

71. *Congressional Record,* May 20, 1963, 8945–8946.

72. *Houston Post,* April 7, 1961.

73. Letter from John P. Patrick to Edwin Walker, July 8, 1966.

74. Weekly messages, August 2, 1975, Edwin A. Walker Papers, box 2005-084, folder 1. A reporter for the *Oklahoma Courier* who listened to both Welch and Walker at the Christian Crusade convention in 1963 said that, compared to Walker, the "avuncular Welch sounded like a retired candy salesman (which he is)." *Oklahoma Courier,* August 9, 1963, in *Congressional Record,* August 15, 1963, 15131

75. *Tampa Times,* March 5, 1963.

76. Text of Edwin Walker interview with KTVT, Fort Worth, August 5, 1962, Edwin A. Walker Papers, box 96-30, folder 37.

77. *Tampa Times,* March 5, 1963.

78. *Dan Smoot Report,* Edwin A. Walker Papers, August 28, 1961.

79. Smoot, *Invisible Government,* 25, 67.

80. Anti-Defamation League, in *New York Times,* September 30, 1962.

81. *Daily Oklahoman,* September 28, 1962; *New York Times,* September 30, 1962.

82. William F. Buckley, in Bendersky, *Jewish Threat,* 420.

83. Simonelli, *American Fuehrer,* 41; Special Agent in Charge, Dallas, "Robert A. Surrey," October 27, 1964, FBI Memorandum 157-416-3372.

84. Simonelli, *American Fuehrer,* 2.

85. Special Agent in Charge, Dallas, "Robert A. Surrey," October 27, 1964.

86. Simonelli, *American Fuehrer,* 41.

87. United Press International, April 4, 1962.

88. *Newsweek,* December 4, 1961.

89. "Alleged Klan Participation in Insurrection Plot," November 5, 1964, FBI Report 116-1654-9.

11. The Outing of General Walker

1. Faderman, *Gay Revolution,* 191.

2. Peiss and Simmons, "Homosexual Menace," 59.

3. *Congressional Record,* July 31, 1961, 14174–14175.

4. Ibid.

5. Simonelli, *American Fuehrer,* 79.

6. Draft of statement to Senate Armed Services Committee, October 24, 1961, Edwin A. Walker Papers, box 93-402, folder 2.

7. *New York Times,* July 9, 1976; *San Francisco Chronicle,* July 9, 1976.

8. *San Francisco Chronicle,* July 9, 1976.

9. *Time,* July 26, 1976.

10. *New York Times,* March 18, 1977.

11. *New York Times,* September 29, 1962.

12. "Edwin A. Walker. Obstruction of Justice," November 2, 1962, FBI Memorandum 157-401-1218.

13. "Desegregation University of Mississippi," November 9, 1962, FBI Memorandum 157-401-1432.

14. *Congressional Record,* September 20, 1961, 20517.

15. To the Director: "Subject: *Congressional Record,*" September 21, 1961, FBI Memorandum 116-1654-10.

16. Letter from Edwin Walker to General Donald Rosenblum, August 30, 1975, Edwin A. Walker Papers, box 2005-084, folder 1.

17. "Deguello Report," in Kaplan, *Encyclopedia of White Power,* 415.

18. *San Francisco Examiner,* October 25, 1964. The journalist, Jean Campbell of the *London Evening Standard,* who was familiarizing her readers with "controversial Texans," also observed that a portrait of Walker's mother "dominates the room."

19. *Time,* February 16, 1976.

20. Ibid.

21. Mason, *Oklahomo,* 84–85, 100.

22. David Noebel, *Homosexual Revolution,* in Gallagher, *Law & Sexuality,* 126.

23. Press release, December 7, 1965, Edwin A. Walker Papers, box 96-30, folder 10.

24. Walker, "The Wicked War in South Vietnam," undated, Edwin A. Walker Papers, box 2005-084, folder 1.

25. "Information Concerning General Edwin Walker," August 10, 1965, FBI Memorandum 105-135-1403.

26. Walker, "Will the People of Dallas Be Surprised!," October 1, 1971, Edwin A. Walker Papers, box 2005-084, folder 1.

27. Letter from Edwin Walker to J. Edgar Hoover, October 6, 1970, FBI Memorandum 116-1654-132.

28. Letter from Edwin Walker to Senator Mike Mansfield, May 31, 1972, FBI Memorandum 116-1654-132.

29. Weekly messages, January 12, 1975, Edwin A. Walker Papers, box 2005-084, folder 1.

30. Ashmore, *Hearts and Minds,* 286.

31. *Smithsonian Magazine,* September 2018.

32. *Washington Post,* May 7, 1965.

33. *New York Times,* April 26, 1963.

34. *Dallas Times-Herald,* May 2, 1965.

35. Ibid.

36. *Chicago Daily News,* May 6, 1965.

37. Ibid.

38. Carter, *Politics of Rage,* 139.

39. *Virginian Pilot,* September 3, 1968.

40. Ibid.

41. Letter from George Wallace to Edwin Walker, February 13, 1970, Edwin A. Walker Papers, box 96-30, folder 6.

42. Letter from Edwin Walker to T. Coleman Andrews Jr., August 20, 1969, Edwin A. Walker Papers, box 96-30, folder 6.

43. *New York Times,* May 18, 1972.

44. Weekly messages, July 3, 1977, Edwin A. Walker Papers, box 2005-084, folder 1.

45. Letter from Dal Givens to Edwin Walker, August 28, 1965.

46. Letter from Alexander Page to Edwin Walker, March 3, 1978, Edwin A. Walker Papers, box 2005-084, folder 1.

47. *Dallas Times-Herald,* May 13, 1978.

48. Letter from Neil Hoey to Edwin Walker, undated, Edwin A. Walker Papers, box 2005-084, folder 1.

49. *Texas Monthly,* November 1975.

50. *Dallas Morning News,* May 14, 1978.

51. *New York Times,* November 2, 1993.

52. *Dallas Observer,* November 18–24, 1993.

53. Letter from J. Warren Cassidy, Executive Director, NRA, to Edwin Walker, February 1, 1984, Edwin A. Walker Papers, box 2005-084, folder 1.

54. Letter from Edwin Walker to Representative Guy Vander Jagt, September 14, 1985, Edwin A. Walker Papers, box 2005-084, folder 1.

55. *Dallas Observer,* November 18–24, 1993.

56. Ibid.

57. Ibid.

58. Ibid.

59. Billy James Hargis, in *Smithsonian Magazine,* September 2018.

60. *Dallas Observer,* November 18–24, 1993.

Epilogue

1. Jasper, *United Nations Exposed,* ix–xi.

2. Ibid., 8.

3. Congressional Record, May 20, 1963, 8959; *New York Times,* July 21, 1963.

4. *New York Times,* May 7, 2015.

5. Ibid.

6. Quoted in Savage, "The John Birch Society Is Back."

7. Cox et al., "Focus on Agenda 21 Should Not Divert Attention from Homegrown Anti-Growth Policies."

8. Republican National Committee, "Republican Party Platform 2016," 51.

9. *New York Times,* November 26, 1961.

10. Congressional Record, May 20, 1963, 8947.

11. *Atlantic Monthly,* June 2020.

12. Weekly messages, July 13, 1975, Edwin A. Walker Papers, box 2005-084, folder 1.

13. *Free Men Speak,* February 15, 1955.

14. Jodi Dean, "If Anything Is Possible," in Knight, *Conspiracy Nation,* 92.

15. *Sunday Oklahoman,* August 6, 1972.

16. Walker, speech delivered December 29, 1961.

17. *Miami Herald,* August 23, 2018.

18. "Address of the President at the Dinner Honoring Him," November 18, 1961.

19. *Washington Post,* April 5, 1962.
20. *Washington Star,* April 5, 1962.
21. *Time,* March 10, 1961.
22. Oklahoma Courier, August 9, 1963, in Congressional Record, August 15, 1963, 15130.
23. *The Remarker,* November 15, 1963.
24. "Johnson and Eisenhower: Moscow Doves," Edwin A. Walker Papers, box 96-30, folder 10.
25. *Washington Post,* December 17, 2021.
26. *New York Times,* November 26, 1961.

BIBLIOGRAPHY

Archival Sources

American Jewish Historical Society Archives: Anti-Semitic Literature Collection
Anti-Defamation League of B'nai B'rith
CIA Historical Review Program
Dwight D. Eisenhower Library
    Records as President, Official Files
    Records as President, White House Central Files
    Kevin McCann Collection of Press and Radio Conferences and Press Releases
Heritage Foundation
John F. Kennedy Presidential Library
    John F. Kennedy Assassination Records Archives 1 (1964–1968).
    Lee White Papers.
    President's Office Files
    The Presidential Papers of John F. Kennedy
    White House Central Files
Burke Marshall Papers. John F. Kennedy Presidential Library.
Mississippi Department of Archives and History
Mississippi State University Libraries, Special Collections Department, Manuscripts Division
National Public Radio
The Presidential Papers of Dwight D. Eisenhower. Johns Hopkins University Digital Collection. National Historical Publications and Records Commission of the Archives.
Edwin A. Walker Papers. Dolph Briscoe Center for American History at the University of Texas at Austin.

US Department of Justice, Federal Bureau of Investigation Files

Christian Crusade
Desegregation University of Mississippi
Billy James Hargis
John Birch Society
Ku Klux Klan
Minutemen
National Indignation Convention
Edwin A. Walker

Books

Ambrose, Stephen E. *Eisenhower: The President.* New York: Simon & Schuster, 1990.

Ashmore, Harry. *Hearts and Minds: A Personal Chronicle of Race in America.* New York: McGraw Hill, 1988.

Barrett, Russell. *Integration at Ole Miss.* Chicago: Quadrangle Books, 1965.

Bendersky, Joseph. *The Jewish Threat: Anti-Semitic Politics of the US Army.* New York: Basic Books, 2000.

Blossom, Virgil T. *It Has Happened Here.* New York: Harper & Brothers, 1959.

Blumenson, Martin. *United States Army in World War II: The Mediterranean Theater of Operations, Salerno to Cassino.* Washington, DC: Office of the Chief of Military History, 1969.

Bogle, Lori L. *The Pentagon's Battle for the American Mind: The Early Cold War.* College Station: Texas A&M University Press, 2004.

Breuer, William B. *Operation Dragoon: The Allied Invasion of the South of France.* Novato, CA: Presidio Press, 1987.

Brownell, Herbert. *Advising Ike.* Lawrence: University of Kansas Press, 1993.

Buckley, William F. *Flying High: Remembering Barry Goldwater.* New York: Basic Books, 2008.

Carter, Dan. *The Politics of Rage: George Wallace, the Origins of the New Conservatism, and the Transformation of American Politics.* New York: Simon & Schuster, 1995.

Chalmers, David. *Hooded Americanism: The History of the Ku Klux Klan.* Durham, NC: Duke University Press, 1987.

Courtney, Kent, and Phoebe Courtney. *America's Unelected Rulers.* New Orleans: Conservative Society of America Publications, 1962.

Critchlow, Donald, T. *The Conservative Ascendancy.* Cambridge, MA: Harvard University Press, 2007.

Cullen, David O'Donald, and Kyle G. Wilkison, eds. *The Texas Right: The Radical Roots of Lone Star Conservatism.* College Station: Texas A&M University Press, 2014.
De Mohrenschildt, George. *I Am a Patsy.* Jane Lew, WV: New Age Press, 1976.
Doyle, William. *An American Insurrection: The Battle of Oxford, Mississippi, 1962.* New York: Doubleday, 2001.
Eagles, Charles W. *The Price of Defiance: James Meredith and the Integration of Ole Miss.* Chapel Hill: University of North Carolina Press, 2009.
Eisenhower, Dwight. *Waging Peace: The White House Years, 1956–1961.* New York: Doubleday, 1965.
Faderman, Lillian. *The Gay Revolution: The Story of the Struggle.* New York: Simon & Schuster, 2015.
Fisher, Ernest F., Jr. *United States Army in World War II: The Mediterranean Theater of Operations, Cassino to the Alps.* Washington, DC: Center of Military History, 1977.
Fleming, Karl. *Son of the Rough South.* New York: Public Affairs, 2005.
Forster, Arnold, and Benjamin Epstein. *Danger on the Right.* New York: Random House, 1964.
George, John, and Laird Wilcox. *Nazis, Communists, Klansmen, and Others on the Fringe.* Buffalo, NY: Prometheus Books, 1992.
Goldwater, Barry. *The Conscience of a Conservative.* New York: MacFadden Books, 1960.
Grose, Peter. *Continuing the Inquiry: The Council on Foreign Relations from 1921 to 1996.* New York: Council on Foreign Relations, 1996.
Gugeler, Russell. *Combat Actions in Korea.* Washington, DC: Center for Military History, 1987.
Hemmer, Nicole. *Messengers of the Right: Conservative Media and the Transformation of American Politics.* Philadelphia: University of Pennsylvania Press, 2016.
Hixson, William B., Jr. *Search for the American Right Wing.* Princeton, NJ: Princeton University Press, 1992.
Huntington, John. *Far-Right Vanguard: The Radical Roots of Modern Conservatism.* Philadelphia: University of Pennsylvania Press, 2021.
Jacoway, Elizabeth. *Turn Away Thy Son.* New York: Free Press, 2007.
Jasper, William. *The United Nations Exposed: The International Conspiracy to Rule the World.* Appleton, WI: John Birch Society, 2001.
Kaiser, David. *The Road to Dallas.* Cambridge, MA: Harvard University Press, 2009.
Kaplan, Jeffrey, ed. *Encyclopedia of White Power: A Sourcebook on the Radical Racist Right.* Walnut Creek, CA: Altamira Press, 2000.
Knebel, Fletcher, and Charles W. Bailey II. *Seven Days in May.* New York: Harper and Row, 1962.

Knight, Peter, ed. *Conspiracy Nation: The Politics of Paranoia in Postwar America.* New York: New York University Press, 2002.

Levitas, Daniel. *The Terrorist Next Door: The Militia Movement and the Radical Right.* New York: St. Martin's Press, 2002.

Lowndes, Joseph. *From the New Deal to the New Right: Race and the Southern Origins of Modern Conservatism.* New Haven, CT: Yale University Press, 2008.

Manchester, William. *American Caesar: Douglas MacArthur, 1880–1964.* Boston: Little Brown & Co., 1978.

Mason, Carol. *Oklahomo: Lessons in Unqueering America.* Albany: State University of New York Press, 2015.

Massengill, Reed. *Portrait of a Racist: The Man Who Killed Medgar Evers?* New York: St. Martin's Press, 1994.

McKeever, Porter. *Adlai Stevenson: His Life and Legacy.* New York: William Morrow & Co., 1989.

Meyer, Karl, ed. *Fulbright of Arkansas: The Public Positions of a Private Thinker.* Washington, DC: Robert Luce Inc., 1963.

Miller, Edward. *A Conspiratorial Life: Robert Welch, the John Birch Society and the Revolution of American Conservatism.* Chicago: University of Chicago Press, 2022.

Miller, Edward H. *Nut Country: Right Wing Dallas and the Birth of the Southern Strategy.* Chicago: University of Chicago Press, 2015.

Nichols, David A. *A Matter of Justice: Eisenhower and the Beginning of the Civil Rights Revolution.* New York: Simon & Schuster, 2007.

Norrell, Robert. *The House I Live In: Race in the American Century.* New York: Oxford University Press, 2005.

The Ole Miss Annual. Oxford: University of Mississippi Student Media, 1962, 1963.

Peiss, Kathy, and Christina Simmons. "The Homosexual Menace." In *Making Trouble: Essays on Gay History, Politics, and the University,* edited by John D'Emilio, pp. 57–73. New York: Routledge, 1992.

Reed, Roy. *Faubus: The Life and Times of an American Prodigal.* Fayetteville: University of Arkansas Press, 1997.

Rusher, William. *The Rise of the Right.* New York: William Morrow, 1984.

Ryan, James. *Early Browder: The Failure of American Communism.* Tuscaloosa: University of Alabama Press, 1997.

Scheips, Paul. *The Role of Federal Military Forces in Domestic Disorders, 1945–1992.* Washington, DC: United States Army Center of Military History, 2012.

Schlesinger, Arthur Jr. *Robert Kennedy and His Times.* Boston: Houghton Mifflin, 1978.

Shawn, Eric. *The UN Exposed.* New York: Penguin Group, 2006.

Sherwin, Mark. *The Extremists.* New York: St. Martin's Press, 1963.

Silver, James W. *Mississippi: The Closed Society.* New York: Harcourt, Brace & World, 1966.

Simonelli, Frederick. *American Fuehrer: George Lincoln Rockwell and the American Nazi Party.* Chicago: University of Illinois Press, 1999.

Smoot, Dan. *The Invisible Government.* Los Angeles: Western Islands Publishers, 1962.

Stockley, Grif. *Daisy Bates: Civil Rights Crusader from Arkansas.* Jackson: University Press of Mississippi, 2005.

Szasz, Thomas. *Psychiatric Justice.* Westport, CT: Greenwood Press, 1978.

Webb, Clive. *Rabble Rousers: The American Far Right in the Civil Rights Era.* Athens: University of Georgia Press, 2010.

Welch, Robert. *The Life of John Birch.* Chicago: Henry Regnery Company, 1954.

Journal and Magazine Articles

Abcarian, Gilbert, and Sherman Stanage. "Alienation and the Radical Right." *Journal of Politics* 27, no. 4 (November 1965): 776–796.

Banks, Helene, R. "Immediate Appeal of Pretrial Commitment Orders: 'It's Now or Never.'" *Fordham Law Review* 55, no. 5 (1987): 785–808.

Bele, Jean. "The Legacy of the Involvement of the Democratic Republic of the Congo in the Bombs Dropped on Hiroshima and Nagasaki." *MIT Faculty Newsletter,* January–February 2021.

"Bob Jones University Apologizes for its Racist Past." *Journal of Blacks in Higher Education* (Winter 2008/2009): 22–23.

Broyles, J. Allen. "The John Birch Society: A Movement of Social Protest of the Radical Right." *Journal of Social Issues* (April 1963): 51–62.

Cope, Graeme. "Dedicated People: Little Rock Central High School's Teachers during the Integration Crisis of 1957–1958." *Arkansas Historical Quarterly* 70, no 1 (Spring 2011): 16–44.

Cox, Wendell, Ronald D. Utt, and Brett Schaefer. "Focus on Agenda 21 Should Not Divert Attention from Homegrown Anti-Growth Policies." *Backgrounder* no. 2628 (December 1, 2011).

"Defamation a Deux: Incidental Defamation and the *Sullivan* Doctrine." *University of Pennsylvania Law Review* 114, no. 2: 241–248.

Eisenberg, Lawrence D. "Constitutional Law of Defamation and Privacy: Butts and Walker." *Cornell Law Review* 53, no. 4 (April 1968): 649–662.

"First Special Service Force." *On Point* 7, no. 2: 1.

Gallagher, Michael J. "Amendment 2." *Law & Sexuality: A Review of Lesbian and Gay Legal Issues* 4 (1994): 123–194.

Godfrey, Phoebe. "Bayonets, Brainwashing, and Bathrooms: The Discourse of Race, Gender, and Sexuality in the Desegregation of Little Rock's Central High." *Arkansas Historical Quarterly* 62, no. 1 (Spring 2003): 42–67.

Goodrich, Leland. "Review: Hammarskjöld, the UN and the Office of the Secretary-General." *International Organization* 28, no. 3 (Summer 1974): 467–483.

Gross, Neil, Thomas Medvetz, and Rupert Russell. "The Contemporary American Conservative Movement." *Annual Review of Sociology* 37 (2011): 325–354.

Hartley, Margaret. "Whose Mental Health? The Psychology of Suspicion." *Southwest Review* 46, no. 4 (Autumn 1961): 269–279.

Holland, Max. "After Thirty Years: Making Sense of the Assassination." *Reviews in American History* 22, no. 2 (June 1994): 191–209.

Kimble, James. "Mutually Assured Disparagement: Enmification and Enlightenment in Early 1950s *Mad.*" *Studies in American Humor* no. 30 (2014): 123–134.

Koeppen, Sheilah. "The Republican Radical Right." *Annals of the American Academy of Political and Social Science* (March 1969): 73–82.

Kovaleff, Theodore. "Review: JFK Assassination Books." *Presidential Studies Quarterly* 24, no. 4 (Fall 1994): 901–910.

Moore, Donald L. "The Bay of Pigs: An Analysis." *Naval War College Review* 19, no. 3 (November 1966): 1–35.

Naske, Claus. "Bob Bartlett and the Alaska Mental Health Act." *Pacific Northwest Quarterly* 71, no. 1 (January 1980): 31–39.

Nichols, Dale K. "The Involuntary Public Figure Class of *Gertz v. Robert Welch*: Dead or Merely Dormant." *University of Michigan Journal of Law Reform* 14, no. 1 (Fall 1980): 71–85.

Peel, Roy V. "The Wackacobi: Extremists of Our Times." *Western Political Quarterly* 16, no. 3 (September 1963): 569–597.

Peters, Shawn F. "Did You Say That Mr. Dean Acheson Is a Pink? The Walker Case and the Cold War." *Vietnam Generation* 6, no. 3–4 (1994): 12–23.

Pratt, Ray. "Theorizing Conspiracy." *Theory and Society* 32, no. 2 (April 2003): 255–271.

Raikka, Juha. "On Political Conspiracy Theories." *Journal of Political Philosophy* 17, no. 2 (2009): 185–201.

Ruotsila, Markku. "'Russia's Most Effective Fifth Column': Cold War Perceptions of Un-Americanism in US Churches." *Journal of American Studies* no. 47 (2013): 1019–1041.

Savage, John. "The John Birch Society Is Back." *Politico Magazine*, July 16, 2017.

Silver, James. "Mississippi: The Closed Society." *Journal of Southern History* 30 no. 1 (February 1964): 3–34.

Sunstein, Cass, and Adrian Vermeule. "Conspiracy Theories: Causes and Cures." *Journal of Political Philosophy* 17, no. 2 (2009): 202–227.

Szasz, Thomas. "Psychiatry's Threat to Civil Liberties." *National Review,* March 12, 1963.

Szasz, Thomas. "The Shame of Medicine: The Case of General Edwin Walker." *Freeman* 59, no. 8 (October 2009): 1–10.

Vacha, J. E. "It Could Happen Here: The Rise of the Political Scenario Novel." *American Quarterly* 29, no. 2 (Summer 1977): 194–206.

Vinz, Warren. "The Politics of Protestant Fundamentalism in the 1950s and 1960s." *Journal of Church and State* 14, no. 2 (Spring 1972): 235–260.

Walsh, William, F. "A Postscript to the Meredith Case." *Case Western Reserve Law Review* 15, no. 3 (1964): 461–478.

Dissertations

Edmondson, Aimee. "In Sullivan's Shadow: The Use and Abuse of Libel Law During the Civil Rights Movement." PhD. diss., University of Missouri, 2008.

Huntington, John. "Right-Wing Paranoid Blues: The Role of Radicalism in Modern Conservatism." PhD. diss., University of Houston, 2016.

Films, Recordings, and Interview Transcripts

Bergquist, Laura. Interview by Nelson Aldrich. December 8, 1965. John F. Kennedy Library Oral History Program.

Decker, George H. Interview by Larry J. Hackman. September 18, 1968. John F. Kennedy Library Oral History Program.

HelmerReenberg. "April 11, 1963—General Edwin Walker Interviewed After Shooting Incident." YouTube video, 1:56. December 24, 2012, https://www.youtube.com/watch?v=yCjahRnkQfk.

HelmerReenberg. "December 2, 1963—General Edwin Walker After the Assassination of President John F. Kennedy." YouTube video, 1:40. February 13, 2013, https://www.youtube.com/watch?v=mx_-K4jCpm8.

Frankenheimer, John. Director. *Seven Days in May.* Paramount Pictures, 1964. 118 minutes.

Knebel, Fletcher. Interview by Sheldon Stern. August 1, 1977. John F. Kennedy Library Oral History Program.

McNamara, Robert S. Interview transcript. NBC *Today.* February 17, 1961.

NBC News. Evening news transcript. October 1, 1962.

Pearson, Drew. Transcript. WTOP radio, Washington, DC. January 20, 1962.

Trump, Donald. "Remarks by President Donald J. Trump to the 74th Session of the United Nations General Assembly." Transcript. United Nations. September 25, 2019.

Walker, Edwin. Interview by Charles Ray. Transcript. WNOE radio, New Orleans. September 28, 1962.

Walker, Edwin. Interview by Eddie Barker. Transcript. KRLD television, Dallas. September 27, 1962.

US Government and United Nations Documents

"Assistant Secretary of Defense for Public Affairs." Department of Defense Directive. Washington, DC: Department of Defense, 1961.

Citizenship Training Manual. Washington, DC: War Department, 1928.

Congressional Record Permanent Digital Collection. Government Printing Office.

Curtis Publishing Co. v. Butts. 388 US 130 (1967).

Hearings Before the Select Committee on Assassinations. US House of Representatives. Vols. 1 and 12. Washington, DC: Government Printing Office, 1979.

Hearings Before the Special Preparedness Subcommittee of the Senate Armed Services Committee January 23, 24, 25, 30, 31, 1962. Congressional Record Permanent Digital Collection. Government Printing Office.

Hearings Before the Special Preparedness Subcommittee of the Senate Armed Services Committee April 4, 5, 6, 10, 11, 12, 13, 1962. Congressional Record Permanent Digital Collection. Government Printing Office.

Hearings Before the Special Preparedness Subcommittee of the Senate Armed Services Committee September 6 and 7, 1961. Congressional Record Permanent Digital Collection. Government Printing Office.

Hearings Before the Subcommittee on Territories and Insular Affairs of the Senate Committee on Interior and Insular Affairs February 20, 21, and March 5, 1956. Congressional Record Permanent Digital Collection. Government Printing Office.

Investigation of the Assassination of President John F. Kennedy. *Hearings Before the President's Commission on the Assassination of President John F. Kennedy.* Vols. 1, 9, 11, 12, 22, 23. Washington, DC: Government Printing Office, 1964.

"Principles of Public Information Policy." Department of Defense Directive, May 31, 1961. Washington, DC: Department of Defense, 1961.

Report of the President's Commission on the Assassination of President John F. Kennedy. Washington, DC: Government Printing Office, 1964.

Reuther, Victor. "The Radical Right in America Today." Memorandum submitted to the United States Justice Department, December 19, 1961.

United Nations. *Transforming Our World: The 2030 Agenda for Sustainable Development.* General Assembly Resolution, September 25, 2015.

United Nations. "United Nations Sustainable Development. Agenda 21." United Nations Conference on Environment & Development, Rio de Janeiro, June 3–14, 1992.

Pamphlets

Dan Smoot Report 1961–1962.

Hargis, Billy James. *The National Council of Churches Aids and Abets Communism 1957–1960.* Tulsa, OK: Christian Crusade, 1960.

Hargis, Billy James. *The Truth About UNESCO.* Tulsa, OK: Christian Crusade, undated.

Hargis, Billy James. *United Nations: A Confidential Report.* Tulsa, OK: Christian Crusade, 1958.

Noebel, David. *Communism, Hypnotism, and the Beatles.* Tulsa, OK: Christian Crusade, 1965.

Newspapers

Albuquerque Journal

Amarillo Daily News

Arkansas Democrat

Arkansas State Press

Augusta Chronicle-Herald

Birmingham News

Cincinnati Enquirer

Citizen-News (Hollywood, CA)

Daily Breeze (Redondo Beach, CA)

Daily Oklahoman

Daily Worker

Dallas Morning News

Dallas Times-Herald

Deseret News

Fort Worth Press
Fort Worth Star-Telegram
Free Men Speak
Greenville News
The Guardian
Houston Chronicle
Houston Post
The Independent American
Jackson Clarion-Ledger
Kansas City Star
Los Angeles Herald Examiner
Los Angeles Times
Louisville Courier-Journal
Manchester Union-Leader
Miami Herald
Miami News
Milwaukee Journal
Mississippi Free Press
Montgomery Advertiser
Nashville Tennessean
National Enquirer
New York Daily News
New York Herald Tribune
New York Mirror
New York Times
Overseas Weekly
Palm Beach Post
Pittsburgh Press
Rocky Mountain News
San Francisco Chronicle
St. Louis Post-Dispatch
Tampa Times
Virginian Pilot
Wall Street Journal
Washington Daily News
Washington Post
Washington Star

Magazines

Air Force Magazine
American Opinion
Atlantic Monthly
Dallas Observer
Look
National Review
Newsweek
The New Yorker
Saturday Evening Post
Smithsonian Magazine
Texas Monthly
Time Magazine

INDEX